THE SEX KILLERS

Norman Lucas

W H ALLEN

This edition published in 1991 by
W. H. Allen
An imprint of Virgin Publishing
338 Ladbroke Grove
London W10 5AH

First published in Great Britain by W. H. Allen & Co PLC in 1974
First published in paperback by Star Books

Copyright © Norman Lucas 1974

Printed in Great Britain by
Cox & Wyman Ltd, Reading

ISBN 0 352 32248 9

Contents

For a typically British family radiating kindness, fun and happiness—the Spurrings—Cecil, Connie, Richard, Margaret, Quentin, Tessa, Jane, Lesley, Charles and my Godson Tim.

Author's Acknowledgement

I am indebted to Dr Arthur Hyatt Williams, MD, DPM, Consultant Psychiatrist at the Tavistock Clinic, London, and Visiting Psychotherapist at H. M. Prison Wormwood Scrubs, who kindly acted as medical adviser during the compilation of *The Child Killers* and who has again fulfilled that role in the compilation of this book.

During his studies of murder cases, Dr Williams has interviewed many killers and sexual deviates. By sharing with me the vast knowledge he has acquired in his field and giving me his highly specialised advice he has made my task of attempting to understand the minds of the sex killers so much simpler.

Foreword

During the past twenty years the annual number of sex offences in Britain has steadily increased. Despite the present permissive age they are almost double what they were in the fifties: 1950—13,000; 1972—23,500.

Why? This is a question that is baffling top medical experts, top police officers and social workers. They would dearly love to find an answer.

Society now exercises far greater tolerance towards soft porn, sex films and homosexuality. Masturbation is no longer considered to be a private perverse act, practised only by the inhibited and repressed, but a normal physical outlet to relieve stimulation.

Few youths are frustrated. Most before reaching the age of sixteen have no difficulty in finding a girl willing to allow intercourse. To cater for a situation in which a girl is unwilling to ask her GP for the Pill, more and more public houses are installing contraceptive machines and sales are soaring.

Why, then, do men risk their liberty and reputation by raping girls or indecently assaulting females?

Statistics for these offences, and for indecent exposure and sex murders, continue to escalate. In 1972 there were 893 cases of rape; 5,129 of unlawful intercourse with a girl under sixteen; and 256 of unlawful intercourse with a girl under thirteen. All reached a new high.

Minor indecent assaults upon females are countless. As a senior detective in the Home Counties told me, the actual recorded figures 'are but the tip of the iceberg'. Many women are too bashful to report their experiences.

One of the truly black areas exists in suburban train travel. Major police investigations into such cases as murder and muggings in trains and tube stations have produced countless stories of these assaults. There are men who coolly kneel on the floor to peer between the legs of lone, mini-skirted girls, and then before the train stops masturbate in front of them.

Many more men attempt to fondle breasts or indecently expose themselves. Others follow women off trains and across open spaces and attempt rape or indecent assaults. Such incidents frequently go unreported.

There are two major aspects to the problem. The most predominant from the point of view of the police and the medical profession, is the danger that 70 per cent of minor sex offenders eventually 'escalate' and finally commit really serious sex crimes—in some cases brutal and sadistic murders. Therefore it is imperative that ALL offences be reported, and that the detection rate should rise to a high level.

The second important feature is dependent to some extent upon the police for early detection contributes to the prevention of more serious crimes in the future. It is vital that the minor sex offender should receive psychiatric treatment in the early stages of his sexual deviation so that the possibility of 'escalation' can be minimised or even eradicated.

Detection is often dependent upon the relatives of the offenders. Police records show that all too often the man who has committed the crime is protected by those close to him—sometimes deliberately, sometimes unwittingly.

Those wives, mothers and fathers who wittingly give protection by confirming fake alibis do so because of misplaced loyalty and because of ignorance of the possible dangers and tragic circumstances that could arise in the future. Far better that they accept the problems that must arise from the conviction of a husband or son for a minor offence, and hope that psychiatric treatment will cure whatever peculiar sexual deviation possesses the mind of the subject, than that they should close their eyes and later be bathed in shame and remorse when that loved one receives a heavy jail sentence for a violent sexual crime.

More sympathy is generated and can be dispensed for those who unwittingly protect offenders. This situation usually arises because they have too readily dismissed from their minds descriptions and Photofits of wanted men. They convince themselves that, despite obvious similarities, their husband or son would be incapable of committing the published offence. They accept their loved ones' stories of their movements on the day or night of the crimes without giving the matter deep thought. Often they have still been totally unsuspicious when clothing has vanished from the house—despite police statements that a killer or a brutal attacker 'had bloodstained clothing'!

People in this group can perhaps be forgiven for not suspecting members of their families if the police have been unable to produce good descriptions, Photofits, or details of clothing, because the behaviour of sex offenders is so often completely normal in the home environment.

As one Scotland Yard detective said: 'Really, just how well does a woman know the man with whom she shares the marital bed? How well does a mother know a son she may only see at the breakfast table? How well does a girl know her boy friend, and how well does a sister know her brother?'

Mothers pressed me to write *The Child Killers* in 1970 (which is, incidentally, why child murders are not included within the pages of this book) for the purpose of somewhat horrifically and dramatically hammering home the dangers that young unescorted daughters at play face today.

I quickly discovered that it was not only British mothers who were roused by the book's publication. Publishers in many other countries, including the terror-torn USA, received heavy demands for the book.

In writing *The Sex Killers* with the valued assistance of Dr Arthur Hyatt Williams, I have sought to illustrate, with the cases I have selected, the formidable difficulties that relatives face in finally suspecting a member of the family as the guilty party in a revolting sex crime because, in so many instances, there was little reason in the home setting to suspect that a killer was within the family group.

So often a 'family face' bears little resemblance to the face contorted with brutal sexual desire that is seen by the unfortunate victim of an attack.

But despite this, I will be happy if the women who read this book think more than once or twice about the habits, characteristics and temperaments of husbands, sons and brothers when a policeman knocks at the door during a local sex offence enquiry with a questionnaire about the movements of male members of the household, or when a description or Photofit appears in the Press.

Members of the medical profession believe that the increasing incidence of sexual crimes is a hangover from the days of sexual inhibition which preceded this decade. They consider that another six years of permissiveness must elapse before men repressed in their childhood and teens adjust their minds and attitudes to the acceptance that no longer is there a need to fight for sexual pleasures, or to lock up in their minds their secrets of pleasurable deviations. Those people who are genuine deviates have to be educated by psychiatrists to a point where they realise that no desires for apparently abnormal deviations are exclusive to any individual. They have to be convinced that, just as millions of people suffer the same types of physical illness that require treatment, so do thousands of men and women experience sexual desires of somewhat less common kinds—desires which can be explained and treated and removed from the mind.

Psychiatrists specialising in the sex-offence problem also strongly maintain that their casebooks do reveal a pattern in the lives of many sex offenders. The pattern springs from a lack of love in the lives of culprits during their very important formative years.

Often the sex attacker has come from a home in which he has been reared by a latch-key mother who has always gone out to work. Often, too, bad foster-parents can be blamed for failing to demonstrate that parental love which begets security.

While accepting that violent sex scenes on the cinema and on the television screen do excite the susceptible individual, and that even in the present age more censorship should be exercised, the medical profession are at present concentrating upon stabilising family life as a preventive measure for the future.

More and more, psychiatrists are seeking ways of welding together the agencies of law enforcement, the medical profession and social workers' organisations. All bodies concerned with this major problem in modern society must work together so that potential offenders can be recognised and treated during childhood and in their teens. Where it is considered that a bad home environment will almost certainly aggravate latent abnormal sexual tendencies, action should be taken to change the environmental atmosphere—viz, improving housing conditions and improving child care.

One thing has become most apparent since, with Dr Hyatt Williams, I began studying the problem three years ago. It is not one to which there is a quick solution. It is part of the pattern of violence which is reflected alongside the increased incidence of murder: 1969—182; 1970—186; 1971—247; 1972—251.

The upsurge in sex crimes will be halted only when the public demonstrates a more acute awareness of the disturbing situation, and when the bodies responsible for dealing with sex offenders and potential offenders develop a closer liaison, and concentrate upon prevention and early detection and treatment of those sick persons likely to exacerbate the national problem.

1

The Train Wrecker

Psychiatrists know, and the general public are quickly learning through the now largely uninhibited medium of plays, films and books, that the methods by which sexual gratification or release can be obtained are manifold. Other chapters of this book deal with what, for want of a better phrase, must be described as deviations from the norm, but there can be little doubt that the most complex—and in its effects the most tragic—perversion was that practised by a sadist whose crimes shocked all the nations of Europe forty years ago.

The story began on New Year's Eve 1930, when an attempt was made to wreck the Vienna–Passau express train near the station of Anzbach, twenty-two miles from Vienna. Only a few minutes before the train was due it was discovered that a section of rail had been damaged and obstructions placed on the line. Fortunately the driver was alerted in time and managed to stop the train with only yards to spare.

One month later, on 30th January 1931, a second attempt at derailment was made at the same place, this time by the lashing of a steel bar to the rails. Again the train involved was the Vienna–Passau express. On this occasion the warning came too late for the driver to halt before reaching the obstruction, but he had started to brake and, although the engine was derailed, no carriages were overturned and the passengers escaped with a shaking.

There was absolutely no clue either to the identity of the would-be wrecker or to the motives behind the attempts.

At the time these incidents received little publicity outside Austria—until more than seven months later when the evening express from Basle, Switzerland, speeding towards Berlin, crashed at Juterbog, forty miles from the German capital, on 8th August. Seven coaches and the dining car left the rails and toppled over a thirty-foot embankment. Miraculously, no one was killed, but more than a hundred passengers were injured, many of them seriously.

The cause of the disaster was clear. Home-made bombs had been placed on the line and detonated by an arrangement of fuses and batteries from a crude hideout close to the scene of the derailment.

Both the Austrian and the German police thought it likely that the wrecking was the work of the person who had made the previous attempts near Vienna, but the most intensive enquiries and weeks of investigation failed to give any useful lead. There were four theories as to possible motives:

In a time of great political unrest in Europe, the wrecker could be a tool of Communists attempting to stir up trouble.

He could be a man with a real or imagined grudge against the railways seeking revenge.

The man may have had one person as a murder target and conceived the diabolical plan of wrecking any train on which he knew his intended victim to be travelling.

He may have been a maniac with a blood lust that could be satisfied only by mass disaster.

Every possibility had to be examined. The only tangible evidence, that of the equipment found in the hideout near Juterbog, led them on a gigantic wild goose chase which resulted in the arrest of an innocent man.

This unfortunate fellow was an Irishman who, after serving with the Royal Flying Corps in the First World War, was earning a comfortable living as a translator and English tutor in Berlin. He was in a café one day early in August, 1931, when he was approached by a well-dressed man who said he was a German baron and owned a large factory in Vienna. The Irishman, thinking the stranger could be a potential customer, gave his name and full details about himself. He thought no more of the encounter until three days after the Juterbog crash when police officers came to his house and told him he was to be arrested for wrecking the train.

They had discovered that part of the detonating equipment had been bought at a shop in Berlin and the proprietor had given them a full description of the purchaser—an Irish ex-officer who had obligingly supplied his name and address and quite a lot more information about himself.

Fortunately for the Irishman, he was able to provide an absolute alibi for the night of the crash. The shopkeeper, when confronted with the arrested man, was in no doubt at all.

'That is definitely not the man who bought the equipment,' he said.

It was clear to the infuriated detectives that the 'baron' was the train wrecker. Anticipating that some of his equipment might be traced to its source, he had selected a suitable victim whose identity he could assume. The ruse was completely successful, for by the time the innocence of the Irishman had been established the trail was cold—and the wrecker had vanished.

Rewards for information that would lead to the capture of this dangerous man were offered both in Austria and Germany. The police felt convinced that the man's mental state was such that he would continue to cause train crashes until he was caught. Although rail security had been tightened, it was obviously impossible to police every mile of track in two countries. And had such a course been taken it would have been to no avail, for when the next crash came it was neither in Austria nor Germany but over the border in Hungary.

It was 11.30 p.m. on Saturday, 13th September 1931—five weeks after the Juterbog crash—and the Budapest–Ostend express was approaching the railway viaduct of Biatorbagy between Budapest and Vienna. Suddenly there was a vivid flash and a tremendous explosion. The engine reared up into the air before crashing eighty feet into the valley below the bridge, dragging the first five coaches with it and leaving the rest teetering precariously on the edge of the embankment.

Twenty-five people were killed instantly and another

hundred and twenty seriously injured. Many lost limbs and others were so maimed that they did not survive for many months after the crash. A number of British people were among the victims, including a party of students. Two of those who were killed in the first coach were Miss Hilda Fowlds, head-mistress of Gibbs School for Girls, Faversham, Kent, and Mr Harry Clements, a London businessman, who lived at Links Avenue, Gidea Park, Essex.

It did not take police and railway experts long to discover the cause of the crash. Sixteen sticks of dynamite, packed tightly into iron tubes, had been lashed to the rails. Nearby were remnants of an electric cable leading to a hideout among some bushes.

A week passed and the police—this time of three countries— were as baffled as they had been on the previous occasions. They might well have remained in frustrated ignorance had it not been for an employee of the Budapest Ministry of Rail-ways who noticed something odd about one of the many claims for damages received after the crash. This request for com-pensation came from a forty-year-old Hungarian, Sylvestre Matuschka, living at Hofgasse 9, Vienna, who claimed in re-spect of facial injuries and loss of luggage. A perfectly normal application—except that Matuschka stated that he had been in the first carriage of the train. Knowing that all those in this carriage had been killed, the railway investigator passed the claim to the police.

Matuschka had already drawn attention to himself on the night of the tragedy, having called out to rescuers and asked for medical attention. Those who attended him found only the most superficial scratches on his face and, in view of the needs of the seriously injured, he was dealt with rather brusquely. Later, at an inn nearby, he told railway officials that he had been pulled out from under the ruins of a carriage in the front of the train.

Initially he was thought to be at best an exhibitionist, or at worst a cheat who was trying to collect compensation to which he was not entitled. Routine enquiries into his background, however, yielded some interesting facts. Matuschka was a man with many business interests, including a house-building society, timber firm, corn merchants and a delicatessen. He travelled quite a lot in Europe, but seldom told his wife, Irene, where he was going, or the nature of his business. It was established that he had been absent from home on the nights of both the wrecking attempts at Anzbach and had been in Berlin at the time of the Juterbog crash.

The Irishman who had been wrongly arrested was shown a selection of photographs and asked if there was a face he could recognise. He immediately picked out Matuschka as the 'baron' he had met in the cafe. Further identification came from a chemical factory at Wollersdorf, near Vienna, where Matuschka had bought explosive materials on 30th July and 3rd August.

In his pleasant suburban house, where he lived quietly and apparently happily with his wife and thirteen-year-old daughter, detectives found a map on which certain places were marked with dates in red ink. The wrecker had evidently planned one rail crash a month, the selected sites including places near Amsterdam, Paris, Marseilles and Ventimiglia (Italy).

It was clear that every detail of his activities had been planned with the greatest care. He had even bought a stone quarry near Vienna in which to test the explosive powers of his home-made bombs.

He was taken into custody and for ten days persisted in vehement denials. Then, quite suddenly, he admitted everything, and told detectives, 'I wrecked trains because I like to see people die. I like to hear them scream. I like to see them suffer.'

At his first trial in Vienna, where he was sentenced to six years' imprisonment for attempting to wreck two trains, he was said by a mental expert to be a sadist with a lust for power and sensation, but not insane. Other doctors who examined him decided that he was only able to obtain full sexual satisfaction when he saw trains crashing, and it was this overpowering need that drove him to perpetrate these crimes. Matuschka claimed that when he was a boy he had been perverted by a fairground hypnotist who had suggested train disasters to him.

He made no attempt to deny his crimes, either at his trial in Vienna or later in Budapest, where he was separately charged with the murder of each of those killed at Biatorbagy. He admitted he had watched that crash from some bushes, having fixed the dynamite to the rails after enjoying a gay evening with two English girls in Budapest. He had scratched his own face with a penknife to create the impression that he had been injured in the crash.

This extraordinary killer, who had been decorated for bravery as an Army officer in the First World War, did his best to confuse both courts as to his motives. In Vienna he claimed to be extremely pious—certainly he was a regular churchgoer—and said that he wanted to save the world from atheism. He was also motivated, he said, by a desire to draw the attention of the world to his many inventions, all of which would benefit mankind. He spoke of a project for making the Niagara Falls navigable and of others for balancing the adverse budget of the Austrian railways, relieving the world crisis by a 'gold inflation', and of a device which would make all rail travel absolutely safe!

He was sentenced in Vienna in June 1932, and had served more than a year in prison when he was extradited to Hungary for trial in Budapest on the greater charge.

Here he pleaded guilty but declared that he had acted under the irresistible influence of a spirit called Leo.

'Leo has never left me in peace,' he said. 'I have wanted to fight against evil all my life but there has always been a Leo to prevent me.'

He spoke of five people called Leo who had influenced him—including one who had prevented him from profiting by his inventions by forestalling him with patents, another who had hypnotised him, and a third who had used his evil influence to prevent Matuschka from fulfilling his ambition to become a priest. One Leo had influenced him for good, however—Pope Leo XIII.

He told the judge: 'I was upbraided by the spirit Leo for failing in my attempts to wreck the Austrian trains. I tried to shoot myself, but Leo caught the bullet and told me I must go on living in order to blow up trains. He was always with me on my journeys and said he would watch me throughout my enterprise.'

Matuschka did his best to convince the jury that he was insane.

Asked his profession, he replied, 'I am a professional wrecker of express trains.' To the question, 'Where were you born?' he retorted, 'I was born in a pair of pants.'

The infuriated judge shouted, 'Enough of this tripe!' Matuschka wagged a finger at him and said, 'What a shame that a Hungarian judge should use such a low expression. I really cannot allow it to continue.'

At another point in the trial the judge was questioning Matuschka when a pretty girl reporter entered the court. The accused man turned towards her, winking and waving.

'While I am speaking to you, you flirt with women—it is intolerable,' rebuked the judge, who ordered Matuschka to be taken to a cell until he had 'cooled off'.

After a trial which dragged on for weeks, Sylvestre Matuschka was sentenced to death and the sentence was later confirmed by the Supreme Court of Hungary. Matuschka, however, was not executed. His sentence was commuted by the Regent of Hungary to one of penal servitude for life in view of the fact that he was arrested on Austrian territory when capital punishment had been abolished in that country; he had in fact been extradited only on condition that he did not receive the death penalty.

It was 1935—four years after his greatest train disaster— before Matuschka began his life sentence. Ten years later, when the Second World War was still raging, he took advantage of the general confusion in Europe to escape from prison. He was never caught and has not been heard of since.

There is no doubt that Matuschka was a megalomaniac rather than a pervert, although the repetitive pattern of his crime may be associated with a recurrent sadistic sexualisation of destructiveness.

The essential feature of his crime was the destruction of trains containing people. His wish to be regarded as one of the victims indicates that the megalomaniac murderous action may have served to direct the killing from himself to others. Therefore in some way the mass murder could be regarded as part of a self-preservative urge. One can assume that the people in the train were mainly if not entirely unknown to him. To a child part of himself, these people involved in an exciting activity were targets for his envious attacks.

There seems to have been a profound psyche splitting between the family man with his teenage daughter and the ruthless criminal planner who worked out the mass killing with obsessional precision.

How he switched, he explained quite clearly. The 'fiend' Leo made a take-over bid, and temporarily subverted all his energy for a purely destructive purpose. The bad Leo seems to be the polarised bad aspect of father. Pope Leo XIIIth also had a good aspect.

Matuschka was a little before his time; a decade later he could have expressed the same kind of destructiveness in the Nazi death camps, or even in the war itself, and have been acclaimed for it.

Arguments about his sanity or insanity and his motives for pursuing his terrible occupation have continued to fascinate criminologists, but it may be that Matuschka was close to the truth when, at the end of his trial, he crossed himself and murmured, 'I am sorry for having done it, but I acted under some irresistible influence.'

Another sex murderer who claimed to be influenced by an alter ego was a young medical student who, just after the end of the Second World War, killed three people in Chicago. Matuschka spoke of his controller 'Leo'. The American youth maintained that all his crimes—he was charged with twenty-nine cases of assault and burglary in addition to the murders—were committed by an 'other self' called 'George'.

This young man, a brilliant student at the University of

Chicago, was William Heirens, aged eighteen at the time of his arrest. He was caught because he made too much noise burgling the flat of a family who were out of town. Neighbours called the police—who were mildly surprised at the tremendous resistance put up by Heirens when they tried to take him into custody. The explanation for his fight for freedom came from the finger-print department of the FBI in Washington—Heirens' prints matched those of a hitherto unidentified killer they had been seeking for six months.

In January 1946 a six-year-old child named Suzanne Degnan was sleeping peacefully in her bed in a Chicago apartment when she was snatched by an intruder who took her to a nearby basement to rape and kill her. The child's body had been dis-membered and the various parts dropped into sewers and man-holes. A ransom note demanding twenty thousand dollars was sent to the victim's parents, but was not followed up by the writer. There was a clear set of fingerprints on the note—matching those of Heirens the burglar.

The same prints had been found in the room of a nurse who had interrupted an intruder in her apartment in October 1945. She had made a remarkable recovery after the burglar had fractured her skull with an iron bar.

Heirens was charged with the murder of Suzanne and the assault on the nurse. While in custody he was given a 'truth drug' and under its influence confessed to two further murders.

Early in 1945 he had broken-into the apartment of Josephine Ross, a widow aged forty-three. He stabbed her in the throat and then strangled her by knotting her nightdress round her neck. In December of the same year he killed a thirty-three-year-old Wave (American equivalent of a British Wren) named Frances Brown. This woman was found dead in bed, having been raped and mutilated. Scrawled in lipstick on the wall above her body were the words, 'For God's sake catch me before I kill again. I cannot control myself.'

Heirens made no attempt to deny the murders or any of the assaults and burglaries and in September 1946 was sentenced to life imprisonment.

The murders represented the culmination of a life of crime started at the age of twelve. By the time he was thirteen Heirens had broken into at least a dozen houses or apartments and stolen a great deal of property, most of which he had thrown away immediately afterwards. He was sent to a corrective training school where he behaved so well that he was returned home after less than a year. Within weeks he committed more burglaries and was soon caught. This time he was sent to another correctional school for eighteen months. The first time he resorted to violence was when he attacked the nurse and from that point on he rapidly progressed to murder.

Heirens told doctors that all his crimes built up from the discovery that he could obtain sexual satisfaction by putting on women's panties. He had been stealing panties for this purpose since he was about eleven and had graduated from taking them from washing lines to breaking into houses to get them. Police officers who searched his home found forty pairs hidden in an attic.

Soon, he said, it was necessary for him to break into houses in order to experience orgasms and sometimes the sight of an open window was enough to excite him. He insisted that he had tried desperately to overcome this tendency, but that he suffered violent headaches when he resisted a burglary impulse.

He continued: 'George was always with me. I know he was in my mind, but he seemed real to me. When I committed a crime it seemed that George was doing it.'

Heirens, who was a handsome youth of good physique, said he murdered only when he had been disturbed during his nocturnal escapades. The child Suzanne had woken up and spoken to him and this had put him 'in a state of high tension' which could be relieved only by killing her.

The son of Roman Catholic parents, he had a strong religious background. Although always rather unsociable, he had never been shy or nervous, and psychiatrists who examined him said that he was of above average intelligence and not suffering from any psychosis.

It is highly probable that Heirens was shocked by what he

had to see as a medical student and that surgical horrors became associated in his mind with a pre-existent destructive murderous constellation.

The killing and dismembering of a six-year-old child makes it appear that he felt he was attacking a young sibling—his mother's other baby. It seems that females had to be murdered, and that Mrs Ross probably stood for his mother.

The wearing of women's panties suggests that he wanted to get 'inside' the woman and become her. Breaking-in seemed to be very important. 'George', whoever he stood for, was the split-off murderous figure, inside the mind of William and from time to time 'George' simply had to break loose into action.

2

The German Butchers

On a bleak, black night early in February 1929, fifty-year-old Frau Appelonia Kuehn was hurrying home along a lonely road in the Flingen district of Dusseldorf, Germany, when suddenly she became aware that someone was walking alongside her.

A pleasant male voice wished her 'good evening' . . . but before she had time to reply the stranger had grabbed her roughly by the lapels of her coat and stabbed her with a pair of scissors. Nobody heard her cries for help as her attacker ferociously plunged the scissors into her twenty-four times before leaving her lying by the roadside. The final stab snapped one blade of the scissors, leaving the point embedded in her back. Fortunately for Frau Kuehn another stranger passed that way and found her before she died. She was taken to hospital where doctors won the fight to save her life.

A few days later, on 9th February, workmen on a building site near St Vinzenz Church, Flingen, found the mutilated body of a nine-year-old girl, Rosa Ohliger, who had also suffered multiple stab-wounds. Rosa had been missing from home for three days. Although the child had not been raped, there had been some attempt at sexual assault and the body had been partially burned.

On 12th February of the same year a middle-aged mechanic named Rudolph Scheer was found dead in a ditch in the Dusseldorf suburb of Gerresheim. He had been stabbed twenty times —again apparently with scissors—as he had been making his rather unsteady way home after a bibulous evening with friends.

Dusseldorf's reign of terror had begun . . . .

Because the weapon and pattern of attack had been similar in all three cases, it was assumed that one man had been responsible for the three crimes. But what kind of creature would choose as victims, on three separate occasions, a man, a middle-aged woman and an innocent child? The police of Dusseldorf were forced to believe that they were hunting for a homicidal maniac who would kill indiscriminately whenever opportunity offered. Not one person in the city or suburbs, of any age or either sex, could be considered safe, and panic began to mount when it became obvious that there was not a single clue to the identity of the killer.

Agitation increased and criticism of the police intensified when on 2nd April, two months after the attack on Frau Kuehn, a sixteen-year-old girl, Erna Penning, was pursued by a man who threw a noose over her head. Fortunately she was a strong girl; she fought so fiercely and yelled so loudly that her attacker ran away. The next night her assailant was looking for another victim. A young married woman named Flake was lassoed from behind as she walked along a quiet road. She was dragged over rough ground into a field and would almost certainly have been killed had not a man and a woman heard her cries and run forward to investigate.

The attacker left the woman as soon as he saw the couple approaching and they were only able to tell the police that he seemed to be a young man because he was a very fast runner.

It was a very slight clue, but it was better than nothing. Living in the Dusseldorf area was a mentally retarded epileptic who was known to run away very quickly whenever anyone approached him in the street. Not very hopefully, detectives interviewed this young man, Johann Staussberg, and asked him if he knew anything of the attacks or the murders. Yes, he replied cheerfully. He claimed responsibility for all the crimes. He boasted that he was the 'Monster of Dusseldorf', as the newspapers had been quick to christen the maniac who had been terrorising the city. For good measure he also confessed to a number of cases of arson of barns and haystacks which had been

13

baffling the police in January 1929, just before the murderous attacks began.

It is doubtful if the police believed the whole of his story, but they were taking no chances. Staussberg was plainly unfit to stand trial, so he was committed to a mental hospital and kept under close guard.

'Monster confesses' ran the headlines, and the people of Dusseldorf, secure in the belief that the murderous attacker was safely under lock and key, began to enjoy their normal lives again.

For a while it seemed that the police hunch had been an inspired one and that the simple Staussberg, who had a hare lip and cleft palate in addition to his other disabilities, was in fact the 'Monster'. Then, after four months of freedom from fear, the whole area was thrown into a state approaching hysteria by a further series of murders and attempted murders.

Towards the end of August 1929, a young married woman named Mantel was stabbed in the back as she was walking home from a fair in the Dusseldorf suburb of Lierenfeld. She was not seriously hurt and immediately turned round in an attempt to identify her assailant, but all she saw was a figure running swiftly into the darkness. Less than twelve hours later there were two further stabbing incidents, one victim being a young girl, Anna Goldhausen, attacked from behind as she walked along a quiet street in the same suburb, and the other a man, Gustav Kornblum, stabbed in the back as he sat quietly in a Lierenfeld park. Both victims survived, but neither was able to give any description of their attacker.

The rising wave of terror reached its crescendo on 28th August when the bodies of two children, six-year-old Gertrud Hamacher and Louise Lenzen, aged fourteen, were found in an allotment near Dusseldorf. The little girls, who had last been seen two days earlier at a fair at Slehe, had been strangled and had their throats cut. They had not been sexually assaulted.

On 27th August, before the discovery of these murders, a young servant girl, Gertrude Schulte, was walking along a river bank on her way to a fair at Neuss, when she was approached by a man who persuaded her to go for a walk with him. When they reached a wood he tried to have sexual intercourse with her, but Gertrude told him that she would rather die than submit.

'Well, die, then!' he said quietly—and stabbed her fourteen times with a small knife.

The girl survived the attack and was able to give some sort of description of the man, but it was not very much help because she could only say that he had 'flaming' eyes and that she thought she was looking into the face of a devil.

Fraulein Schulte spent nearly six months in Dusseldorf Hospital. When she recovered she was given a job as typist in a police office in order that she should always be available when suspects were lined up for identification. This proved to be a clever move on the part of the police, because after saying 'No' to some dozens of men who were paraded before her during a period of three months, she eventually made a positive identification which helped to convict the 'Monster'.

But before that confrontation took place there were three more murders and a series of sadistic attacks on women and girls in the Dusseldorf area.

Early in September two cases of attempted strangulation were reported, in each case the young girl victim being approached from behind and left unconscious without a chance of seeing her assailant. A third girl was at first believed to have fractured her skull in a fall from her bicycle, until it was found that the wounds on her head were much more consistent with blows from a hammer.

Then at the end of September, a thirty-two-year-old domestic servant, Aida Reuter, failed to return from her Sunday afternoon walk. Her body was found next day in a meadow beside the Rhine just outside the city. There were thirteen separate marks of hammer blows on her head. Her knickers were missing and she had been raped.

Within ten days another servant girl, Elizabeth Dorrier, aged twenty-two, was battered to death by hammer blows as she walked along the banks of the River Dussel at Grafenberg. In this case there was no sign of sexual violation.

Frau Elizabeth Meurer, aged thirty-four, was walking alone on the outskirts of the city, on 25th October, when a man approached her and asked: 'May I accompany you on your way home, young lady?' She saw his face in the light of a car's headlamps and thought him 'a handsome young man'. In spite of the publicity given to the activities of the 'Monster', Frau Meurer was unafraid because the stranger was so pleasant and well spoken. She thought he was just making conversation on the number one news topic of the time when he pointed out that they were close to the spot where Rudolph Scheer had been murdered.

'Are you not afraid of being attacked?' asked her companion. Frau Meurer assured him that she was not nervous, but began to wonder when the man continued, 'There are no policemen here. They are drinking their beer in the public house far away.'

As she quickened her steps the woman said that her husband was coming to meet her and would doubtless soon appear. She felt some relief when the man dropped behind—and remembered no more until she regained consciousness in hospital some hours later. She had been hit on the head with a hammer.

Within a few hours of this attack another woman, a waitress named Wanders, was found unconscious in a park in the centre of Dusseldorf. She, too, had been struck several blows with a hammer.

The next victim was another child, Gertrud Albermann, aged five, who was reported missing from home on 7th November 1929. The following morning one of the Dusseldorf newspapers received a note stating that the child's body would be found 'by the Haniel Wall'. It was, in fact, lying among nettles and rubble beside a wall of Haniel and Luig's engineering works in Dusseldorf. The child had been strangled, then stabbed thirty-six times after death.

Accompanying this message to the newspaper was a sketch map which referred to 'the murder near Pappendell' (an estate about a mile from the city) and purported to show the burial site of another murder victim. No name was given, but the police recalled that on 11th August a domestic servant, Maria Hahn, had been reported missing and that shortly afterwards a farmer had found a woman's hat, a handbag and a bunch of keys near Pappendell. A first search of the area revealed nothing and this fact was duly reported in the newspapers. Next day a postcard arrived at the police station. 'Go on digging' was the cryptic message. The police returned to Pappendell and there, after five days, Maria's body was found buried under nearly six feet of heavy soil. She was completely naked, had been stabbed twenty times, and sexually assaulted both vaginally and anally.

It is not unusual for police and newspapers to receive anonymous letters during a murder enquiry and more than two hundred such communications had been received in Dusseldorf since the attacks began early in 1929. They increased in volume after the discovery of Maria Hahn's body, and although there was never any proof that the later communications were written by the 'Monster', they added to the alarm of the already terrified citizens.

'Drink blood to the next victim' was one message. 'Blood, blood, I must have blood' ran another. In a letter to one newspaper, the writer, referring to the women victims, said, 'All of them were honest girls. I only delivered their poor souls from poverty.' And another, posted early in December, 'Seek farther. Come sweet death. Blood! Blood! Blood! How happy the dead! Get the bodies. Death rejoices!' Later the anonymous correspondent announced that he would be transferring his activities to Berlin and that his first victim in that city would be the Chief of Police.

It was not long before almost any murder or attack, committed in any part of Germany, was being attributed to the 'Monster'. In Ratibor, an industrial town in Upper Silesia, a lad aged fifteen was found dead with a dagger wound beneath his heart, a tailor was similarly stabbed to death, a tradesman attacked with a knife and an old farm labourer killed by savage hammer blows to the skull. As the tension eased in Dusseldorf, so it mounted in Ratibor—until it was discovered that the boy had committed suicide and that three separate arrests had been made in connection with the other three crimes.

In Eschweiler, a town about forty miles from Dusseldorf, a young dressmaker was attacked and badly wounded with a hammer, a nineteen-year-old girl was found unconscious, bound and gagged, and an elderly woman reported that she had been accosted by a strange man who had attempted to stab her. Again the 'Monster' was blamed, and again all three incidents were quickly cleared up to the satisfaction of the local police. It was the same in Dortmund, where the body of a woman was found with her throat cut by a meat knife, but this murder, too, was proved to be unconnected with the Dusseldorf attacks.

As the months passed and the 'Monster' remained un-identified, panic spread beyond the frontiers of Germany to Holland, Belgium and Poland. In April 1930 a hospital nurse was stabbed to death and her girl companion attacked near Bennekom in Holland. There was terror in the town until a man—only just released from prison after serving a sentence for rape—was arrested for the crimes. An aunt of Gertrud Albermann, the last of the Dusseldorf child victims, received an unsigned letter describing, in revolting detail, the manner of the little girl's death. It bore the postmark 'Dortmund-Aachen-Express'. As Aachen is a border town between Germany and Belgium the Dusseldorf police feared that their quarry might have escaped across the frontier, and it was not long before any attack on anyone in Belgium was being attributed to the mass killer.

Poland was drawn into the net of fear when it was suggested that seven unsolved murders, all of girls between five and twenty years of age, committed in Warsaw in 1926, could have been the work of the Dusseldorf 'Monster'. If so, might he not return to Poland in search of fresh victims? The rumour that he was actually in Poland, ready to strike again, was strengthened by the news that teams of Polish police were searching the forests along the frontier.

Meanwhile in Dusseldorf the police were having to cope with something approaching mass hysteria. More than thirteen thousand letters had been received from members of the public, and the police had followed up 2,650 clues. Nine thousand people had been interviewed—many of them men who had been accused of being the Monster. The innocent actions of ordinary, law-abiding citizens were often misinterpreted. One evening in November 1929, not long after the murder of little Gertrud Albermann, some schoolboys noticed a man, accompanied by a child, walking towards allotments near the scene of Gertrud's killing. They told some labourers, who informed the police, and the man was taken to the police station for questioning. It was quickly established that the man was the child's father and that they were on their way home, but the crowd gathered outside the police station refused to believe this. The unfortunate man had to be smuggled out by a back entrance while hundreds of people filled the road at the front, shouting abuse at the police and threatening to lynch the man they believed to be the Monster.

Then there was the story of a mysterious deep-voiced woman, believed to be a man in disguise, who had been seen giving sweets to children—including Gertrud Albermann—on the day before she disappeared. As soon as this item of news appeared in the papers a woman called at the police station to explain that it was she who gave the sweets—for the innocent reason that she loved children and wanted them to like her. She allowed herself to be physically examined to prove that she was, in fact, a woman.

Edward Soermus, the internationally famed violinist, was the centre of another incident which showed the extent to which unreasoning panic had taken hold of the whole nation. On a very cold December night in 1929 he was driving near Cologne when he drew up at the side of the road and after walking briskly for a few yards in either direction, waved his arms vigorously to improve his circulation. A woman who saw him decided that he was about to attack her and ran swiftly to call the police. The unfortunate Mr Soermus was obliged to go to the police station and produce evidence to prove his identity.

Although popular opinion held that one man was responsible for all the murders and attacks in Dusseldorf, the police for some time believed that there were two or three killers at large. There was no pattern to the crimes. Most of the victims were women, but there was no connecting link. They were of all ages and came from different walks of life—unlike, say, the prostitute victims of Jack the Ripper, the never-caught mass murderer who terrorised London in 1888. There were also four children and one man. In some cases there had been rape or attempted rape, in others no sign of sexual violation. The weapon, too, had varied. Scissors, a stiletto, a hammer and a rope had all been used, and in one case at least the victim had died from manual strangulation.

Was it likely, asked the police, that one man had been responsible for such a variety of crimes?

In the last months of 1929 and early in 1930 a number of men were arrested in connection with the Dusseldorf attacks. A farm labourer who had worked at Pappendell and had been seen in the company of Maria Hahn shortly before she disappeared was arrested on suspicion in Berlin, but after hours of close questioning the police decided that he had no connection with that murder or of any of the other outrages.

In Czechoslovakia a chauffeur who was being detained on some minor charge was thought to bear a strong resemblance to the description given of the Dusseldorf killer and his handwriting was said to tally with the writing on the notes sent by the Monster to the newspapers. He was released when it was discovered that he had been in custody in Prague on another charge during the period of the first five murders.

A male dancer was arrested after a tip-off sent detectives to his house. There they found a series of macabre sketches, one showing the sorrowing mother of Gertrud Albermann looking at the mutilated body of her child and another depicting the dancer stabbing a girl. He, too, was proved to be unconnected with the crimes.

Two homosexuals came under suspicion because women's clothing was found at their homes and it was thought it might have belonged to some of the murder victims. Both men were obliged to confess that they often dressed in female attire.

A Czech butcher's assistant who had been charged with one of the Ratibor murders was closely questioned about the Dusseldorf crimes after a ticket collector at Ratibor railway station said he recognised him as having several times travelled from Dusseldorf. There was really little to link the two affairs. The butcher bore no resemblance to the description given of the Monster and spoke so little German that he could not have conversed, as the mass murderer did, with a number of his German victims.

So the hunt went on. Arrests were made and suspects released. Every tiny clue was followed. No hint, however nebulous, was ignored. But at the beginning of 1930 the police seemed no nearer to a solution of the crimes than they had been twelve months before.

Oddly enough, it was a former Scotland Yard man who made the most accurate prediction of the way in which the mystery would most probably be solved.

Ex-Chief Inspector Gough made his own investigations into the crimes on behalf of a British newspaper. Pointing out that the Dusseldorf police had no solid basis on which to build their enquiries, he commented:

'I have often said that the most successful detectives in such cases are Inspector Luck and Sergeant Chance. I do not see how any hope can be entertained of clearing up the mystery in the immediate future unless something occurs which is at present unforeseen.'

Inspector Gough was proved right. It was eventually pure chance, an unforeseeable stroke of luck, that led his Dusseldorf colleagues to the man they were seeking.

It was 14th May 1930. A girl named Maria Budlich travelled from her home in Cologne to Dusseldorf, where she was to take up a new job as housemaid. In view of the stories she had read about the Monster, Maria was nervous when her new employer failed to meet her at the railway station as arranged. She became even more apprehensive when a strange man, whom she thought looked rather sinister, tried hard to persuade her to let him be her guide. It was with some relief that she turned to a neatly dressed, softly spoken man who intervened when he heard her protesting.

'You are wise to be careful,' said this second man. He seemed so pleasant and respectable that she happily accepted his offer of refreshment at his home at 71, Mettmannerstrasse. Here he treated her with absolute propriety and she enjoyed a glass of milk and a ham sandwich before they set off together to find— as she thought—the home of her new employer.

Her first doubts came when, instead of taking her along the well-lighted roads, the man led her into the Grafenberger woods, but he assured her that the house she wanted was near the Wolf's Glen in the woods. As soon as they were out of sight of the road, the man grabbed her by the throat and attempted to have sexual intercourse with her standing up. She pleaded with him and he released her.

'Do you remember where I live?' he asked her.

'No,' replied Maria, 'I have not the slightest idea.'

That answer almost certainly saved her life. The man pushed her aside and ran away.

It did not occur to the somewhat simple Maria that she should have reported this incident to the police. Instead she wrote about it, in half-joking vein, to a woman friend. The letter was never delivered because Maria made an error in the address and the missive found its way to the dead-letter office. Here it was opened by an official, who immediately handed it over to the police.

Maria was soon traced and taken by detectives to Mettmannerstrasse. She could not remember the number of the house, but took the officers into one that looked similar. The landlady showed them rooms occupied by a lodger—and Maria immediately recognised the furnishings of the place in which she had enjoyed her milk and sandwich.

The lodger was a forty-seven-year-old factory labourer, Peter Kuerten, who on the face of it seemed an unlikely candidate for the title of Monster. He was known as a quiet, well-mannered man who, in spite of his menial job, took a great pride in his appearance. He looked younger than his years and was fussy about his appearance. He was apparently kind to his wife—a drab, bony woman of fifty who looked even older—and their landlady regarded them as ideal tenants. Too aloof and superior to be popular with his workmates, he was regarded by his employers as an unusually good workman with an intelligence far keener than the job required.

Could this be the man who had been terrorising the city?

The police, who still held the view that more than one killer was at large, thought it unlikely and believed that a charge of attempted rape against Maria Budlich was the most that could be proved against him.

He was taken into custody on this charge and, like every other man who had committed even the smallest misdemeanour during the year of the Monster, was asked if he had any knowledge of any of the murders or other attacks.

'Yes,' he replied. 'I am the man you want.'

He then confessed not only to the recorded crimes but to a number of other attacks in 1929 and 1930 of which the police had until then no knowledge. As this was by no means the first 'confession' the police had heard—there are always plenty of unbalanced people who like to put themselves in the limelight by confessing to crimes they have not committed—his lengthy statement was treated with some caution. It soon became clear, however, from details he was able to give, that he was responsible for at least some of the attacks.

Confirmation came from Gertrude Schulte, the girl who had been given a job at the police station after recovering from the attack on her life. She was called in from an outer office and confronted with Kuerten.

'Oh yes, oh dear yes, that's the man . . .' she cried, and fainted at the feet of the interrogating officer.

Kuerten was also positively identified by Frau Meurer, the

only other victim who had actually seen and spoken with her attacker.

While he was in custody awaiting trial Kuerten confessed to many more crimes. He told detectives that:

When he was nine years old he pushed a boy off a raft on the banks of the Rhine. A second boy jumped into the river to help his companion, but Kuerten held them both under the raft until they drowned.

In November 1899, when he was sixteen, he strangled a girl while having sexual intercourse with her in the Grafenberger woods.

In May 1913 he broke into a public house with the idea of robbery, but found a thirteen-year-old girl, Christine Klein, asleep in one of the bedrooms. He strangled her, cut her throat with a penknife and then sexually assaulted her. He dropped an initialled handkerchief, with the result that the child's uncle, Peter Klein, was arrested and charged with her murder. He was released for lack of evidence and was later killed in the First World War, many people still believing him guilty of the crime of which he was innocent.

In August 1929, Kuerten said, he strangled a girl he knew only as 'Anni' and pushed her body into the river.

In March 1930 he attacked a girl named Irma and threw her down a ravine near the Grafenberger woods.

Between 1925 and 1928 he had attempted to strangle four women.

Kuerten also admitted a number of frauds and robberies and about twenty cases of arson. He had set fire to barns and haystacks and two houses.

Some of these incidents were verified, others were not. Police records showed, however, that Kuerten had spent a number of years in prison—for fraud, theft, for attempting to shoot a girl with a rifle, for assaulting servant girls and for discharging firearms in a restaurant when a waiter tried to stop him accosting a woman.

There was such a complex mass of evidence to be sifted that it was nearly a year from the date of his arrest before Peter

24

Kuerten stood his trial at Dusseldorf in April 1931. He was charged with nine murders—Christine Klein in 1913 and the other eight in or near Dusseldorf between February and November 1929. There were seven other charges of attempted murder.

This incredible man—who asked for a shave, massage and manicure and a careful pressing of his best blue suit before he appeared in court—stood apparently unmoved as nearly two hundred witnesses gave evidence.

He stared straight at his seventy-one-year-old father as the old man, leaning heavily on a stick, described his son as 'a bad lad, spoiled by his mother'. There was not a flicker of emotion when he heard that one of his brothers and one of his sisters, called to give evidence, had refused to testify.

Something approaching interest showed on his face when the evidence of his wife, who had divorced him shortly after his arrest and did not attend his trial, was read in court.

Frau Kuerten said that during the seven years they had lived together she never suspected that her husband was leading a double life. He went frequently to church, was keenly interested in his trade union and preferred to work as a labourer rather than 'go on the dole'. He loved children and liked to romp and play games with the little ones in the neighbourhood. She had suspected, however, that he was 'intriguing' with other women and once, when she questioned him about this, he struck her. He then apologised and vowed never to strike her again. He kept his word.

On one occasion he had joked with her about the Dusseldorf murders, saying, 'The description of the criminal corresponds exactly with myself, with the exception that the murderer is said to be about thirty while I am already forty-six.' She added that her husband was something of a dandy, a rather vain man who used to make up his face with cosmetics before going out in the evenings.

When Frau Kuerten told her husband that the police had called at their apartment he took her for a walk along the river bank and told her that he had 'done everything'. She was stupefied and asked him, 'Did you also kill the children?' He replied, 'Yes, I felt I had to.' He then told her to keep his secret unless she wanted to meet the same fate as his victims. Afterwards they went into a café for a meal, but she was too upset to eat anything. Her husband ate her portion as well as his own.

The biggest sensation of the nine-day trial was caused by the accused man's own story of his life and crimes, given in such sickening detail that the public was excluded for part of the two days he spent in the witness box.

It is from that evidence, and from further information given to Professor Karl Berg, a leading German psychiatrist who came to know Peter Kuerten well during his time in prison and believed him to be an unusually truthful man, that this almost unbelievable saga of sex and sadism can be pieced together.

Peter was the third of a family of thirteen children and for a time the whole family lived in one room, so it is hardly surprising that the boy became sexually aware at a very early age. The father was a violent, boastful, heavy-drinking man, who served a term of imprisonment for the rape of one of his daughters. Peter also attempted incest with this girl and had sexual advances made to him by another of his sisters. It was not an uncommon occurrence for the father, after an evening out in the beer gardens, to force his wife to have intercourse with him in front of the whole family.

Living in the same tenement building was a man who rounded up strays for the dog pound. He taught the child Peter how to masturbate the dogs and the boy often watched him torturing the poor creatures. Soon after his twelfth birthday Peter was pestering schoolgirls to have intercourse with him and in his early teens he practised bestiality with farm animals. A later development of this perversion was to stab the beast as he was having intercourse with it.

Sex was closely involved, for him, with the suffering of animals, particularly if blood was shed. Kuerten told Professor Berg that the sight of a horse injured in a street accident precipitated his orgasm and that with the same object he had cut the head off a sleeping swan and drank the blood.

He had run away from home when he was eight years old, and 'lived rough' for some time. He returned, but left again when he was about fourteen. At that time he supported himself by robbery, and was first sent to prison when he was fifteen, serving two years for theft. During this and later periods of imprisonment he used to dream of killing 'to revenge himself on society', and found that his visions of violence sexually excited him.

Later he discovered that the sight of fire could have the same effect and he became an arsonist. He chose mainly to ignite barns and haystacks because he imagined that tramps were roasting to death in the flames—a fantasy that heightened his excitement.

Telling the court about the murders to which he had confessed, Kuerten said that even after the killings the bodies of his victims fascinated him and he often returned several times to gaze upon them, the sight of the blood giving him great sexual satisfaction. When the body of Aida Reuter was discovered he managed to get through the police cordon by posing as a Press photographer. He felt he had to see the corpse once more before it was taken away.

He said the reason he killed the two children Gertrude Hamacher and Louise Lenzen at the fair was because the display of fireworks had sexually aroused him.

'I asked the older girl to buy me some cigarettes,' he said. 'When she had gone I killed the younger. I killed the other girl when she returned with my cigarettes, then I went home and enjoyed my lunch.'

When he reached his description of the murder of Maria Hahn, Kuerten said that for a time he felt he could not kill 'this carefree girl on a starry night', but he eventually decided to do so.

'Afterwards everything was silent,' he continued. 'I sang and found my song wonderful. It was a beautiful night.'

He added that after he had buried this victim he thought of digging up her body and crucifying it on a tree, but found the girl was too heavy to lift. During the three months in which

27

the body remained undiscovered he often returned to her grave and masturbated over it.

In a final, impassioned plea for clemency, this monstrous man blamed his crimes on the influence of his early life and his experiences in prison.

'With what silent longing I often in my youth looked at other families and wished that all was so in my own,' he said. 'Every man has in his life a day which he regards as its happiest. I know such days only from hearsay, for I have never lived them.'

Any feeling of sympathy that this outburst might have engendered was destroyed, when he continued: 'I should like to say that many of my victims made things very easy for me, not merely by their willingness to go into the dark woods at night but also by their readiness to meet my wishes in other respects. Doubtless, many a one thought that I should become her bridegroom. The hunt for husbands has today become general and this cannot have good results. The pursuit of men by women has assumed many forms. . . .'

Kuerten took the hint when the presiding judge raised his hand as if to stop him and changing his tactics, went on: 'I am sorry for my victims, I am sorry for their relatives, I beg their forgiveness and I am ready to accept all the consequences of my deeds. The death penalty can only be executed once, but believe me, I have suffered that penalty a dozen times already in mind and soul.'

In conversations with Professor Berg the mass murderer confessed to a great admiration for Jack the Ripper and said that stories of the Ripper's crimes had fascinated him.

'If I had the means I would have killed whole masses of people,' he told the psychiatrist. 'The sex urge was always strong in me, particularly towards the last years. But it was increased by the deeds themselves. That was why I had to go out again and again to look for another victim.'

His wife was apparently the only person for whom he felt normal feelings of affection, but he told Professor Berg that he had to imagine sadistic violence in order to enjoy sexual intercourse with her.

The defence plea of insanity was not upheld by the many mental specialists who examined Kuerten. One of them, Professor Soili, said that neither Kuerten's brain nor his body showed any signs of organic defects. He had a vivid imagination and had only been able to commit so many crimes without detection because of his considerable intelligence.

Dr Raethert, director of a mental institution, described the killer as 'a man capable of remaining perfectly cool in difficult situations . . . a cruel egoist and a neurotic subject who desired to play a role'.

On 23rd April 1931, Peter Kuerten was sentenced to death nine times. After the announcement of the verdict his defending counsel said, 'This is surprising neither for me nor for Kuerten. We have had a long discussion on the matter and I have come to the conclusion that Kuerten wishes to accept the sentence. This declaration is not the result of an impulsive decision, but of serious reflection.'

Even so, there was for some time considerable doubt as to whether or not the death sentence would be carried out. At that time there was a Bill before the Reichstag recommending the abolition of the death penalty and the last execution in Germany had taken place in January 1928. Public opinion, however, was so strong that it was decided that Kuerten must die.

He was guillotined at Cologne in the early morning of 3rd July 1931, having so greatly enjoyed his last meal of wiener schnitzel, chips and white wine that he asked for second helpings.

London psychiatrists studying the pattern of murderers liken Ian Brady, the Moors killer, to Kuerten. Both men had an enormous appetite for killing.

Examining the Kuerten case in the context of advances made in psychiatric research they find the fact that Kuerten was able to have a reasonably normal sexual life with his wife somewhat baffling.

One of the most interesting psychiatric facets of Kuerten was the 'externalisation' of his panic. Doctors today see Kuerten as a perverse psychopath who experienced an internal panic which he discharged from his mind by creating panic among the people of Dusseldorf and district.

No killer is more dangerous than that of Kuerten's type, who experiences a sense of triumph from killing, delights in humiliating his victims, is sexually stimulated by the sight of blood and gratified by acts of mutilation.

Fortunately, persons with such an uncontrollable urge to murder without any desire to discriminate among their choice of victims are little short of unique.

Although the doubtful distinction of being the most wholesale sexual criminal of all time probably goes to Peter Kuerten, two of his own compatriots came very close to equalling the grisly record of the Monster of Dusseldorf.

One of them boasted that he was a greater sex killer than Britain's notorious Jack the Ripper, and was anxious that his self-styled title of 'best death-maker of Germany' should be included in the official court records. He was Rudolf Pleil, who had been a sailor, a waiter, a soldier in Hitler's army and a policeman in post-war Western Germany before he killed a salesman with an axe in 1947 and was sent to prison for twelve years for manslaughter.

While in jail he kept a diary which he titled *Mein Kampf* (My Struggle) in imitation of his erstwhile Fuehrer. But in Pleil's case the book was largely a record of sex murders he claimed to have committed. He signed the diary 'by Rudolf Pleil, death dealer (retired)' and arranged for it to be sold at about £1 a page to pay for his defence after he was charged with mass murder.

Much of the evidence was taken in camera when the nineteen-day trial was held in Brunswick in November 1950. Chief Justice Leuttich deciding to exclude the public 'for moral reasons'. Pleil, aged 26, a short, tubby man with a round, friendly face, was charged with the murders of nine women, but he repeatedly interrupted court proceedings with shouts of 'It is twenty-five . . . I had twenty-five victims but they can find only nine bodies . . . you underrate me. I am Germany's greatest killer. I put others, both here and abroad, to shame.'

All the crimes of which he was accused were committed in 1946 and early 1947 and the victims were refugee women trying to cross alone from East Germany into the Western zone. Pleil lay in wait for them and won their confidence by offering, as a policeman, to escort them to safety. He then raped them, robbed them and finally killed them, using variously hatchets, hammers, stones and knives. The identity of five of the women remained unknown.

One woman he attacked was lucky enough to live to tell her tale—Frau Lydia Schmidt, aged forty-five. She said in court, 'Pleil beat me over the head and did indescribable things to me. I pretended to be dead and managed to crawl away after he had left me.'

Peering benignly through his steel-rimmed spectacles, Pleil told the judge that his lust for murder dated from the time he was seven when he tortured and killed a cat. His first killing of a human being was, he claimed, accidental, but he found it very satisfying. His first chosen victim was a thirty-seven-year-old woman named Eva Miehe whom he killed in March 1946.

'I came up behind her with an axe and finished her with one blow,' he said. 'I did not rob her but found it very satisfactory. I threw her body into a canal. I never killed for material gain . . . it was necessary for my sexual satisfaction.'

Pleil described in detail the manner in which he ravished and murdered each of the twenty-five women he claimed had been his victims, continuing to protest vehemently every time the prosecuting counsel or the judge mentioned the nine charges of the indictment.

'No, not nine, it is twenty-five,' he insisted. 'Remember that I am the champion death-maker of all. I am allowed to kill because my conscience orders it. What I did is not such a great harm, with all these surplus women nowadays. Anyway, I had a good time.'

In his diary Pleil stated that he had wanted to be a professional hangman, and it was established that he had written to the Soviet Zone police for a job as executioner, saying that if they wanted proof of his qualifications they should look into a certain well. When they looked a strangled body was found in the well!

Continuing his story in court, this deceptively cherubic-looking little man said that his greatest sexual satisfaction had been achieved not by any one personal rape but by the sight of a number of dead bodies.

'A train with concentration-camp inmates was passing through the place where I worked in Saxony towards the end of the war,' he said. 'It stopped for a few hours. Those who had died of hunger during the last stages of the journey were stripped by the Gestapo and thrown into a special wagon. That was my finest sexual experience.'

Dr Gottfried Jungmichel, the court psychological expert, said he thought the decisive factor in Pleil's life had been his repeated failures in attempts to have sexual intercourse with a waitress when he was fourteen years old. Other medical witnesses testified that the accused man was sexually abnormal.

Pliel himself said that he committed the crimes while he was epileptically semi-conscious, but his plea was rejected as incompatible with the detailed descriptions he had given of how the murders were carried out.

Two accomplices were in the dock with Pleil. One, thirty-six-year-old Karl Hoffman, denied helping with six of the murders. The other, Konrad Schuessler, aged twenty-two, admitted participating in two killings and one attempted murder.

Pleil said he broke with Hoffman because the latter had insisted on cutting off the head of one of the victims.

'I told him it was a disgusting practice and refused to be connected with such behaviour,' he said. 'In any event, Hoffman and Schuessler have no right to kill. I am permitted because it is dictated by my most innermost feelings.'

All three men were found guilty and sentenced to life imprisonment. The judge told them, 'You have acted like beasts. Only the fact that I am not empowered to pass the death sentence saves you from hanging.'

Pleil was arrogant to the end. 'These stupid laws want to set me behind iron bars for the rest of my life,' he said to the judge. 'I am not going to put up with this, and will hang myself one day.'

He was as good as his word. He was found hanged in his prison cell in February 1958.

Just ten years after the Pleil affair, the exploits of another multiple sex killer aroused such strong feeling that the sentence of life imprisonment imposed on him resulted in agitation, albeit unsuccessful, for the restoration of the death penalty in West Germany.

Heinrich Pommerencke was tried at Freiberg, in October 1960, on four sex murder charges, twelve cases of attempted murder and twenty-one rapes, attempted rapes and other sexual assaults against women. The charge sheet, a hundred and thirty-seven pages long, also included indictments for robbery with violence, larceny and blackmail.

Like Kuerten and Pleil, he confessed to many more crimes than those with which he was charged, claiming to be the author of sixty-five assorted offences, many of them sexual assaults in the Black Forest. Looking younger than his twenty-three years, and with his fair hair, wide blue eyes, slight build and girlishly soft features, it was difficult to identify him with the man of whom the prosecutor said, 'Human language is inadequate to describe the horror and misery Pommerencke has brought to so many people.'

Dubbed by the German newspapers 'The Beast of the Black Forest', Pommerencke boasted that he had seduced his first girl when he was only ten. At the age of fifteen he used to wait outside the local dance hall in the village of Bentwich, near Rostock, where he then lived, to 'try his luck' with young girls. According to his own story, those who were not willing were knocked down and raped.

In 1953 he fled from Germany to Switzerland because he was afraid of being prosecuted for a sexual offence he had committed, but was deported from the latter country after

33

serving a prison sentence for another crime. From 1955 to 1957 he had lived in Hamburg, where he committed seven rapes before being sent to jail for robbery.

He attacked two English girls on holiday in Austria in the summer of 1958. They were saved from rape and possibly murder by other tourists who rushed to their help when they screamed. Pommerencke escaped in the general confusion.

He told the court, 'When I was a boy I never had a friend in the world. After a while I got the urge to assault females. I had a girl friend once, but we split up and I went back to my old ways. One night I went to the pictures to see *The Ten Commandments*. I saw women dancing round the Golden Calf and I thought they were a fickle lot. I knew I would have to kill.'

He went on to describe how, after leaving the cinema that night in 1959, he saw a girl, eighteen-year-old Hilde Knothe, and decided to kill her.

'She appealed to me,' he said. 'I had bought a razor and I followed her. I hit her and placed my hands around her throat, then dragged her into a park where I raped her and cut her throat.'

Questioned by prosecuting counsel. Pommerencke said that sex films made him 'so tense inside' that he felt he had to do something to a woman. A lust he could not control came over him.

On 1st June 1959 he again decided to commit murder. He had once worked as a steward on holiday trains and knew from his experience that 'trains were good places for doing the job'. So he bought a platform ticket and slipped into the rear carriage of a train bound from Germany to Italy. It was late at night and most of the passengers were sleeping. He walked along the train, peering into the compartments, until he saw a pretty girl student, Dagmar Klimek, who was asleep and alone.

He lay down close to the girl and was overcome with lust and the urge to kill. The girl awoke and ran from the compartment, and he thought she had gone to raise the alarm, so followed her into the corridor. When he realised that she had only gone to the lavatory he removed the bulb from the corridor light, and as she emerged in the darkness he opened a door and pushed her onto the track.

Pommerencke then ran along the corridor and pulled the communication cord two carriages ahead. As the train slowed he jumped clear and made his way back to his victim. It took him half an hour to reach the unconscious girl. He raped her as she lay beside the track, then stabbed her to death and walked away.

A week later he raped, stabbed and strangled an eighteen-year-old hairdresser in the Black Forest, and ten days afterwards similarly killed a girl student named Rita Waltersbacher.

Asked by Judge Friedrich Kaufmann why he had attacked and killed women, Pommerencke replied, 'Other men always had girl friends with them. I wanted a friend, too, but I never succeeded.'

Although the German police had been searching for more than a year for 'The Beast of the Black Forest', it was, ironically, a careless slip linking him with a non-sexual crime that led to Pommerencke's arrest.

In the summer of 1960 he went into a tailor's shop in Freiberg to enquire about a suit—he was a dapper young man and careful about his appearance—and mistakenly left a small parcel on the counter. The tailor felt the packet and thought it might contain a gun. Knowing that there had been an armed hold-up at a bank in the town the previous day, he informed the police.

The parcel did indeed contain a gun, and ballistics experts established that it matched the bullets fired in the raid. Pommerencke was traced and arrested. There was already a suspicion, from descriptions given by victims of sex assaults and by people who had been robbed, that many of the crimes had been committed by the same man. Questioned about the murders and rapes, the bank robber made a full confession.

Pommerencke differed from Kuerten and Pleil in one respect—he expressed regret for his actions.

'Everything I did was cruel and bestial,' he said in court. 'From the bottom of my heart I would like to undo all this.'

3

Menace in the Black-out

When several women are murdered in a specific area within a comparatively short space of time—and particularly if there is mutilation of the bodies—it seems inevitable that the old 'Jack the Ripper' tag should be attached to the killer.

Peter Kuerten was Germany's 'Ripper' before he was rechristened 'The Monster of Dusseldorf'. The man responsible for the slaughter of a number of prostitutes in London in 1964–5 also earned the 'Ripper' title—though he was later referred to as the 'Stripper', because all the bodies were nude. (That killer committed suicide before the police could arrest him.)

But one man whose crimes really did mirror those of the unidentified 'Ripper' was the slayer who created a minor panic in London during the Second World War. Like the Ripper killings of 1888, the crimes were confined to one small area of the Metropolis, most of the victims were women who walked alone after dark, and three of the bodies were savagely slashed.

Unlike the original Ripper, however, his twentieth-century counterpart made one mistake, and it was to lead him eventually to the hangman's noose.

The gruesome story began quietly enough early in the morning of 9th February 1942. A postman delivering letters in Montague Place, Marylebone, London, WI, noticed a bicycle lamp lying just inside the entrance to a brick air-raid shelter. Such lamps were highly prized in those blackout days and the postman stooped to pick up his find. He jumped back in horror as his hand brushed against the feet of a woman. The lamp illuminated the scene. A red and green knitted scarf was knotted tightly around the woman's neck.

Detective Chief Inspector Sydney Birch, Detective Inspector Percy Law, the Yard's top fingerprint expert, Chief Superintendent Fred Cherrill and a pathologist decided that the woman had been dead about eight hours. She had been manually strangled and the scarf twisted round her neck after death. Although her clothes had been disarranged there was no evidence of rape. Her empty handbag was found in nearby Wyndham Street, so it looked very much like another case of blackout robbery—a common enough crime in the days when all street lights and shop illuminations were banned—but one which had ended, perhaps accidentally, in murder, because the victim had fought too hard to foil the would-be bag snatcher.

The woman was quickly identified as Miss Evelyn Margaret Hamilton, aged 42, who until three months before her death had lived with her widowed mother and two sisters at Howlett Hall Road, Denton, Newcastle upon Tyne. She was a qualified chemist who had taken honours at Durham University and was known as a quiet, reserved woman with intellectual interests.

By one of those bitter tricks of fate, Miss Hamilton was only passing through London. She had been working at Hornchurch, Essex, and was on her way to Grimsby, Lincolnshire, to take up a new appointment. She had arrived at Baker Street station at 10 p.m. on 8th February and taken a taxi to a Marylebone boarding-house. There was not a vacant room, however, so she continued in the same taxi to the Three Arts Club in Gloucester Place, where she booked in for the night. She went out for a late supper and was only about thirty yards from the club on her way back when she was attacked, probably at about midnight.

It seemed to be a thoroughly nasty, but by no means remarkable, case of murder in the course of robbery. There was little to help the police in their investigations. The only fingerprints on the handbag, a powder compact and matchbox which had been turned out of the bag and left by the body, and the bicycle lamp, were those of Miss Hamilton.

The killer had left only one clue—the bruises on the dead woman's neck had been made by the strangler's left hand. The police were frankly not very optimistic about their chances of

37

tracing a left-handed killer who had struck unseen and disappeared into the sheltering blackness of wartime London, and it is doubtful if they would have done so had the murderer been content with one victim.

But Birch, Law and Cherrill had only just reached their offices the following morning, 10th February, when a call came through from Divisional Detective Inspector Gray at West End Central police station. A former Windmill Theatre showgirl, Mrs Evelyn Oatley, who was also known as Nita Ward, had been found dead that morning in her Wardour Street flat. Her naked body was spreadeagled across the divan bed. Her throat had been slit and a tin opener had been used on the lower part of her body in the way it would have been utilised to open a can. This weapon, covered in blood, lay near her body.

Mrs Oatley, a very pretty woman of thirty-five, had been married for six years to Harold Oatley, a poultry farmer living in Lyddesdale Avenue, Cleveleys, Blackpool. The couple had been separated for some time because Mrs Oatley had been bored by life in the provinces and felt she could be happy only in the West End of London.

On the evening before the discovery of her body, Mrs Oatley had been seen by a number of people in the West End of London. She was last noticed, accompanied by a young man with brown wavy hair, getting into a taxi near the Café Monico in Piccadilly Circus and asked to be driven to Wardour Street. Neighbours told the police that they heard a man's voice in the flat that night and thought that the radio was turned up to full volume.

There seemed nothing to connect this ghoulish killing with the murder and robbery of Evelyn Hamilton twenty-four hours previously—until Fred Cherrill got to work. On the handle of the tin opener which had been used to mutilate the body he found a set of fingerprints which did not belong to the dead woman. There was also an unidentified thumbprint on a small mirror found beside Mrs Oatley's opened handbag.

All these prints had been made by a left hand.

In the Fingerprint Department at Scotland Yard there were at that time the complete prints of about a million and a half convicted criminals. Those from the tin opener and the mirror were not among them. So again only one vague clue remained —that the murderer was a left-handed man who had no previous criminal record.

Three days later, on 13th February 1942, a woman living in a flat at Gosfield Street, near Tottenham Court Road, reported to the police that a neighbour, Mrs Margaret Campbell Lowe, had not been seen for some days. The neighbour was concerned because Mrs Lowe had not taken in a parcel left outside her flat and had failed to answer repeated knocks on the door.

When detectives forced the front door and entered the flat there was at first no sign of the missing woman. On the floor of the bedroom they saw a hat with a big feather—fashionable at the time—and on the bed, as if flung there in a hurry, there was a woman's skirt, sweater and coat. The bed was covered with a big black eiderdown—and under that covering lay the naked body of Margaret Lowe. She had been strangled with a much-darned silk stocking and, as in the case of Evelyn Oatley, had been viciously mutilated about the lower part of the body. A macabre selection of weapons that had apparently been used to satisfy the abnormal sexual lust of her killer were close beside the dead woman—a bread knife, two kitchen knives, a thin iron poker and a candle.

The seemingly innocent candle proved to be of the greatest interest to Fred Cherrill because the glass candlestick from which it had been taken bore some very clear finger impressions on its base. The prints on the candlestick had been made by fingers of a right hand. Cherrill deduced that if a left-handed person were to snatch the candle from its holder, he would steady the base with his right hand while he seized the candle, his main objective, with his left. A right-handed person would have used his right hand on the candle and his left on the holder.

A glass containing beer dregs and a nearly empty quart bottle of stout bore out Cherrill's suspicion that the left-handed killer had claimed yet another victim. Both revealed finger-prints and thumbprints of a left hand.

Margaret Lowe, who also called herself Peggy Campbell and was sometimes known simply as Pearl, was a tall, dark, good-looking woman in her early forties. Little was known about her except that she had owned a boarding-house in Southend, Essex, before the war and had given it up for what she had thought would be the gayer life of London.

The fingerprint team was still working in Mrs Lowe's flat when the doorbell rang. A uniformed policeman stood there with a message from Detective Superintendent George Yandell at Paddington.

Would they please go as quickly as possible to Sussex Gardens, W2—where yet another woman had been found dead.

Victim No. 4 was Mrs Doris Jouannet, a Newcastle woman married to a Parisian who was a naturalised British subject. Aged forty, she was tall, slim and elegant, with blonde hair and blue eyes.

The Jouannets had been married for six years, had at one time controlled a cafe at Cornfield Road, Eastbourne, Sussex, and later managed the Queen's Hotel, Farnborough, Hampshire. In January 1942 Mr Jouannet took over the managership of the Royal Court Hotel, Sloane Square, and he and his wife had moved into the Sussex Gardens flat only three weeks before her death.

Except when he was off duty, Mr Jouannet slept at the Royal Court, but usually went home for a few hours during the evening. His wife had a responsible job as manageress of another hotel, working during the day, but she was always home to cook supper for her husband.

Detectives soon discovered, however, that she rarely stayed in the flat after her husband returned to the Royal Court. Calling herself Doris Robinson, she joined in the night life of the West End, where there were always plenty of British and American servicemen looking for feminine company to brighten their time on leave.

Mr Jouannet had taken supper at home as usual on 12th

February, and his wife had walked a little way with him as he returned to work at about nine o'clock.

The following day, 13th February, he reached Sussex Gardens at 7 p.m. and was surprised to see the morning milk still on the doorstep. In the sitting-room the supper dishes from the previous night were unwashed and obviously untouched since the meal. There was no reply to his shouts of 'Doris!'—and the bedroom door was locked.

He called the police and they forced the door of the bedroom. This time there were no fingerprints, but there was little doubt that the left-handed killer had been at work yet again. Doris Jouannet was dead on the bed, her white-lined, quilted black satin dressing-gown flung open to reveal the sadistic slashing of the lower half of her body. On the floor was a blood-stained razor and round the woman's neck was a tightly knotted scarf.

Four women murdered within four days. The 'Ripper' headlines were inevitable. Three victims had been slashed, and all had been killed within a circumscribed area—the original Ripper had confined his vicious activities to a square mile of the East End, while the four 1942 crimes had been committed within a two-mile circle at the opposite end of the city.

The police were faced with what looked like a hopeless task. Although they had a number of matching fingerprints, they were not the prints of any known criminal—and it was hardly feasible to consider fingerprinting every man who had been in London during the vital four days.

Their greatest fear was that this vicious killer, having once given way to the perverted lust which might have been lying dormant within him for some time, would seek and find fresh victims before the police could track him down.

Fingerprints found at the scene of any recent crime of violence anywhere within the Greater London area were checked to see if they matched the murder prints. Comparisons were made with the prints of some quite unlikely candidates—drunks involved in public house brawls, men who had beaten their wives or ill-treated dogs. There was even a check with prints found in a public park—where the insignificant victim of brutality was a sad little tabby cat.

Nothing fitted. The killer was as little known after the fourth murder as he was after the first.

Then, a few days later, Mrs Greta Heywood, of Glenton Grove, Kingsbury, Middlesex, became engaged in conversation with a young airman in a Piccadilly brasserie where she was going to have a meal. A handsome man with thick, wavy brown hair, dark eyes and well shaped, rather full lips, he was charming, friendly and seemed to be lonely.

He asked if she would have a drink with him in a cocktail bar and Mrs Heywood agreed, on condition that she returned to the brasserie in time to meet a friend she was expecting shortly. They had their drink and were walking back towards the brasserie when the airman said, 'You must let me kiss you goodnight'. He drew her into the doorway of an air-raid shelter and put up his hands as if to hold her face while he kissed her. Then suddenly he grabbed her by the throat and she realised that she was losing consciousness.

Greta Heywood was lucky. Her gasp of terror was heard by a lad who was delivering wine to a nightclub, and the flash of a torch in the blackout sent the airman running swiftly down the street. The woman was unconscious by this time, but she recovered and reported the incident at Jermyn Street police station.

Officers who raced to the air-raid shelter found that the would-be strangler, in his haste to get away, had left behind his respirator—with his name, number and rank stamped inside.

Only two hours later another attack was reported. This time the victim was Mrs Catherine Mulcahy, also known as Kathleen King, who told Paddington police that a man who had accompanied her to her flat in Southwick Street, W2, had attempted to strangle her. She had kicked him and screamed so loudly that he had run from the flat, leaving his RAF belt behind. From Mrs Mulcahy's description, it seemed that he was the same airman who had tried to kill Mrs Heywood.

Chief Inspector Ted Greeno was in overall charge of the teams investigating the four murders. He decided that he would personally interview the dual attacker who had so obligingly left his name and number behind him. There was no reason to suppose that the airman had anything to do with the series of murders, but Greeno was taking no chances . . .

It was a simple matter to find the suspect—Aircraftman Gordon Frederick Cummins, aged twenty-eight, a married man billeted at St John's Wood, NW8.

Questioned by Greeno about the attack on Mrs Heywood the airman did not attempt to deny it, but said he had been accosted by the woman and had lost his temper and struck her when she demanded money. He had run away to avoid a scene. He said he knew nothing of the attack on Mrs Mulcahy.

It seemed a reasonable explanation and it could have been true. But Greeno noticed that when Cummins signed his written statement he did so with his left hand.

He was charged with assaulting Mrs Heywood and, as a matter of routine, his fingerprints were taken. His left little fingerprint matched that on the tin opener found by Mrs Oatley's body, his left thumbprint corresponded with that on the mirror from her handbag. His right fingerprints checked with those on the candlestick in Mrs Lowe's flat and the prints on the tumbler and bottle of stout had undoubtedly been made by his left hand.

Detectives searched his billet and found, among other property, a metal cigarette case which had belonged to Mrs Lowe, a fountain pen with the initials D. J., stolen from Mrs Jouannet, and a ration book taken from Evelyn Hamilton's handbag. Another link with Miss Hamilton was forged by samples of brick dust taken from the seams of Cummins' respirator case—identical in colour and constitution to a small scoop of dust from the air-raid shelter in which her body had been found.

Cummins was closely questioned about his movements during the week of the four murders—which he denied committing. He said that on the night of 8th February, when Miss

43

Hamilton was killed, he and another airman, named Johnson, had been drinking together in West End bars, and that they were both so drunk when they reached their billet that other airmen had to put them to bed. Johnson's story, however, was that Cummins did not turn up for the appointment they had previously made and he (Johnson) eventually went drinking alone. He found Cummins asleep in bed when he arrived back at the billet at six o'clock next morning.

Cummins then produced a leave pass which seemed to show that he was miles from London during the period of the other three murders. It was a clever move, but not quite clever enough. Tests under ultra-violet rays revealed the pass as a forgery—evidently prepared by Cummins in case the police should catch up with him and he needed an alibi.

At Bow Street Magistrates' Court, in March 1942, Gordon Cummins was committed for trial on charges of murdering Evelyn Hamilton, Evelyn Oatley, Margaret Lowe and Doris Jouannet, and attempting to murder Greta Heywood and Catherine Mulcahy. Although accused of those six crimes, he was tried at the Old Bailey a month later for one murder only—that of the first victim, Mrs Oatley.

There was little doubt of his guilt and the jury took only thirty-five minutes to return the inevitable verdict. Sentencing him to death, Mr Justice Asquith described the killing of Evelyn Oatley as 'a sexual murder of a ghoulish type'.

Some of the police officers involved in the case were not so certain that the murders were committed solely to satisfy an abnormal sexual appetite. While the hunt for the killer was going on they believed they were looking for a second Jack the Ripper, but they speculated later on the possibility that Cummins had mutilated his victims in order to create just that impression—hoping that their search for a sex maniac would lead them away from a man who killed for gain.

If Cummins was sexually abnormal then quite clearly he was anti-woman and the 'game'—the strange injuries he inflicted—was purely symbolic and token. He could have been a maniac, grandiose psychopath, in which case the homicidal

44

current of his mind would have been split off from an apparently normally functioning self—the self that could be married and live conventionally and happily.

His indulgence of this split-off, murderous part of himself would have stimulated his appetite for more killings.

But one question must remain unanswered. When confronted by the enormity of his crimes, did he then experience a feeling of guilt, then persecution and then anger with womankind so that to annul the guilt he killed another woman?

That is one of two alternative psychological explanations. The other is that a killing may have constituted an important split-off part of his sexuality as with the notorious 'Moors killer' Brady, whose sexuality was one of death and not of life.

If, on the other hand, robbery was his main objective, he was singularly unsuccessful. He is believed to have stolen about twenty pounds from Miss Hamilton and possibly another thirty pounds from the other five victims. The small items of personal property he took would have raised little more than five or ten pounds.

Certainly he needed money, for he maintained a curiously pathetic make-believe life in order to impress his friends. He called himself 'the Hon. Gordon Cummins' and often showed a photograph of a member of the House of Lords who, he claimed, was his father. This romantic story varied slightly. Sometimes Cummins was the legitimate son of a nobleman. On other occasions, with a wry smile he would admit to some slight irregularity of birth and say that his noble father made him a handsome allowance as compensation for the embarrassment of illegitimacy.

At one time he was billeted in Wiltshire, where he borrowed a horse from a farmer. He used to ride round the local inns, ostentatiously tying the horse outside before swaggering in and inviting all the locals to 'have one on me'.

He was known to his Air Force comrades as 'The Count' or 'The Duke', but his endless boasting—of his noble birth and his easy conquests of women—made him unpopular.

The truth about Gordon Cummins is that he was born at

New Eastwick, Yorkshire, and was the reasonably well educated son of the headmaster of a Home-Office-approved school. He trained as an industrial chemist and worked in a laboratory before joining the RAF in 1935, when he was twenty-one. He did well in the service, was recommended for a commission and at the time of the murders had just started training to become a Spitfire pilot.

In 1936 he had married a girl of his own age who was private secretary to a London theatrical producer, and there is no evidence that the marriage was other than happy. Certainly his attractive young wife, like his father, continued to believe in his innocence and made great efforts to save him from the gallows.

He appealed against conviction on the grounds that 'the verdict was against the weight of evidence', but the Lord Chief Justice, Mr Justice Humphreys, declared, 'There was no "scamping" of the evidence in this case.'

His appeal was dismissed on 8th June 1942. A last-minute attempt to save him was made by The People's Common Law Society, who sent a petition with 10,000 signatures to the Home Secretary, asking for the execution to be delayed so that new evidence might be examined. The Home Secretary replied that he had failed to find sufficient grounds to advise interference with the sentence.

He was hanged, during an air-raid, on 25th June 1942, with one question still unanswered: Did he kill for sex or money—or both?

4

Death Before Dishonour

It is a curious anomaly that the victims of sex killers are most likely to be either completely immoral or, conversely, highly virtuous women who will fight like tigresses to evade what used to be described in the pre-permissive days as the fate worse than death.

Prostitutes, by the very nature of their lives, are in constant danger of violence and are frequently the victims of sadistic assaults. Black eyes, smashed teeth and bruised bodies are their accepted occupational hazards, and because they attract perverts who cannot satisfy their abnormal lusts in any other way, these women stand a greater than average chance of finding an early place in the mortuary. A classic example is that of the unsolved 'Nudes Murders' case of 1964–5, when at least six prostitutes were choked to death during the course of excessively violent oral intercourse.

On the other side of the picture are those girls and women who, ironically, might have saved their own lives had they resisted rape with less vigour. Often the victims of such sexual assaults are killed only to silence their screams or because the very violence of their resistance further excites the already uninhibited passions of their attackers.

'I did not mean to kill her' is a plea frequently heard in such cases and it is probably sometimes true in that the original intention was rape and not murder. None the less, if a person intentionally commits an act likely to kill another and if death does in fact result from that act, then the perpetrator is legally guilty of homicide.

There was a spate of such cases during the Second World War. Families were separated, many girls were away from home

47

for the first time, moral standards relaxed, and there were enough so-called 'good-time girls' around to create the impression among often bored and frustrated servicemen that it was worth pursuing any woman who was out alone at night.

Two very similar cases occurred within a few weeks of each other in 1944, the victims each being strangled with their own scarves and their attackers both pleading that they had not intended to murder.

Late in the evening of 13th February Leading Aircraftwoman Iris Miriam Deeley, a twenty-one-year-old WAAF, left her parents' home at Blake Hall Road, Wanstead, E11, after weekend leave. Her fiancé, Pilot Officer Quill, kissed her goodnight at Bow Road Underground Station and she arrived at Lewisham, about four miles from her camp at Kidbrooke, shortly before midnight. There was no public transport to take her beyond this point, so she set out to walk and was accompanied part of the way by a Mrs MacGregor and this lady's brother. The trio was later joined by a young soldier, who continued to walk beside Miss Deeley after her other companions had gone their own way.

At 8.35 the following morning, St Valentine's Day, the girl's body was found on allotments in Sherard Road, near Well Hall railway station at Eltham, SE9. She was wearing only a shirt and pullover and had clearly put up a fierce fight before she was raped and then strangled with her Air Force scarf. Dr W. T. Milton, of West Mount Road, Eltham, estimated the time of death at between midnight and 2 a.m.

Detective Chief Inspector (later Detective Chief Superintendent) Ted Greeno, of Scotland Yard, organised an immediate hunt for the soldier who had been seen with Iris Deeley the previous night. He was traced ten days later— Gunner Ernest James Harmon Kemp, a deserter from the Royal Artillery, Woolwich. When arrested, this twenty-one-year-old soldier was wearing a Commando beret, with the badge of a physical training instructor, and had on his khaki uniform RAF wings and sergeant's stripes. He was also displaying ribbons of the Military Medal, 1914–18 war medals and South African war medals, and was carrying an American kitbag. Yet in spite of these obvious irregularities of uniform he had moved freely about London since the day of the murder without once being challenged.

There was little doubt that he was the killer. He had kept the dead girl's wallet, fountain pen and keys, and readily confessed to the murder.

'I put my hand over her mouth and pulled her to the ground,' he said. 'She tried to struggle, so I twisted her scarf round her neck and pulled it too tight. She went out . . . I felt her heart and found she was gone. I got the wind up and dragged her into the cabbages and left her there.'

At the Old Bailey trial in April 1944, Mr Justice Cassels said nobody could doubt that Miss Deeley met a violent death. Turning to the jury, he added, 'You may think she died after exerting all the resistance of which she was capable, probably in defence of her honour, possibly in defence of her life.'

Finding Kemp guilty of murder, the jury added a recommendation to mercy.

There was later an appeal against conviction on the ground that the judge had misdirected the jury as to the meaning and nature of the presumption that a person *intends* the natural consequences of his own acts. Mr F. H. Lawton, for Kemp, maintained that the judge had, in effect, told the jury to disregard the appellant's defence that he had pulled the scarf round the girl's neck to stop her from screaming or struggling and that he had no intention of causing her grievous bodily harm.

The Lord Chief Justice, dismissing the appeal, said that the judge had accurately stated the law to the jury and had properly left the question of guilt to them.

Ernest Kemp was hanged at Wandsworth in June 1944.

On 19th March of that year another girl was killed in almost identical circumstances in another part of the country. She was Gladys May Appleton, aged twenty-seven, who was walking to her home at Bishop's Road, St Helens, Lancashire, after spending the evening with her fiancé. She failed to arrive and early the following morning a postwoman found her body on the lawn of a house called The Elms in Cowley Hill Lane, St Helens. She too had been raped and most of her clothing ripped from her body. Her scarf was wound three times round her neck and the ends thrust into her mouth.

There was no clue to the identity of her killer, but in the course of house-to-house enquiries the police learned of an attempted assault on another woman earlier on the evening of the murder. A Mrs Galvin was approaching her own home in Gamble Avenue, St Helens, when she was accosted by a soldier who spoke with a pronounced Scottish accent. The man tried to kiss her, but she broke away and ran towards her front door. The soldier pursued her across some flower beds, but ran away when she shouted loudly—leaving on the soft earth footprints of square-toed size nine boots with metal plates on the heels.

Hundreds of soldiers' kits were examined and on 31st March a pair of boots which fitted exactly the footprints was found in the kitbag of eighteen-year-old John Gordon Davidson, a Scot stationed at a camp in the St Helens' area. Davidson admitted walking beside Mrs Galvin, but at first denied all knowledge of Gladys Appleton. He then began to cry and said, 'I did it . . . that poor girl—my God, what made me do it?'

He told detectives that he asked the girl to show him the way, pretending that he was lost.

'I took her in a gate and kissed her,' he continued. 'She did not like it and she struggled . . . I tore her clothes and I killed her.' When charged with murder, he replied, 'I did not mean to do it.'

At Manchester Assizes in May, defending counsel Mr Kenneth Burke pleaded that Davidson was drunk and was suffering from minor epilepsy at the time of the attack and that he was insane at the time, but the jury rejected this plea and found him guilty of murder.

The sentence was upheld by the Court of Appeal, Mr Justice Humphreys saying that the defence of insanity was unsupported by any evidence, medical or otherwise.

Davidson, whose home was at Kerse Road, Grangemouth, Stirlingshire, was hanged at Walton Jail.

'She cut up rough, so I bashed her', was the simple explanation given by Terence Casey, a twenty-two-year-old private in the RAMC who killed a woman at Putney, South West London, in the summer of 1943.

There was never any doubt about his guilt because he was actually seen attacking his victim and made no attempt to run away. Two air-raid wardens on patrol, hearing gasps and groans, shone their torches into the garden of a house in Gwendolen Road. They saw a man and a woman lying on the ground, apparently having sexual intercourse. Thinking the couple were probably drunk, the wardens signalled to a passing police patrol car. Mrs Bridget Nora Milton, an Irishwoman aged forty-five had been raped and strangled and was already dying when the officers ran into the garden.

As Casey was taken into custody, detectives pieced together the story leading up to the murder. The young soldier was on nine days' leave and had been staying with his brother Albert at Hannell Road, Fulham. On the evening of 13th July the two brothers and another man had visited several public houses and Terence Casey had drunk about twelve pints of beer. While they were in the Quill Tavern at Quill Lane, Putney, Mrs Milton—who lived at Cambalt Road, Putney, and was known locally as 'the little Irish lady'—slipped into the bar to buy a bottle of stout but stayed only a few minutes.

Terence Casey began chatting to one of the barmaids, Mrs Freda Gibbons, of Fanthorpe Road, Putney, and told her he would be waiting for her when she finished duty. Mrs Gibbons told him not to be so silly. As she left the public house at 11 p.m. she noticed a soldier hanging about outside, so decided to take a different route home and hurried away in the blackout before she could be identified.

A few minutes later Mrs Gibbons saw Bridget Milton and noticed a soldier following closely behind. No one knows exactly what happened after that, but it was suggested at

Casey's trial that in his befuddled drunken state he thought Mrs Milton was the barmaid and was determined to make love to her.

In a statement made to Detective Inspector A. Phillpott, Casey said that the woman started to scream and he put his hands round her throat to quieten her.

In an attempt to prove that the accused man was not responsible for his actions at the time of the murder, the jury at the Old Bailey trial in September 1943 were shown graphs of Casey's 'brain waves' as recorded on an electro encephalograph while he was in custody.

Dr J. D. N. Hill, chief of a London County Council neurosis centre, said that in the first tests, records of the waves given out by the brain showed an abnormality in its rhythm. It was then decided to carry out another test to examine Casey's brain in approximately its state on the night of the murder, when he had drunk twelve pints of beer. Consumption of large quantities of liquid induced epileptic-like behaviour among abnormal people, so Casey was given twelve pints of water at the rate of four pints an hour. This was approximately the rate at which he had consumed the beer. At the end of each hour he was taken for a few minutes' stroll to simulate the exercise he took in going from pub to pub.

After an hour had elapsed, said Dr Hill, the accused man's brain showed instability following three minutes' deep breathing. When he had drunk the twelve pints the instability was apparent after one and a quarter minutes' breathing. Dr Hill concluded that Casey had an abnormal brain predisposed to epileptic-like states of a kind which commonly led to aggressive crimes, and that the automatism began when the man entered the garden where the woman died and ended when he was found beside her.

He added: 'Yet these tests do not provide any evidence that he did not know what he was doing or that it was wrong.'

Referring to the 'brain waves' in his summing-up, Mr Justice Singleton commented: 'I daresay it shows a great advance in some ways, but if the medical witness who made the test thought the man knew what he was doing . . . are we very much further?'

The jury of ten men and two women decided that Casey had known what he was doing when he raped and killed the Irishwoman and found him guilty of murder, with a recommendation to mercy.

At the Court of Criminal Appeal in November, Mr Justice Charles said that the crime was plain, stark murder and the verdict a proper one. Casey was hanged at Wandsworth three weeks later.

Medical evidence ensured Casey's hanging because the abnormal electroencephalograph did not illustrate a defect of reasoning.

Without doubt the test did reveal that the murderer suffered from an undue lack of control.

At any stage in his life, he was liable to act out sexual and aggressive impulses and once again, as in so many similar cases, alcohol activated the impulses.

His excuse for murder was no more valid than those submitted by Kemp and Davidson. It is too easy for sexual killers to say, after they have murdered, that they really did not intend to take life.

The majority of murders in Britain are unpremeditated 'family' murders which occur during heated quarrels. Often the person who kills in these circumstances commits suicide before arrest, contacts the police at once and confesses to the crime or, when finally charged and committed, knows no peace of mind for the rest of his or her life.

But in a sexual killing, the death itself results from what is, at the very outset, an act that is as aggressive as that of a man who enters a bank with a loaded gun, to carry out a hold-up.

Only in a very few cases can legitimate medical evidence be produced to convince a jury that in such murders—those committed by the sexual offender, the mugger or the gunman—a state of insanity caused the guilty person to take life.

It is a matter of great regret that too many lawyers, finding themselves with nothing upon which to build a defence for their guilty clients, scratch around for some member of the medical profession who can be bamboozled into standing in the witness box to advance complex arguments about the prisoner's mental state that might confuse the jury.

One of the earlier victims of a wartime sex killer was an unusually attractive young WAAF corporal, Margaret Mary Rice, who had been married only a few weeks when she was sadistically raped and killed on her way back to billets after weekend leave with her husband.

The elder daughter of Mr L. W. Liell, a solicitor and magistrate of Wintory Park, Epping, Essex, twenty-four-year-old Margaret had been married at St Mary's Church, Loughton, in April 1942, to Second Lieutenant Patrick Rice of the Royal Artillery. She was stationed at Kenton RAF Camp, near Newcastle upon Tyne, and it was at her billet at The Uplands, Kenton, that she was joined by her husband on his forty-eight-hours' embarkation leave. The young couple left the house at 11.30 p.m. on Friday 12th June, and took a taxi to Newcastle railway station, where they sat in the refreshment room until Lieutenant Rice caught the 12.40 a.m. train to London.

He advised his wife to take a taxi for the four-mile journey back to her billet, but she said she would prefer to walk. She had often covered the distance on foot and thought on this occasion that it would help to take her mind off the worry and sadness of their separation.

Eight hours later a milkman, from his high seat on a delivery truck, glimpsed the legs of a woman in the grass at the edge of the Town Moor. The rest of her body was concealed behind some big emergency water pipes which had been laid ready to repair blitz damage in Claremont Road. The milkman jumped down to investigate. He found Margaret Rice, her skull smashed, her grey check suit and most of her WAAF issue underclothing torn from her battered body.

It was estimated that she had been killed between 1.15 and 2 a.m. Professor Louis Nickolls, of the Home Office Forensic Laboratory, who was staying as a guest at the home of Mr

F. J. Crawley, Chief Constable of Newcastle, examined the girl's body shortly after its discovery and gave his opinion that it had been disturbed about two hours after death.

There was some delay in the identification of the body because Mrs Rice's identity card and leave pass were missing and her wedding and engagement rings and personal trinkets had been stolen.

Detective Sergeant John Barrett, of Newcastle, in charge of enquiries, checked every service camp in the area, but no absentees were reported. A description of the dead girl was published in local newspapers, and it was then discovered that she had not been listed missing from camp because a sympathetic woman officer knew that Margaret's husband was on embarkation leave. She assumed that the young corporal had overstayed her leave and did not want to get her into trouble.

A few feet away from the body, police searchers discovered two ragged scraps of black vulcanite which a gunsmith said had come from the butt of an old-fashioned revolver. It was thought that the fracture to the skull could have been caused by the lanyard ring of such a weapon. When the drain grids in Claremont Road were removed it was found that the metal grilles underneath had trapped a silver bangle, one glove, a powder compact and other items which Patrick Rice identified as belonging to his wife.

It is not unusual for sex killers to implicate themselves by purporting to 'help' in the solving of their own crime, perhaps to gain some vicarious satisfaction by reliving the horror, possibly to enjoy the limelight of publicity, or even—who knows?—because subconsciously they want to be caught and punished. Neville Heath and Peter Manuel both tightened the net around themselves in this way, but one murderer who might never have come under suspicion had he not offered unsolicited assistance to the police was the man who killed pretty Mrs Rice.

While detectives were busy in Claremont Road they were approached by William Ambrose Collins, a twenty-one-year-old Merchant Navy apprentice who was on sick leave at his home in Framlington Place, no more than fifty yards from the murder scene. Collins volunteered the information that he had been in Claremont Road in the early hours of that morning and offered to make a statement regarding his movements.

At the police station later that day he told Chief Inspector Jake Smith that he had spent the evening with a friend who had given him a lift in his car to the corner of Claremont Road at about midnight. He had walked straight home and had not seen or heard anything.

Smith was not altogether satisfied and ordered a search of Collins' home. Under the pillow of his bed police officers found a revolver from which the vulcanite grip was missing. One complete part of the grip was discovered in another part of the room—and the pieces of black vulcanite recovered from the site of the murder were pieced together like a jigsaw to complete the grip.

Part of Collins' story was true. He *had* spent the evening with a friend, mainly in public houses, and he had had a great deal to drink. Some time before midnight the two men visited the railway station buffet for coffee and a snack and it was there that Collins first noticed Margaret Rice. He saw her again after he left his friend's car in Claremont Road.

'I do not know what happened,' he said. 'We had a bit of a struggle and I must have hit her with the gun. I took a bangle and a few odds and ends and then beat it. I shoved the things down a drain.'

He went home to bed but could not sleep, and felt he had to go back to Claremont Road to see if he had in fact killed his victim.

'I shone a torch on her . . . then I fainted . . . I must have stripped her. I took some rings off her fingers and I ran like hell. I put the rings down a drain . . .'

There were two theories for the seemingly motiveless theft and subsequent disposal of the girl's jewellery and other items. Collins might have hoped to deceive the police into believing the murder was incidental to robbery. Or, as John Barrett believed, he was a fetishist who took the trinkets for the perverted pleasure of possessing them as souvenirs of his crime—and, after keeping them for a little while, threw them away in a panic. There was some support for the theory of fetishism in the discovery of women's panties and brassières in Collins' bedroom. None of the underwear belonged to Mrs Rice and it might well have been stolen from clothes lines or taken as trophies of previous sexual adventures.

Collins gave no explanation. When told he would be charged with murder, he simply replied, 'There is something wrong with the charge because there was no aforethought.' At his trial at Newcastle Assizes in August 1942 it was pleaded in his defence that the frenzy with which his victim was attacked was due to temporary insanity caused by drink. The jury did not accept this plea and neither did the Appeal Court. Collins was executed at Durham Jail on 28th October that year.

The minds of sex killers were not so extensively understood by the medical profession thirty years ago as they are today.

For some reason which members of the medical profession do not yet understand, there has been a great escalation of all types of sexual offences despite the permissive age.

Hundreds of cases of 'pantie pinchers' are dealt with by magistrates every year. Most offenders steal underwear from clothes lines and are charged with theft. Most, on their first court appearance, are put on probation. Most, happily, even though they may repeat their offence, live out their lives without physically harming members of the community. But, regrettably, a small percentage 'escalate'.

As with those mentally disturbed but not insane men who become Peeping Toms, a time arrives when they can no longer contain their sexual aggression by simple fetishism. They then turn to sexual violence to gain satisfaction.

In the police file on Collins he is described as a fetishist but, of course, he was not insane. Collins was a pervert whose aim was to get possession of the coverings or belongings of a woman, a condition which today is recognised as entirely usual with such fetishists.

Once again during a sex murder trial at the Old Bailey in 1937 the jury raised the question: 'If, as the result of an intention to commit rape, a girl is killed—although there is no intention to kill her—is a man guilty of murder?'

Lord Hewart, then the Lord Chief Justice, replied, 'Yes, undoubtedly.'

An appeal was lodged on the grounds of misdirection, the defence maintaining that the answer to the jury's question was inadequate, but His Lordship's view was upheld and the appeal dismissed.

In most rape-and-murder cases the victim and her killer are unknown to each other, but in this instance they were well acquainted and had at one time enjoyed at least a romantic relationship. The girl, Ruby Keen, who lived in Plantation Road, Leighton Buzzard, Bedfordshire, was provokingly attractive and enjoyed using the powers of her charms on the many young men in her circle. When she was seventeen she met Leslie Stone, then eighteen, and for some months devoted most of her attention to this handsome young man, who lived in the nearby village of Heath and Reach.

Then Leslie joined the Army and, although they corresponded and met when he was on leave, Ruby's enthusiasm waned after he was posted to Hong Kong. There were plenty of other boy friends—including two or three policemen—and Ruby enjoyed quite a gay life until she became engaged to one of the police officers and decided to settle down.

She was making plans for a June wedding in 1937 when Stone reappeared on the scene, after an absence of five years. The couple met by chance in the town and Ruby agreed to spend an evening with him 'for the sake of old times'.

All the early magic returned for Leslie Stone as he sat with Ruby in the saloon bar of the Golden Bell Hotel in Leighton Buzzard on the evening of 11th April. He pleaded with her to forget her policeman and marry him instead. His insistent proposals and her 'we can still be friends' responses were overheard by a number of people in the hotel and by others at the Cross Keys public house they visited later in the evening.

They were seen walking together towards a secluded coppice of fir trees and it was there, not far from the Keens' home, that the girl's body was found early next morning. Her yellow dress had been ripped from neck to hem and she had been strangled with her black and white scarf. The disturbed state of the ground bore witness to the vigour with which Ruby had unsuccessfully attempted to resist rape.

Stone at first denied any knowledge of the attack, saying that he had left Ruby near her home only fifteen minutes after closing time at the public house. Later, faced with irrefutable forensic evidence linking him with the murder, he said that they had quarrelled and he had pulled her scarf round her neck. He did not think he had killed or badly injured her.

'I was in a kind of rage,' he said.

It was a rage that cost him his life. He was hanged at Pentonville on 13th August 1937.

Yet another girl who might well have saved her life had she not fought so vigorously to save her virtue was pretty Veronica Eleanor Foy, who was little more than a child when she was killed soon after midnight on 11th December 1960.

Veronica, aged fifteen, had gone with a friend, Pamela Cooksey, to a two-shilling Saturday night dance at the Palais de Danse, Barrow-in-Furness, Lancashire. The two girls enjoyed themselves and Veronica was seen by two other fifteen-year-olds, Carol Mowbray and June Beckman, still whirling gaily round the floor a few minutes before the dance ended at midnight. Veronica, a shop assistant, and fourteen-year-old Pamela both lived in Worcester Street, Barrow, but Pamela walked home alone because Veronica left the hall with a young man.

At 3.40 a.m. Mr Edward Foy reported his daughter missing.

An immediate police search was organised and within an hour the first clues were found—the girl's left shoe, one glove, a comb and some bloodstains, near an outhouse of Risedale County Secondary Modern School in Risedale Road. It did not take the police long to follow the trail to the girl's body. Part of a nylon stocking, pieces of underclothing and blue threads from a man's overcoat caught on some iron railings showed that her killer had carried Veronica's body 220 yards to a pond, partly covered with ice, in a public park. When she was pulled out of three feet of water it was clear that she had been raped and afterwards strangled with one of her stockings.

The picture of events was completed by a police constable who saw the girl and a young man going towards the school at 12.15 a.m., a youth who spoke of hearing voices from the out-house five minutes later, a cyclist who heard a girl screaming just before 12.30, and someone awakened by the quacking of ducks on the pond at 12.45.

There was little doubt about the identity of Veronica's escort. Seen and later identified by a number of witnesses, he was a butcher's assistant, Jack Colin Knight, aged twenty-one, who lived in Greengate Street, Barrow, and was engaged to be married to a girl in Plymouth, Devon. When first interviewed by Detective Inspector David Barr, Knight said, 'No, not me. I don't even know a girl of that name.' He could not explain how blood of the girl's group came to be on his clothing, nor the origin of recent scratches on his hands.

When charged with murder he admitted that he had lied, adding, 'I cannot remember much, but I'll tell you some things . . . I walked with Veronica into a school doorway and we both kissed. She pushed me away and I think I hit my head on the wall. I can't remember anything else until I was leaning on a tree near a fence round the park lake.'

He said he remembered passing a sandpit, then nothing else until he was near an hotel on his way home. He was 'puffed' and thought he must have been running. When he arrived home he made some coffee and then noticed a scratch on his hand which was bleeding. He washed his hands, put his shirt and pullover into some water, then went to bed.

In January 1961, at Lancaster Assizes, Jack Knight was sentenced to life imprisonment, the jury rejecting his plea that, having drunk fifteen or sixteen pints of beer at the dance, he had 'blacked out' and had no knowledge of the rape and murder.

It is very difficult to believe Knight's story that he could remember nothing of the rape and killing.

He was probably unaware, however, of the murderous component of himself which was stimulated into action by a combination of alcohol and the consequential bulk of fluid taken into the bloodstream.

In other similar cases—where a person commits a sexual crime, but not necessarily murder, while under the influence of a heavy alcoholic intake—the memory of the actual incident has never been completely eradicated. It remains in the mind, rather like an unrealistic bad dream.

Nobody knows precisely what happened on the night Flora Jane Gilligan was raped by an intruder who broke into her home—because the man who was accused of killing her after the assault never admitted that he was her assailant.

One thing is certain. Miss Gilligan, a spinster aged seventy-six, known as a woman of strict moral standards, would have resisted violation with all the strength she could muster. She was, in fact, unusually strong and active for her age and undoubtedly fought back with a vigour that must have surprised the intruder and may have led him to kill in order to quieten her.

It was a sex murder with a difference in several respects—not the least, apart from the age of the victim, being that the police at first thought it might be a case of accidental death or suicide.

Miss Gilligan, a retired cook, had lived alone in a terraced house in Diamond Street, York, since the death of her sister some years earlier. During the afternoon of 9th March 1953 she was seen by her next-door neighbours, Mr and Mrs George Laughton, taking in some washing from her clothes line. The following morning Mr Laughton found that the wooden shutter with which he covered his scullery window each night had been taken down and placed against the back door. He also noticed that Miss Gilligan's back bedroom window was wide open. It was not until three o'clock in the afternoon of 10th March that Mrs Laughton saw another open window at Miss Gilligan's house, this time on the ground floor. The weather was very cold and it was unusual for the old lady to let so much air into the house at that time of year, so Mrs Laughton decided to investigate. She peeped through a key-hole in a garden door and was horrified to see the naked body of her elderly neighbour spreadeagled on the flagstones of her back yard.

Police officers who arrived at the house soon afterwards were puzzled by a number of inconsistencies. Miss Gilligan had died from multiple injuries clearly caused by a twelve foot fall from the bedroom window. In the scullery downstairs all the shelves had been removed from the gas oven, possibly indicating the preliminaries to an attempt at suicide. Had the old lady planned to gas herself and then for some reason changed her mind and killed herself by jumping from the upper window?

The front of Miss Gilligan's hair was singed and there were signs of recent burning on a hearthrug in the living room. Had she rushed upstairs when a fire started and jumped in panic from the bedroom to the yard below?

Both theories seemed unlikely. If she had wanted to commit suicide—and there was no evidence that she was unhappy—the gas oven would have been the most likely way. The signs of fire were quite slight and there would have been nothing to prevent Miss Gilligan from walking out of her front door to summon help if she felt unable to deal with the outbreak.

But the most telling factor against such possibilities was the absolute certainty of all her neighbours and friends that she would never have walked around the house naked, whatever the weather, and would in no circumstances have removed her vest and nightdress as a preliminary to jumping from a window. She was a very modest and proper woman and such an action would have been quite out of character.

An added mystery was created by the discovery of her day clothes in her bedroom and her nightgown in the sitting-room below.

A pathological examination of her body provided the answer to some of the questions. The fall from the window had killed her, but she had first been raped and injuries to her throat and lips were the result of severe pressure. Detectives reconstructed the probable sequence of events.

A prowler had attempted to enter the house next door, but had found access difficult, so he had broken into Miss Gilligan's home. The old lady, already in bed, heard noises and had gone downstairs to investigate. She was attacked and raped, her nightclothes being left in the sitting-room, where they had been removed by her assailant. In an attempt to fake a suicide, the killer removed the shelves from the gas oven, but for some reason changed his mind, carried the injured woman upstairs and flung her out of the window. He then set fire to the hearthrug to make it look as if she had been running from an outbreak of fire, no doubt hoping that the flames would spread widely enough to give credence to this supposition.

He was not very successful as an incendiarist, for the fire died very quickly. He was careless in other ways, too, leaving a fingerprint on a brandy bottle and another on a bedroom door, as well as footprints made by army boots in the soil of a flower bed outside a window.

The police decided to check the fingerprints of all soldiers in camps in the area, going first to Strensall, six miles from York, from which personnel were frequently posted overseas. It was a lucky choice, because the prints found in the Diamond Street house matched those of Private Philip Henry, a twenty-five-year-old coloured man of Rathnew Avenue, Stockton-on-Tees, Durham, attached to the King's Own Yorkshire Light Infantry, stationed at Strensall.

By the time the prints were identified Henry was on board the troopship *Empire Halladale*, about to leave Liverpool for Hong Kong with a draft for Korea. Two hours before the ship sailed on 17th March, however, Henry was taken back to York by Detective Superintendent John Black and Detective Sergeant Neil Sutherland. He denied all knowledge of the crime, saying that he had never been to Diamond Street and did not know where it was.

There was plenty of evidence against him. The footprints outside the house had been made by boots recently repaired with distinctive toes and heels. This repair was identified by Mr Frederick Marley, of Stockton-on-Tees, who said the work had been done for Philip Henry, who was known to him. But when asked about the boots he had been wearing on the night of 9th–10th March the soldier said he had lost them in camp.

Detectives found a tiny splinter of pinewood, similar to the rotting wood of the bedroom window sill at Miss Gilligan's home, caught in the fabric of Henry's khaki shirt. The soldier lied about his movements. He said that on 9th March he had caught the last bus from York Railway station to Strensall, but it was established that he had not returned to camp until reveillé on 10th March, and soon afterwards was seen cleaning his uniform and washing his underclothes.

Henry stuck to his story when he stood in the dock at East Riding Assizes in June 1953, saying he had had nine pints of beer before boarding the bus back to camp. He did not remember the journey because he was drunk and ill and his next recollection was waking up in the camp cookhouse early next morning.

Asked by Mr G. R. Hinchcliffe, QC, for the Crown, how he could explain his fingerprints in Miss Gilligan's house, Henry replied, 'They were not mine.'

His appeal against conviction for murder failed and he was hanged at Leeds Jail in July 1953.

The motive was clearly sex and not robbery because money kept in the house had not been taken and there were no signs of a search. It is possible, when Henry tried first to enter the house next door, that something alerted him to the presence of a man on the premises and that he decided to investigate further until he found a woman living alone.

5

Con Man, Casanova—Killer

There was no reply when the young chambermaid knocked on the door of room No. 4 at the Pembridge Court Hotel, Notting Hill, London. The girl hesitated a few seconds, then opened the door quietly and peeped inside. The curtains were drawn across the windows, but in the shaded morning light she was able to see the outline of a figure under the coverings of one of the two beds. Not wishing to disturb a visitor who evidently wanted to sleep late, she closed the door and went about her duties in other rooms.

By two o'clock that afternoon of Friday 21st June 1946, there was some concern about the non-appearance of the occupant of room No. 4, and Mrs Alice Wyatt, who assisted her father-in-law in the management of the hotel, decided to investigate. She drew back the curtains and moved the bed-clothes a little from the shoulders of the figure in the bed. To her horror she saw the badly bruised and blood-flecked face of a woman who was quite plainly dead.

The room had been let on Sunday 16th June to a couple who registered as Lt-Colonel and Mrs N. G. C. Heath and gave their address as Black Hill Cottage, Romsey. The woman in the bed was not the girl who had called herself 'Mrs Heath'—and the mysterious 'Colonel' had disappeared.

Mrs Wyatt telephoned the police and the first officers to arrive at the hotel– Detective Inspector Shelley Symes and Sergeant Frederick Averill, both stationed at Notting Hill, and Detective Sergeant William Cramb, of Scotland Yard's photographic department—were left in no doubt that the woman had been murdered in a hideously ferocious and sadistic manner. When they pulled back the bedclothes they saw the weals of seventeen whiplashes across her naked body. The nipples had been practically bitten from her breasts and there were extensive genital injuries. Her ankles had been tied together with a man's handkerchief and there were marks on both wrists indicating that they too had been tied, probably behind her back. An attempt had been made to wash away the blood resulting from the injuries to her face, but some remained in her nostrils and eyelashes.

The second bed in the room had been roughly covered with the bedclothes, as if they had been pulled up hurriedly, and there were extensive blood stains under the coverings, suggesting that the victim had been attacked on one bed and had then been moved to the other. On the pillowcase of the second bed the detectives found criss-cross interlacing marks in blood that matched the whip marks on the woman's body.

Dr Keith Simpson, the pathologist, estimated the time of death at about midnight or the early hours of that morning. The woman, he said, had died from suffocation, possibly by having her face pressed into the pillow. All her injuries had been caused before death.

The victim of this barbarous attack was a woman named Margery Aimee Brownell Gardner, a creature of mystery who was well known in the so-called 'Chelsea set' of that period but was apparently without relatives or close friends. She was known to be married, but separated from her husband, and it is perhaps indicative of the lonely road she walked that she was not officially identified until five days after her death—and then by a solicitor from Sheffield who had not seen her for nearly a year.

Even her age was uncertain, but she was thought to be thirty-two. Certainly she was a strikingly handsome woman, with her finely chiselled Grecian nose, well-shaped mouth and arched eyebrows. She scorned the curly 'permed' styles fashionable just after the war and wore her long dark hair drawn smoothly back into a bun on the nape of her neck. Her unusually long, slender fingers were often adorned with heavy rings and she loved to wear earrings and wide, ornate bracelets.

66

She was an artist of some considerable talent and when she was not working as a film extra, earned a living as a freelance commercial illustrator.

Detectives also established that she was sexually promiscuous with a masochistic streak which made her a popular partner for certain types of deviates.

On the evening before her death, 20th June, Margery Gardner had spent some time at the Panama Club, Cromwell Place, South Kensington, where she had shared a table with a tall, fair-haired man. She exchanged a few friendly words with an acquaintance, Miss Winifred Humphrey, and was noticed by the club's receptionist, Solomon Joseph, as she and her companion left soon after midnight. Outside the club the couple hailed a taxi. The driver, Harold Harter, took them to Pembridge Gardens and saw them strolling—the man with his arm round Mrs Gardner's waist—towards the gate of the Pembridge Court Hotel.

All these people were able to give detectives a good description of the man—and it was clear that he was the visitor who had booked room No. 4 at the hotel.

From the police point of view this was merely corroborative evidence, for they were already sure they knew the identity of the murderer. Although he had in the past used a number of aliases, on this occasion he had obligingly signed the register in his true name—Neville George Cleveley Heath.

At this point Scotland Yard officers were faced with a terrible dilemma. Heath had to be found, and found quickly. All the evidence pointed to him as the killer, a man of such violent propensities that it was reasonable to assume him to be a sexual maniac. The surest way of finding him would be to publish his picture in the national newspapers. But if as a result of the publication of such photographs, Heath had been caught and put on trial for Mrs Gardner's murder, his defenders would be able to argue that he had been identified by witnesses as the companion of the murdered woman only because they had seen his picture in the papers. The police knew that in those circumstances any defence lawyer would destroy the identification evidence of Winifred Humphrey, taxi-driver Harter and Mr Joseph of the Panama Club.

The Yard officers had to make a tremendously difficult decision. If they authorised the publication of Heath's picture, would they see a sadistic murderer acquitted to kill again? Should they run this risk, or trust that the normal machinery of the law would catch up with him before he claimed another victim?

A compromise decision was made. Fleet Street newspapers were forbidden to print photographs of the hunted man, but were permitted to give his name and description and state that he was 'wanted for questioning', and pictures of Heath were sent to every police station in the country.

These measures were not enough. Twelve days after the first murder Heath killed an innocent girl whose life might well have been saved. There was a great deal of criticism of the police ban on the publication of his picture after the killing of Mrs Gardner, but many years later the decision was defended by Sir Ronald Howe, Assistant Commissioner (Crime) at Scotland Yard at the time of the murder, in an article in the American magazine *Saturday Evening Post*.

'In the light of after events, this may seem a difficult decision to take,' he wrote, 'but at the time I did not find it difficult, nor do I now think I was wrong. All we knew about Heath was that he had a criminal record for larceny, housebreaking and false pretences. There was no reason to believe he would kill again. He was not yet convicted of murder, nor is there, as far as I know, any previous record of a murderer of Heath's type committing another murder within a few days of his first crime.'

It is true that until the Gardner murder Heath, then aged twenty-nine, had no official record of violence or sexual crimes. It was not until his trial—in evidence introduced by his own counsel in an attempt to prove him insane—that mention was made of Heath's savage attack on a woman at the Strand Palace Hotel, London, earlier that same year. In that case the victim recovered from her injuries and, for reasons undisclosed, no charges were brought.

After the murder trial a number of stories were circulated which purported to show that Heath had been violent from an early age. He was said to have beaten an eight-year-old girl so severely that she needed hospital treatment, and that he had attempted to rape and choke a girl of fifteen. There were suggestions that he might have been involved in the murder of a young WAAF during the war and there was another story of a nurse who had been found dead in his burned-out car. The truth or otherwise of these rumours must remain a matter for speculation because nothing appeared on police records. Heath was known only as a man who had been in a good deal of trouble during his service career and as a civilian had faced a number of charges for fraud and theft, having twice been sent to borstal and several times fined or placed on probation. He was not entitled to call himself 'Lt-Colonel', or to use any of the other elevated service titles he assumed from time to time, having only reached the rank of captain.

As soon as his name and description appeared in the newspapers, a mass of information—all useless—flooded into police stations all over the country. Heath had been seen at an airport in Scotland, boarding a ship at Southampton, walking in the streets of Chichester . . . he was still in London, he had reached France, he was in places hundreds of miles apart at the same time. . . .

In fact, he left the Pembridge Court Hotel early in the morning of the murder, after having bathed, shaved and dressed, and took a taxi to the Grosvenor Hotel at Victoria. He asked for breakfast, but was told he was too early, so settled for some coffee before catching a train to Brighton from Victoria station. At a hotel facing the sea he ate a good breakfast of bacon and eggs, toast and marmalade, then took a stroll round the town before returning to the station and boarding a train for Worthing. Here he had a few drinks at a public house before telephoning a girl friend.

Pretty, dark-haired Yvonne Symonds had first met Heath only six days previously, at a dance in Chelsea on Saturday 15th June, but such was the man's overwhelming fascination that she had already agreed to marry him and regarded herself as unofficially engaged. There is no doubt that Neville Heath was unusually attractive to women—and understandably so. Well educated and intelligent, he had a man-of-the-world assurance and an air of distinction which was enhanced by the titles he assumed. Six feet tall, with muscular shoulders and slim hips, he had blond, crinkly hair and clear blue eyes. He might have been the prototype for any of the heroes of the popular romantic novels of that period.

So far as Miss Symonds was concerned, he certainly pursued the 'sweep-'em-off-their-feet' technique so often described in romantic fiction. After the dance, at which he was persistently attentive, he took her to the Panama Club for drinks before escorting her to the Overseas Club where she was staying. Early next morning he telephoned her, and during the course of a full and happy day he proposed marriage. On the understanding that they were unofficially engaged, the nineteen-year-old girl agreed to spend that night with him—and she was his companion when they booked into room No. 4 at the Pembridge Court Hotel as Lt-Colonel and Mrs Heath.

He treated her with tenderness and she returned quite happily to Worthing the following day. During the course of that week he telephoned her several times and told her he was anxious to meet her parents, so she was delighted when he rang on the following Friday morning and told her he was in Worthing. They lunched together and Heath booked a room for himself at the Ocean Hotel. The next day, Saturday, they met again in the morning and lunched together, after which Miss Symonds introduced her handsome 'fiancé' to her parents.

That evening Heath took her to the Blue Peter Club at Angmering and it was while they were dining that he asked her if she had read anything about the murder of Margery Gardner in London. Miss Symonds had been too concerned with her own romantic affairs to take any interest in sordid murder cases, and she was shocked when Heath told her that the woman had been killed in the very room that he and she had occupied such a short time previously.

Heath then told her an extraordinary story. He said he had lent his key to room No. 4 at the Pembridge Court Hotel to Mrs Gardner and a man friend and that he himself had slept in North London that night. In the morning, he said, he had been telephoned by Superintendent Thomas Barratt, of Scotland Yard, and the inspector had later taken him to Pembridge Court to see Mrs Gardner's body. Heath told Miss Symonds that it was 'a gruesome sight' and that a poker had been 'stuck up' the woman's body. He offered the opinion that the murder had been the work of a sexual maniac.

The story was entirely untrue. Heath had been in Worthing lunching with Miss Symonds before Mrs Gardner's body was discovered, Superintendent Barratt was not called to the hotel until four o'clock in the afternoon, so far from accompanying Heath to see the body, Barratt was taking all steps to ensure that Heath was found as soon as possible.

There was no poker in room No. 4 and it was later deduced, although never definitely established, that the victim's genital injuries had been caused by the steel-tipped whip which had also been used to lash the body.

Yvonne Symonds was naturally concerned about Heath's involvement in this tragic affair, but it did not occur to her to doubt his story and the couple parted on affectionate terms after he had escorted her home later that night.

It was not until the following morning, when she read in the Sunday newspapers that the police were looking for Heath, that the first awful doubts began to creep into her mind. She telephoned Heath and told him that her parents were rather worried by the news in the papers.

'Yes,' he said, 'I was afraid they would be.'

He was jauntily reassuring, however. He said he had hired a car and was going up to London to sort things out, and promised to telephone her that evening.

Fortunately for this unhappy girl she did not see Neville Heath again until he stood in the dock on a charge of murder.

On Monday 24th June the following letter, postmarked

Worthing, 5.45 p.m., 23rd June 1946, addressed to Superintendent Barratt, arrived at Scotland Yard:

'Sir,

'I feel it to be my duty to inform you of certain facts in connection with the death of Mrs Gardner at Notting Hill Gate. I booked in at the hotel last Sunday, but not with Mrs Gardner, whom I met for the first time during the week. I had drinks with her on Friday evening, and whilst I was with her she met an acquaintance with whom she was obliged to sleep. The reasons, as I understand them, were mainly financial. It was then that Mrs Gardner asked if she could use my hotel room until two o'clock and intimated that if I returned after that, I might spend the remainder of the night with her. I gave her my keys and told her to leave the hotel door open. It must have been almost 3 a.m. when I returned to the hotel and found her in the condition of which you are aware. I realised that I was in an invidious position, and rather than notify the police, I packed my belongings and left. Since then I have been in several minds whether to come forward or not, but in view of the circumstances I have been afraid to. I can give you a description of the man. He was aged approximately 30, dark hair (black) with small moustache. Height about 5′ 9″ slim build. His name was Jack and I gathered that he was a friend of Mrs Gardner of some long standing. The personal column of the Daily Telegraph will find me, but at the moment I have assumed another name. I should like to come forward and help, but I cannot face the music of a fraud charge which will obviously be preferred against me if I should do so. I have the instrument with which Mrs Gardner was beaten and am forwarding this to you to-day. You will find my fingerprints on it, but you should find others as well.

'N. G. C. Heath.'

The instrument to which Heath referred was not sent to Scotland Yard and when eventually it was found it had been cleaned of all fingerprints.

Soon after posting this letter Heath left Worthing, arriving later the same evening at the Tollard Royal Hotel on the West Cliff at Bournemouth. It is perhaps indicative of his own unreal picture of himself that he registered in the name of Rupert Brooke, the romantically handsome and tragic poet who died on active service in the First World War. He could not resist adding the embellishment 'Group Captain' to the name.

Heath was given room No. 71, but four days later he asked for a room with a gas fire and was moved to room No. 81. It was later suggested that he wanted a gas fire because he intended to commit suicide, but he showed no sign of depression during his stay at the hotel. The handsome and charming 'Group Captain' soon became popular with the other guests and joined freely in their social activities. He was also on friendly terms with the staff, making a point of engaging them in conversation. Apart from using an assumed name, he made no attempt to disguise himself.

On the afternoon of Wednesday 3rd July he was strolling along the promenade when he saw two girls, one of whom he had previously met at a dance. She introduced him—'Group Captain Brooke, staying at the Tollard Royal' to her companion, Miss Doreen Marshall. There seems to have been an immediate mutual attraction between Heath and Miss Marshall because within a short while she had accepted his invitation to tea at his hotel. It was a very 'proper' arrangement—tea in one of the public rooms of an hotel, with the good-looking young man showing just the right degree of flattering interest, so that the girl had no reason to decline his further invitation to dinner that evening.

Doreen Marshall was a pretty, soft-featured, wavy-haired brunette, aged twenty-one, recently demobilised from the WRNS. Because she had been ill with influenza and measles, she had been sent by her father, Mr Charles Marshall, of Woodhall Drive, Pinner, to recuperate at the four-star Norfolk Hotel, Bournemouth. By the time she met Heath she had been staying alone at the hotel for five days and probably welcomed the idea of an evening out in the company of such an apparently suitable young man.

After tea she went back to the Norfolk to bath and change, then returned to the Tollard Royal by taxi in time for dinner. Other guests noticed the attractive couple chatting happily during the meal and in the public lounge afterwards. At about 11.20 p.m. they were joined by some other guests, including Mrs Gladys Phillips, on holiday from Cardiff.

Mrs Phillips thought that 'Group Captain Brooke' had been drinking rather a lot and noticed that Miss Marshall looked pale and tired, so she was not surprised when the girl asked Mr Phillips to call a taxi to take her back to her hotel. Mr Phillips arranged this with the night porter before he and his wife went upstairs to their room. When the cab arrived, however, Heath told the night porter, Fred Wilkinson, that they did not need it because Miss Marshall had decided to walk.

'I shall be back in half an hour,' said Heath, but Miss Marshall corrected him with 'No, in quarter of an hour.'

Nobody knows what time Heath did, in fact, return to the hotel because instead of entering by the front door he went round to the back and climbed a ladder, left by workmen, to enter his second-floor room through the window. At 4.30 a.m. the night porter peeped into Heath's room and saw him soundly asleep. The next day Heath told Mr Ivor Relf, joint manager of the hotel, of his unconventional method of entry, saying that he had done it 'as a joke' to confuse the night porter.

At eight o'clock that morning Fred Wilkinson went to room No. 81 with the daily papers and found Heath still asleep. He roused the visitor, who seemed his normal cheerful self. No one, in fact, noticed any difference in Heath's demeanour that day. He mixed as usual with the other guests and made his customary amiable remarks to members of the hotel staff.

On the morning of Friday 5th July the manager of the Norfolk Hotel telephoned Mr Relf at the Tollard Royal to say that a young lady guest was missing from his hotel and that she was believed to have dined at the Tollard on the Wednesday evening. Mr Relf mentioned this to Heath and asked if his guest had been a Miss Marshall from Pinner.

'Oh no,' replied Heath. 'I have known the lady for a long while and she certainly does not come from Pinner.'

Heath then took the extraordinary course of telephoning the local police station on Saturday 6th July and asking if they had a photograph of the missing girl so that he could say definitely whether or not she was the young lady with whom he had dined. He was told that no picture was at that time available, so offered to telephone again later. This he did, and at 5.30 that evening he went, quite voluntarily, to Bournemouth police station to meet Doreen Marshall's father and sister, who had travelled down from London as soon as they learned that Doreen was missing.

Mr Joshua Casswell, QC, who led the defence for Heath at his subsequent trial, said in his memoirs many years later that he believed this direct approach to the police—like the letter Heath wrote to Superintendent Barratt after the killing of Margery Gardner—was prompted by a desire to be caught. He was convinced that Heath wanted to be hanged.

Certainly he walked straight into the arms of the law. He must have known that every police station in Britain had his description and picture and could hardly have been surprised when Detective Constable Souter, whom he saw when he first entered Bournemouth police station, recognised him and challenged him as Neville Heath.

Heath insisted that his name was Rupert Brooke, but Souter detained him at the police station, and an hour later, when Detective Inspector George Gates arrived, Heath was ready to admit his true identity. That evening he was told that officers of the Metropolitan Police were on their way to interview him in connection with the murder of Margery Gardner, and Heath replied, 'Oh, all right.'

When he was asked about his association with Doreen Marshall, Heath agreed that she was the girl with whom he had spent part of the afternoon and the evening of 3rd July. He said that after leaving his hotel they sat on a seat overlooking the sea and talked for about an hour. They then walked down the slope towards the Pavilion and he accompanied her as far

75

as the pier, where they said 'good night' and he watched her cross the road.

'I asked her if she would come round the following day,' said Heath, 'but she said she would be busy for the next few days and would telephone me on Sunday if she could manage it. I have not seen her to speak to since then although I thought I saw her entering Bobby's [a department store] on Thursday morning.'

While Heath was at the police station he complained of the cold and asked if he could return to the Tollard Royal to collect his jacket. Needless to say, this request was refused. Detective Inspector Gates picked up the jacket, and found in the pockets three significant items. One was the return half of the first-class London–Bournemouth railway ticket issued to Doreen Marshall; the second was a cloakroom ticket for a suitcase deposited at Bournemouth West station; and the third was a single artificial pearl.

Among clothing in the suitcase, which was collected by detectives, was a square blue handkerchief scarf and a blue woollen scarf, both heavily stained with blood, and a steel-tipped riding whip which Heath had NOT sent to Superintendent Tom Barratt.

The importance of the single pearl bead did not become apparent until Monday 8th July, when twenty-seven matching beads were found scattered among the bushes in Branksome Chine—part of the gruesome scene uncovered when a girl out walking with her dog noticed a swarm of flies persistently buzzing around one particular section of the copse. Behind some rhododendrons, and further concealed by the broken branch of a fir tree, lay the shattered body of Doreen Marshall. It was naked except for one shoe, but had been roughly covered with the girl's own clothing. Her powder compact and blood-stained stockings were found several feet away from the body and some time later her pocket knife was uncovered on the beach by Miss Patricia Howe, a holidaymaker.

As in the case of Margery Gardner, there was evidence of a sadistic attack, one nipple having been bitten from the breast, the genitals savagely injured by some rough instrument, and the rest of the front of the body deeply cut several times.

Mr Crichton McGaffey, the pathologist who examined the body, said that these injuries had been inflicted after death, which had resulted from knife cuts to the throat. There were signs that the victim's wrists had been tied together, and one of the exhibits produced at Heath's trial was a knotted handkerchief, soiled with blood and earth, which was found in his hotel bedroom by Divisional Detective Inspector Reginald Spooner, from Notting Hill police station, who was in charge of enquiries into the killing of Mrs Gardner.

If further evidence against Heath on this second murder was needed it was provided by a crystal fob watch and a dress ring, both belonging to Doreen Marshall, and sold by Heath to two different jewellers in Bournemouth on the day following her disappearance.

He was charged with both murders—though he subsequently stood trial at the Old Bailey only on a charge of killing Margery Gardner—and was visited by Mr Casswell while on remand at Brixton Jail. Asked by Casswell if he wished to give evidence in court, Heath replied, 'Oh hell, why shouldn't I plead guilty?' When it was pointed out that his parents and younger brother would suffer even greater shame and pain if he admitted that he had killed two women in such a manner while he was in his right mind. Heath hesitated for a second, then shrugged and nodded.

'All right,' he said, 'put me down as not guilty, old boy.'

When the handsome young ex-airman stood before Mr Justice Morris at the Central Criminal Court in September 1946, the only real issue to be decided was whether or not he was sane. The facts of the case were never in any real doubt and it was in an attempt to show that Heath was not responsible for his actions that his defence counsel took the unusual step of telling the jury about the second murder, arguing that no man in his right mind would, without attempting to disguise himself, deliberately savage a second victim when he knew that the police of every county in England were looking for him in connection with the first killing.

Mr Casswell invited the jury to 'step back out of the wood of detail' and look at the case from a distance.

'Say to yourselves perhaps what you said when you first heard of the two terrible crimes committed within a fortnight,' he said. 'What did you say? That the man must be mad? Can you have come to any other conclusion? Can you believe that a man who was merely a brutal sensualist, a mere sadist, was capable of those things? Remember those awful injuries of which you have been told. Picture the scene. Was that the work of an ordinary criminal? Surely that man at that time was as mad as a hatter, absolutely insane, a maniac. Can he have been anything else?'

The chief witness for the defence was Dr William de Bargue Hubert, who for five years was the psychotherapist at Wormwood Scrubs, and was part author of a psychological study of the prevention of crime which was presented to the Home Secretary in 1938. This witness, who had also worked at Broadmoor and at Feltham Prison, expressed the opinion that Heath was not an ordinary sexual pervert, but was suffering from moral insanity and was at times quite unaware that he was doing wrong. He believed Heath to be certifiable as morally insane.

Heath himself appeared to object to this classification because during Dr Hubert's evidence he passed this note to Mr Casswell:

'It may be of interest to know that in my discussions with Hubert I have never suggested that I should be excused or that I told him I felt I should be because of insanity. This evidence is Hubert's opinion—not what I have suggested he say on my behalf.'

Heath need not have worried. Dr Hubert—who six months after this trial was found dead from an overdose of drugs—was unconvincing under cross-examination by Mr Anthony Hawke, who led for the prosecution.

'May I take it that at the time Heath murdered Margery

Gardner he knew that he was doing something that was wrong?'
asked Mr Hawke.

'No,' replied Dr Hubert.

He knew he had bound and tied a young woman lying on a
bed?—Yes.

He knew when he inflicted seventeen lashes upon her with a
thong that he was inflicting seventeen lashes with a thong?—
Yes.

He knew those things, but did not know they were wrong?—
He knew the consequences.

When he suffocated that woman, lashed her, having tied her
up and made her helpless first, he knew it was wrong?—No.

Would you tell me why?—Because people during sexual
behaviour generally consider what they are doing is right and
their own business.

Because he could only satisfy his sexual appetite by inflicting
cruelty, you say that he thought it was right to inflict it, do you?
—Well, he was doing what he wished to do.

The medical witnesses called by the prosecution were positive
in their opinions that Heath was sane. Dr Hubert Young,
senior medical officer at Wormwood Scrubs, said that the man
had a psychopathic personality and was a sadist, but was not
insane and was not a moral defective. Dr Hugh Grierson,
senior medical officer at Brixton Prison, who had reviewed
Heath's history from an early age, said there was no history of
mental abnormality or disordered conduct when he was young.
His offences in later life had been advantageous to himself and
were not of the vicious or senseless kind characteristic of the
moral defective, Heath having always taken precautions to
cover his traces.

Questioned by Mr Hawke about the meaning of the word
psychopath, Dr Grierson said that it was a person who took a
short-term view—a person who did what he felt like doing at
the moment without any thought of what the consequences
might be. He agreed with Mr Hawke that a psychopath was
not suffering from a disease of the mind but rather from an
abnormality of character and temperament.

Under cross-examination by Mr Casswell, Dr Grierson said that Heath had strongly denied being sexually abnormal and insisted that he had no perverted impulses, but was not willing to talk about his sexual relationships. Dr Grierson did not agree that this denial of his perversions was an indication of insanity.

'I suppose you would agree that this man is a psychopathic personality?' asked Mr Casswell. 'He is a most abnormal individual, is he not?'

Dr Grierson replied 'Yes' to both questions.

The jury of ten men and two women took just an hour to decide that they preferred the opinions of Dr Young and Dr Grierson to those of Dr Hubert. They were unanimous in their verdict that Neville Heath was guilty of the murder of Margery Gardner and that he was not insane at the time he committed the crime.

He refused to appeal and was hanged at Pentonville Prison on 26th October 1946.

Mr Casswell, in his memoirs, said he did not share the views of those who thought Heath was enjoying the publicity brought by the trial and wanted 'to make a hero's exit'. He believed that Heath was appalled at the crimes he had committed and realised that it would be best for him, and best for the world at large, if his life were to be ended.

Neville George Cleveley Heath was twenty-nine years of age when he spoke his last words—'Come on, boys, let's be going'—to hangman Pierrepoint and his warders, and in spite of all attempts at his trial to show that he had been morally defective from an early age, there is nothing on record to show that he had been in any trouble until he was twenty.

Born in Ilford, Essex, in June 1917, he enjoyed a comfortable middle-class life with his parents and younger brother. Educated at a Catholic preparatory school and later at a minor public school until he was seventeen, he was a satisfactory if not a brilliant pupil and got his General Schools Certificate. The Heaths had by now moved to Wimbledon and Neville took a job in a City office, but found the work boring and after only a few weeks he left to join the Artists' Rifles. He decided that he was going to enjoy service life, but felt that the Air Force offered more excitement and glamour than the Army, and in 1936 he joined the RAF. After initial training at Cranwell, Lincolnshire, he was given a short-term commission and early in 1937 he gained his wings and was gazetted a pilot officer, serving with No. 19 Fighter Squadron and No. 87 Fighter Squadron.

The uniform of a RAF officer added to the attractions of this tall, fair-haired young man, and wherever he went there were dozens of pretty girls competing for his attentions. His vanity demanded that his social life should match the glamorous standard set by his good looks. He liked to take beautiful girls to the 'best' places and needed fast sports cars to bolster his image in their eyes. His pay as a junior officer did not match the standards he set, so he 'borrowed' from the RAF sports fund of which he had charge, and took a car belonging to an NCO. Later he was charged with those offences and with being absent without leave and escaping while under arrest.

For these misdemeanours he was dismissed from the RAF, but it is perhaps typical of Heath that he insisted that the real reason for his dismissal was because he had flown his plane under a bridge. He never wavered from this romanticised version of his exploits, even attempting to convince those who had access to his records and knew the true story.

'Always I have been dogged by this simple piece of folly that led to my dismissal from the RAF when I was a twenty-year-old pilot officer,' he said in a statement published after his trial.

During the following two years Heath had only one honest job—two weeks as a sales assistant in an Oxford Street store in May 1938. For the rest of the time he lived largely on his wits. He went to Nottingham after his dismissal from the RAF and there, posing as Lord Dudley, he obtained credit by fraud at the Victoria Station Hotel and tried to get a car by false pretences. When he was caught he admitted eight other offences, most of them for obtaining money in the name of Lord Dudley.

These were his first official offences and he was placed on

probation for two years. He did not take the chance offered to him. He returned to London and continued his career of crime. He broke into the house of a friend at Edgware and stole fifty pounds' worth of jewellery, and used a forged banker's order to obtain clothing worth £27. When he was caught he asked for ten other cases, mostly for obtaining money by fraud, to be taken into consideration. He was still only twenty-one and the magistrates took the lenient course of sending him to borstal for three years.

Luck was on his side because after serving fourteen months at Hollesley Bay Colony he was released on the outbreak of war in September, 1939. He immediately tried to rejoin the RAF, but they did not want him, so he enlisted as a private in the RASC. Within four months he was commissioned as a second lieutenant and in March 1940 was posted to the Middle East with the rank of acting captain.

Heath seemed incapable of taking the chances offered him because within a year he was in trouble over bouncing cheques. It was discovered, too, that he had fraudulently obtained a second pay book and that he had told a false story in order to obtain leave to which he was not entitled. He was court-martialled and cashiered in July 1941.

Here again, Heath's later story of events bore little relation to the truth. He said that he was bored with 'enforced inactivity' at his station on the Haifa-Baghdad road, where he was supposed to be in charge of prisoners who had been rounded up as pro-Nazis.

'Then I heard of a raiding party made up of the Arab Legion and men of the Beds and Herts Regiment,' he wrote. 'They were going to attack Fort Rutbah and I decided it would be a good idea to go with them. I did, and we had quite a party. Unfortunately the Commander chose that particular night to visit the station . . . he was very cross when he found I wasn't there and that there were some prisoners waiting. The net result was that I was returned as unsuitable. Still, the gin we found at Spinney's in Rutbah was pretty good, and anyway every officer of the RASC who tried to take part in the war at

Left, Diana Kemp, who hitch-hiked once too often and was found dead in a ditch in December 1969. *Right*, a police mock-up of the appearance of her murderer, from the description given by a shopkeeper to whom the man, Ian Troup, sold Diana's watch.

Above, Dr Peter Drinkwater, from a photograph taken when he played hockey for Cambridge University. *Below*, his girlfriend, Carole Califano, whom he killed with a 'cocktail' of several drugs.

Photographs were forbidden at the trial of 'Jack-the-Ripper' murderer Peter Kurten, the Monster of Dusseldorf, in 1931; this picture (*top*) was taken with a hidden camera. He admitted to 50 atrocities, was charged with nine. *Below left*: Rudolf Pleil, 26, convicted in 1950 of killing and raping 9 women—he claimed there were 25; *right*, Heinrich Pommerencke, the 'Beast of the Black Forest', tried at Freiburg for countless murders and rapes.

Left, Aircraftman Gordon Cummins, whose pleasing expression is belied by th[e] peculiarly brutal series of murders of girls that he committed. He was convicted a[t] the Old Bailey in 1942 and hanged.

Above, Neville Heath, the charming, dapper con-man and sadistic murderer, here seen with police officers after his arrest. *Opposite*, a candid snapshot from more carefree days–serving with the army in the Middle East. *This page, below left*, Doreen Marshall, one of his victims, with her father, mother and sister.

Above left, Alfred Whiteway, who waylaid sixteen-year-old Barbara Songhurst (*above right*) and eighteen-year-old Christine Reed (*below centre*) as they cycled by Teddington Lock, and killed them with an axe and a dagger, committing violent sexual assaults on their corpses.

Peter Manuel presented his own defence when charged with eight murders at Glasgow High Court in May 1958. The judge commended him for his skill in dealing with the evidence, but the jury convicted him just the same.

Above left, Mr William Watt, whom Peter Manuel falsely accused of murdering his own family. But it was Manuel himself who was convicted of slaughtering Watt's daughter Vivienne (*above right*), his wife Marion (*below left*) and his sister-in-law, Mrs Margaret Brown (*below right*) at the Watt family home (*opposite page, above*).

Below, two more of Manuel's victims; Mr Peter Smart and his son Michael, who with Mrs Smart were found shot in bed.

and she said "alright," we walked along the
road up to Maxwelltown Rd. From there we
b... alon...

cannot name. About halfway along this road I
pulled her into a field gate. She struggled and ran
away, and I chased her across a field and over a
ditch. When I caught up to her I dragged her into
a wood. In the wood she started screaming and
I hit her over the head with a piece of iron I picked up.
After I had killed her I ran down a country lane
...
Kilbride Rd. I do not know where I flung the
piece of iron. I then ran down to High Blantyre and
along a road that brought me to Bardykes Rd. I
went along Bardykes Rd and over the railway up
to where I live. I got home about 10.15 p.m.
I went up to East Kilbride from Hamilton about
6.30 p.m. in the evening.

Above left, Anne Kneilands, whom Manuel battered to death on a Glasgow golf course;
and, *right*, Isabel Cooke, whom he suffocated. *Below*, part of Manuel's confession.

Two murderers and their victims; *Above*, Albert Matheson, a fifty-two-year-old Newcastle man, with Gordon Lockhart, the fifteen-year-old boy he killed and mutilated. *Below*, Mustapha Bassaine (*left*), the young Moroccan who stabbed Lord Bernstein's butler, Julian Sesee (*right*) in Belgravia in 1970.

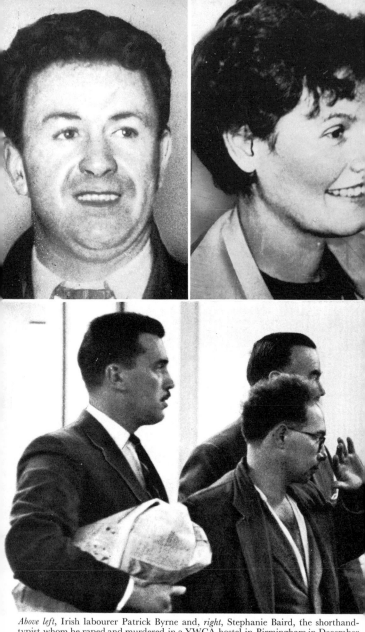

Above left, Irish labourer Patrick Byrne and, *right*, Stephanie Baird, the shorthand-typist whom he raped and murdered in a YWCA hostel in Birmingham in December 1959, entirely severing her head from her horribly mutilated body.

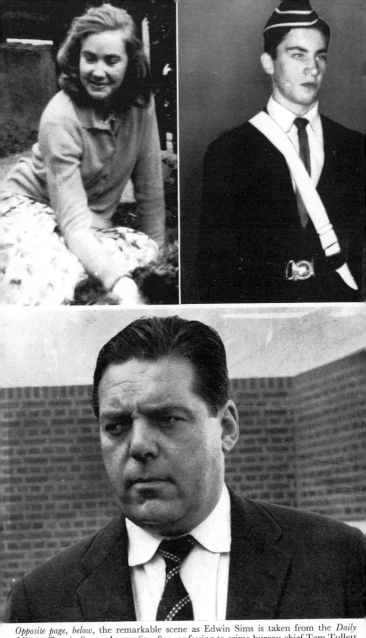

Opposite page, *below*, the remarkable scene as Edwin Sims is taken from the *Daily Mirror* offices in September, 1961, after confessing to crime bureau chief Tom Tullett (*this page*, *below*) to the slaying of Lilian Edmeades and Malcolm Johnson (*above*). A policeman carries the grisly parcel that Sims brought to support his confession.

Above, a policeman finds a pistol near the scene of the crime. *Below*, the lonely canal bank near Gravesend where Sims committed the double murder.

Edwin Sims.

Michael Dowdall, eighteen-year-old Welsh Guardsman, and (*inset*) Veronica Murray, the call-girl he murdered in a London suburb.

this stage was always classified as unsuitable—but they'd never let one of us leave the wretched organisation.'

Heath was put on to the troopship *Mooltan* to be returned to England, but he jumped ship at Durban and made his way to Johannesburg, calling himself Captain Selway, MC, of the Argyll and Sutherland Highlanders. Again he started passing dud cheques, but he eluded the authorities and no charges were brought. With his usual audacity, he then changed his name to James Robert Cadogan Armstrong and joined the South African Air Force. He enlisted as a private, but was soon commissioned and ultimately reached the rank of captain.

There is no doubt that Heath was a trickster, a thief and a complete rogue, but there is equally no doubt that he was a first-class airman. The South African authorities discovered that he was using a false name and found out all about his past misdemeanours, but valued him so highly that they over-looked the whole sorry business and allowed him to remain in the service and to keep his captain's rank.

Official records show that Heath was engaged on transport and instructional duties during the whole of his period of service with the South African Air Force, but he always in-sisted that he was on operational duties in Egypt, Tripoli and Algeria and that he took part in the Battle of Alamein.

Soon after his arrival in South Africa, Heath met an attrac-tive girl named Elizabeth Rivers, daughter of a wealthy Johannesburg couple. Neville and Elizabeth were mutually attracted and were married in February 1942. A son, Robert, was born in September 1944.

Before the birth of this child, Heath (or Armstrong, as he still called himself) was seconded to the RAF with the rank of captain and was posted to England. As the pilot of a bomber he was engaged in raids over enemy countries. In October 1944 his aircraft was hit by anti-aircraft gunfire and the crew baled out. According to Heath he saw his plane disintegrate in flames, but there is no Air Ministry record of this.

Later, he wrote: 'I have done things which I am ashamed of, but never in the air. My war record, as a fighter pilot, is a good one, and it may be that some of the experiences of those frenzied years have played a part in bringing me where I am today. Maybe here, but for the grace of God, might stand other pilots who lived as close to death as I did. Maybe they, too, need sympathy, understanding and help in changing their lives from being wartime killers.'

In other documents published after his murder conviction, Heath blamed his moral disintegration on the break-up of his marriage. He returned to South Africa early in 1945 and in October that year his wife divorced him for desertion and was given custody of their son. There is no evidence that he was ever cruel to his wife or that the marriage was anything but happy in the early days, and no reason for the break-up of the marriage is recorded.

Heath commented, 'Eventually my wife divorced me and that was the end. From then on I lost interest in everything. . . . I have never felt the same since it happened and ever since I have acted in a peculiar way on occasions. . . . From the day of my divorce I have had a couldn't-care-less attitude towards life generally. Everything went wrong.'

Everything, in fact, 'went wrong' very quickly. On 4th December 1945 he appeared before a general court-martial in South Africa and was convicted on three charges of wearing military decorations without authority and three of conduct prejudicial to military discipline.

For the third time in a career of less than twelve years he was dismissed from the service. At the same time he began passing dud cheques again. He was deported from South Africa and returned to London in February 1946.

Flying was undoubtedly an obsession with him because, in spite of a record which would surely have prejudiced his chances of success, he enrolled at the London School of Air Navigation with the idea of getting a commercial pilot's licence to enable him to apply for a post in civil aviation.

Once again he spoiled his own chances. Keeping the name Armstrong, he began to wear the uniform of a lieutenant-colonel of the South African Air Force—complete with an impressive row of medal ribbons. He was quite brazen in this masquerade, frequenting the night spots of the West End and spending a lot of time in Fleet Street drinking-haunts, where he was speedily recognised for the phony he was. On 5th April 1946, at Wimbledon Magistrates' Court, he was fined £5 for unlawfully wearing the uniform and a further £5 for wearing decorations to which he was not entitled.

He was not deterred. Reverting to his true name of Heath, he was still calling himself 'Lieutenant-Colonel' when he took Margery Gardner to the Pembridge Court Hotel on the night of 20th June 1946. . . .

It seems that Neville Heath was a sexually perverse individual with a psychopathic personality. The megalomaniac elements in him were the most dangerous, in that he was constantly contriving to award himself a more grandiose, worthy, dignified or superior rank to the one which he actually occupied. His trouble was that he had to falsify reality in order to maintain this image of himself. Inevitably events caught up with him. He was forced to create even more complex identities to satisfy his ego and maintain his prestige.

He seemed to show little or no capacity to learn from experience. There was profound 'splitting', in that for some time he could sustain the work of a captain in the South African Air Force, but his experiences in the war, or his fantasies of what those experiences might be, brought him face to face with a fear of death which he could neither digest nor metabolise. His moral disintegration is to be ascribed not to the break-up of his marriage but rather the break-up of his marriage and his moral disintegration can both be ascribed to his inability to metabolise, and digest his thoughts about, and fears of, his own death. He externalised the whole business, linked it with what was probably a pre-existent sexual sadism within himself and then proceeded to have unscrupulous sexual relationships with a variety of women. What made him resort to two crimes, the second of which was even more fantastically sadistic than the first, seems to have been the need to exclude a highly pathological part of his inner world, by which he was plagued constantly, into the external world, by enacting it, and then to get himself caught and dealt with.

The affair between the two murders with Yvonne Symonds stemmed from the other side of Heath's character—the desire to show that he could have loving relationships with a woman and get her to love him and promise to marry him, without doing her any grievous harm.

The trouble with Heath was that the two sides of him were never integrated and articulated but remained separate, and therefore the highly pathological, sadistic, murderous side was never mitigated. The relatively benign side of him was probably shocked and horrified at what was perpetrated by the other side. Psychological testing would undoubtedly have revealed the dangerous internal situation, but of course Heath was the kind of person who had to preserve his idealised image of himself—in other words face—at all costs, and it is highly doubtful whether he would have allowed himself to get involved in a meaningful psychotherapeutic endeavour.

6

The Axe-man Killer

Barbara Songhurst and Christina Rose Reed were 'best friends'. They were at that transitional stage between childhood and womanhood when, like thousands of other girls before and since, they needed to share everything. Together they went dancing, to the cinema, on long cycle rides, exchanged confidences about boy friends and spent hours comparing clothes, make-up and hair styles. Barbara read Christina letters she had received from servicemen pen friends in all parts of the world. Christina showed Barbara her ever-growing collection of autographed pictures of film stars.

They were two quite ordinary girls sharing ordinary harmless teenage interests. Barbara, aged sixteen, petite and pretty, friendly, popular with the boys, was the dominant partner of the duo. Christina, although two years senior, was quiet, reserved and shy without her friend's support. It was Barbara who planned all their outings. Attractive, wavy-haired Christina was always happy to follow.

For months they had spent all their spare time together—and they were companions when their short lives were brutally ended one summer night in 1953.

The two girls had enjoyed a happy weekend. On Saturday 30th May they spent the evening at a dance at York House, Twickenham, Middlesex, later joining other friends at the nearby Blue Angel Café. It was 12.45 a.m. when they arrived at Christina's home at Roy Grove, Hampton Hill, to spend the night. They were up by 7.30 next morning and told Christina's parents, Mr and Mrs James Reed, that they were going to cycle to Brighton. They set off full of enthusiasm—Barbara in blue jeans and white jacket, Christina wearing blue slacks and a yellow cardigan—but later in the morning they returned, having changed their minds because the weather was unsuitable.

Barbara, who worked in a chemist's shop at Richmond, Surrey, lived with her parents, Daniel and Gertrude Songhurst, at Princes Road, Twickenham. The girls called there on that Sunday morning to say that Barbara would not be back until about eleven and 'not to worry'.

Cheated of their trip to the coast, Barbara and Christina spent most of the day quite close to home, by the River Thames. Camping in tents in Ham Field, near Teddington Lock, were three youths with whom they were acquainted—John Wells, Peter Warren and Albert Sparkes. The girls decided to take up the lads' casual invitation, issued earlier that week, to visit them. They called at the camp in the morning, went back to Christina's for midday dinner, visited the boys again in the afternoon—when they all sat talking round the camp fire—and left at five thirty, saying they were going to a cinema.

The two girls changed their minds again, however. By eight o'clock they had returned to the camp. The boys teased them by disappearing into the bushes and later hid the girls' cycles in some nettles, but after a good deal of chasing, romping and ragging a mutual truce was called and the five sat quietly chatting round the fire.

At about eleven o'clock the girls left. The boys lent Barbara a lamp for her cycle and they escorted the pair to the towpath.

The girls cycled away along the track beside the river. A few minutes later they were noticed by a courting couple who overheard one girl say to the other, 'We're going to be late.' Some time between 11.30 and midnight one short, sharp scream was heard by two boys out of a party of fifty lads camping three hundred yards from the towpath . . .

Neither Barbara nor Christina arrived home.

At 8.15 next morning Mr George Coster, a Port of London foreman, was inspecting a break in the river wall opposite St Catherine's Convent, Twickenham, when he saw something on the surface of the water. River police patrol boats arrived and found that the 'something' was the ravaged and battered body of Barbara Songhurst, floating face downwards. About a mile away, in a glade of poplars near the towpath close to Teddington Lock, detectives found two pairs of girls' shoes and two separate large pools of fresh blood. There was no sign of Christina and both bicycles had disappeared.

Detective Superintendent Herbert Hannam took charge of investigations, helped by Detective Sergeant Harold Hudson and Detective Chief Superintendent Charles Rudkin. After the river had been intensively dragged for some hours between Teddington Lock and Richmond Bridge the first clue was uncovered. Police in boats reported that an electro-magnet showed a positive reaction about a hundred yards from the bloodstained patches. Christina's silver and blue sports cycle was pulled from the water.

The hunt for Christina continued for almost a week. Detectives with mine detectors, billhooks and scythes slashed their way through the undergrowth along the towpath, while police with dogs scoured adjoining fields and woodland. Mr John West, lock-keeper at Teddington, had heard nothing unusual on the night of 31st May–1st June, but it was evident that the noise of the river rushing through the sluices would have covered most other sounds. Vocal tests carried out at various distances from Mr West's lodge showed only that any sound like a·scream would have had to be very close to be heard.

On 6th June, when the riverside was thronged with holiday-makers—many of them visiting London for the coronation of Queen Elizabeth—the body of Christina was recovered from Duke's Hole, a stretch of water adjoining Glover's Island, two miles away from the point at which her friend had been found.

At the Kingston-on-Thames double inquest on 9th June, the police took the unusual course of requesting publication of full details of the victims' injuries. It was felt that if members of the public were made aware of the dreadful savagery of the killer they would be more likely to cooperate in the search for him.

Dr Keith Mant, pathologist, said that in both cases death had been caused by stab wounds in the chest. Barbara Songhurst had been stabbed three times and Christina Reed ten times. Barbara also had a fractured skull, a stab wound on the face and lacerations of the sexual organs. Christina had two depressed fractures of the skull and a stab wound on one arm probably caused when she tried to ward off her attacker. There had been extensive lacerations caused by sexual assault after death.

'Both girls were virgo intacta before the assault,' said Dr Mant. 'In both cases the injuries were inflicted with great violence and were of similar nature and appeared to be inflicted with the same weapon. In both cases the sexual assault was of the most violent type.'

The stabbing weapon used was thought to have been a double-bladed knife of the dagger type. Injuries to the heads had been caused by a blunt instrument.

The police had little evidence on which to start enquiries. Christina's bicycle bore only her own fingerprints. On the murder night a man was seen riding a woman's cycle along the towpath at Teddington and it was thought likely that he was the killer making a quick getaway on Barbara's maroon and cream machine. The most intensive search was made for this bicycle but it was not—and never has been—found.

Assistant Commissioner Crime Ronald Howe, Scotland Yard's CID chief, issued a direct appeal to the public. He asked them to report to the nearest police station (1) if they knew of anyone living within reach of the Teddington area who was absent from home after 10.30 on the murder night; (2) if they knew of anyone owning a dagger with a heavy handle and a blade about four inches long; (3) if they saw anyone acting suspiciously just before closing time in or near a public house in the area and (4) if they had seen or handled bloodstained clothing.

Detectives made house-to-house visits in the district with questionnaires. On these they detailed the movements between 10 p.m. and midnight on 31st May of every man in every house. Questions were also asked about people visiting the neighbourhood and residents who had gone away since the night of the murders. Other officers visited factories in the area and house-boats moored for a mile along the river.

There was an enormous response to these appeals, producing a great mass of material to be sifted, checked and where appropriate followed up.

Mr Cuthbert Turner, landlord of The Anglers, a riverside public house near Teddington Lock, reported the suspicious behaviour of a tall man dressed in a light grey suit and brown trilby who had been hanging about the car park until well after 11 p.m.; a number of his customers confirmed the report.

Nine hundred men at Bushey Park US Air Force base at Teddington were interrogated. Enquiries switched to Byfleet, Surrey, when detectives were told that a missing airman had been to a Coronation party in a local farmhouse on 30th May but had left before the festivities ended. He had since been seen in Brighton, Sussex, and in Teddington. He was picked up in Southampton and questioned about three knives and a cosh in his possession. It was established, however, that at the time of the towpath killings he had been in Reading, Berkshire.

A middle-aged man in a small beige saloon car was seen near the lock between 11.15 and 11.30 p.m. on 31st May, again at 5.30 a.m. the following day and yet again two hours later.

A report reached Superintendent Hannam that a man missing from his lodgings at Rivermeads Avenue, Twickenham, since three days before the murders, had been found dead by holidaymakers at Onchan Harbour in the Isle of Man.

All these leads were painstakingly followed and all yielded precisely nothing.

The only person to have seen the man who *might* have been the towpath murderer was the witness who spoke of a man riding a woman's cycle; but he could only say that he was 'a fairly big-man, pedalling fast'. There was absolutely nothing on which the police could base a description of the murderer. They did, however, have a good description of a man wanted in connection with another crime and it was this that led them rather belatedly, because of a series of unfortunate incidents, to the killer of Barbara and Christina.

On 17th June, seventeen days after the murders, a scaffolder named Harry Bedford was walking with a friend across Oxshott Heath, Surrey. He noticed a man sitting on a log and hurling an axe at a tree-stump. He wore blue overalls and brown gloves. Bedford thought he bore a resemblance to a man wanted for the rape of a fifteen-year-old schoolgirl at Oxshott on 24th May. This girl, who had been attacked with an axe, had described her assailant and said he was wearing blue overalls and brown leather gloves and was riding a blue bicycle. A 999 call brought a police car to the heath and the man was taken to Kingston police station. After a brief interview he was allowed to leave.

Only a few minutes later information was received by Surrey County Constabulary about a man who had attempted to rape a woman aged fifty-six, Mrs Patricia Birch, at Windsor, Berkshire, on 12th June—twelve days after the killing of Barbara and Christina. He had been dissuaded from his attempt when Mrs Birch offered him the contents of her hand-bag. His description—again a cyclist wearing blue overalls and brown gloves—had already been circulated and new information suggested that he might be a builder's labourer named Alfred Charles Whiteway living at Sydney Road, Teddington.

Alfred Whiteway was the man who had just left Kingston police station!

Detectives raced to the house where twenty-two-year-old Whiteway lived with his parents, a sister and brother and other relatives. He was not at home. Officers finally left a message for him to visit the station for an interview. Whiteway ignored it. On 28th June he was arrested.

He was sent for trial on the Oxshott and Windsor charges and, greatly to the surprise of the police, intimated that he would plead guilty. There was nothing at that time to link him with the murders of the two girls and it seemed unlikely that a man who had committed such crimes would attempt to attack another woman while thousands of policemen were looking for him.

What the murder investigating team did not know was that a

most damning piece of evidence against Whiteway was already in police possession. During the journey from Oxshott to Kingston, after he had been picked up as a man answering the description of the schoolgirls' attacker, Whiteway sat alone in the back of the police car. PC Arthur Oliver was driving and PC Howard, the wireless operator, was in the front passenger seat. During the drive Whiteway leaned forward on the pretext of looking at the speedometer and pushed under one of the front seats the axe he had been concealing inside his shirt.

The interior of the car was not searched that day, although, having carried a prisoner, it would be normal procedure to do so. The following day the axe was found by another constable, who put the weapon in a locker in the garage. This officer was on sick leave between 30th June and 8th July. When he returned he saw that the axe was still in the locker. He took it home and used it for chopping wood. He did not report his find.

It was not until 15th July that the constable took the axe back to the police station and handed it to PC Oliver.

An examination of this axe showed that it matched the crushing lacerations on Christina's scalp and could have been the weapon used to inflict the injuries.

Whiteway was first questioned about the murders while he was in custody awaiting trial on the other charges—to which presumably he had pleaded guilty because he thought he would be sent to prison and be safely out of the way until long after the hue and cry for the towpath killer had ended. He was seen by Detective Constable (later Commander) Wallace Virgo, of Richmond, on 29th June and was asked to account for his movements on the night of 31st May.

Whiteway said that he and his wife lived apart because of housing difficulties. His wife lived with her parents at King's Road, Kingston, and they met nearly every evening, usually in Canbury Gardens, Kingston, where they sat in a shed. They quarrelled during the afternoon of 31st May and he returned home. In the evening he cycled in Richmond Park, but at 10.30 p.m. he went back to Canbury Gardens to meet his wife again. They were together until about 11.30 and then walked back to his wife's home, where he drank two cups of tea while standing in the porch. He cycled home and arrived there about five minutes before midnight.

'I did not go near the towpath at Teddington Lock,' added Whiteway. 'I very rarely go down there and when I do it's only to do a bit of fishing.' He had known Barbara Songhurst when she was about six years old living near his family in Sydney Road, but he had not seen her since and he did not know Christina Reed at all.

Two days later Whiteway was interviewed by Superintendent Hannam.

'I guessed this would come before long,' said Whiteway. 'It looks like me, I grant you, but I can save you a lot of time by telling you now that when that job was done I was with my wife at her home.' Asked if he knew where the girls were murdered, he replied, 'I am going to keep my mouth shut. I know what you coppers are. I had nothing to do with the girls. You are wasting your time. The bloke who did that job was mad.' He admitted that he would 'go any distance' to rape a virgin but not to murder her.

Examining clothing belonging to Whiteway, Dr L. C. Nickolls, head of Scotland Yard's forensic laboratory, found human blood in the stitching of one heavy rubber-soled shoe. He reported that the shoes had been extensively bloodstained and later washed or rubbed in very wet grass.

When Whiteway was told this he said, 'I don't believe it. I think you're putting one over on me.'

In one of a number of statements made to Superintendent Hannam, Whiteway said that he had always been fond of knives. He used to throw them at trees and sometimes threw a chopper in the same way. Usually he carried this weapon in the saddlebag of his bicycle but he thought at that time it was in a cupboard at his home.

When Hannam next saw Whiteway he told him that a search of his home had not revealed the axe. Whiteway then said, 'Kingston police have got it. When I was in the police car

I tucked it under a seat.' The axe was subsequently recovered from Kingston.

On 30th July the superintendent again saw Whiteway. At the beginning of the interview Hannam took the axe from his brief case and placed it on the table in front of him.

'Blimey!' exclaimed Whiteway. 'That's it. It's been buggered about. It was sharp when I had it. I sharpened it with a file.'

He made yet another statement, elaborating on details of times and places given earlier. Just as Hannam and Detective Sergeant Hudson were about to leave, Whiteway asked, 'Were you kidding about the blood on my shoe?'

Told it was a fact that one of his shoes was bloodstained, Whiteway turned very pale and started to tremble, then blurted out:

'You know bloody well it was me. I didn't mean to kill 'em. I never wanted to hurt anybody.'

He then made this statement:

'It's all up. You know bloody well I done it, eh? That shoe's buggered me. What a bloody mess. I'm mental. My head must be wrong. I must have a woman, I can't stop myself. I'm not a bloody murderer.

'I only saw one girl. She came round a tree where I was stood and I bashed her and she was down like a log. The other screamed out down by the lock. Never saw her till then I didn't. I nipped over and shut her up. Two of 'em—and then I tumbled the other one knew me. If it hadn't been for that it wouldn't have happened. Why don't the doctors do something? It will be mental, won't it? It must be. I can't stop it.'

Staring at the axe on the table, Whiteway pleaded, 'Put that bloody chopper away. It haunts me.'

After this statement had been written down by Hannam and signed by Whiteway, the accused man asked, 'Have you got the bike?'

'No,' replied the superintendent. 'We have not found the bike or the knife.'

'So you have done it on me,' exclaimed Whiteway. 'I shall

say it is all lies like the blood. You can tear that last one up. I didn't do it.'

That, in fact, was Alfred Whiteway's defence when he appeared at the Old Bailey in October 1953, charged with the murder of Barbara Songhurst. Through his counsel, Mr Peter Rawlinson, QC (now Attorney General), he denied that he had ever made such a statement and suggested that it had been fabricated by Superintendent Hannam.

Cross-examined by Mr Rawlinson, the superintendent said that every interview with Whiteway was conducted with complete propriety.

'What did you do to get Whiteway's signature?' asked Mr Rawlinson.

'I put the statement in front of him.'

'I suggest he put four signatures and four initiallings on several pieces of paper which you handed over to him?'

'That is a terrible suggestion, it is absolutely without truth.'

Mr Justice Hilbery: 'The suggestion is that the confession statement is a completely manufactured piece of fiction written by the officer?'

Mr Rawlinson: 'That is the suggestion. I put it to you, Mr Hannam, that no such words were ever used by Whiteway on 30th July or at any other time.'

Superintendent Hannam replied that they were Whiteway's own words from his own lips. The suggestion that the statement was invented was a shocking one and he was pleased to deny it.

Three defence witnesses who had given alibis supporting Whiteway's account of his movements on the night of the murders all admitted in court that they had been 'confused' or 'mistaken'. The accused man's eighteen-year-old wife, Nellie, said that her husband had left her at 11.30.

Mr Christmas Humphreys, for the Crown, pointed out discrepancies in times she had given in her statement to the police and times in her evidence. Mrs Whiteway murmured, 'I must have got mixed up.'

The judge, in his summing-up, after a six-day trial, spoke of 'these two light-hearted young people in the very springtime of their lives . . . little thinking of the foul death that awaited them as they went along the towpath'.

Holding up Whiteway's confession, the judge looked directly at the prisoner as he asked: 'Was this the sudden outburst of a man who was deeply conscious of his guilt, and who had kept that consciousness locked in his breast until there came a moment when he must purge his bosom of the stuff that poisons the heart? If it was a concoction by the police—where did they concoct it? Is the theory that this imaginative police officer had written this piece of fiction beforehand and taken it with him so that he could get the prisoner to sign it without knowing what he was signing? And look at the statement . . . do you think that an experienced writer of fiction could have done much better than that? It is said to have been done by a police officer.'

The jury took forty-seven minutes to find Whiteway guilty, and he was sentenced to death. Three other indictments against him—the murder of Christina Reed, the rape of the schoolgirl at Oxshott and the attempted rape of Mrs Birch at Windsor—were ordered to be kept on the file. Detectives believed he was also responsible for the rape of an eleven-year-old girl in Windsor Great Park in 1952 and the rape and severe assault of a woman on Oxshott Heath in March that year.

There was a strong suspicion, too, that he was the man who for more than a year had haunted woods and fields near the Thames wearing only a loincloth. On five separate occasions women had reported that such a man had jumped out of the bushes and threatened them with a knife or chopper. It was thought possible that Whiteway had been naked or near naked when he killed Barbara and Christina, because there was no trace of blood on any of his clothing. The staining of his shoe could have occurred when, having dressed himself after disposing of their bodies, he had accidentally stepped into the blood on the towpath.

Whiteway's appeal against conviction was dismissed on 7th December 1953.

Alfred Charles Whiteway was hanged at Wandsworth

Prison on 22nd December, having first given a warder a Christmas card to be posted 'afterwards' to his tragic young wife.

It was a gesture that typified one side of the man's character. His wife, an unusually pretty, sweet-faced girl, remained steadfastly loyal to the man she knew as a loving husband and devoted father. She found it almost impossible to believe that he could have committed the crimes. She was sixteen and had not long started her first job as a typist when they first met. He apparently fell in love at first sight and was keen to marry her, but told her there were things she should know about his past life in case she thought he was not good enough for her. He confessed that he had been a thief who had spent some time in an approved school and had served a prison sentence. Nellie— or Cherry, as she preferred to be called—believed him when he gave his solemn assurance that he would go straight in future.

Cherry's mother, however, was not so easily convinced and refused to give the necessary consent to the marriage. Even when Cherry became pregnant her mother was reluctant to see her tied to a man with a criminal record, but eventually she succumbed to the inevitable pressures and agreed to the marriage. The baby, a girl named Tina, was born a few months after the wedding ceremony, which took place at Norbiton Register Office, Surrey, in February 1952.

Alfred and Cherry Whiteway moved into furnished rooms at Teddington, paying £3 7s. weekly—nearly half Whiteway's wage as a labourer. They were told to go after their landlady missed some money from a wardrobe. For weeks they trudged around together, but failed to find anyone prepared to let rooms at a low rent to a young couple with a baby on the way. So Cherry went back to her mother's home and Alfred returned to his bed in the kitchen at Sydney Road, Teddington. Usually he shared this room at night with an uncle, but on rare occasions Cherry was allowed to stay there with him. She became pregnant again and their second daughter, Sally, was born while Whiteway was in jail awaiting trial on the murder charge.

According to Cherry, her young husband tried to join the Army because he thought they would be given married quarters, but was turned down because of his criminal record.

To his wife he was always thoughtful and kind. Previous girlfriends described him as 'gentle and sometimes even gallant'. But male friends and workmates found him moody and difficult to get on with and were sometimes impatient with his passion for physical fitness. For several years he had been obsessed with the body-building cult, practising weight-lifting, muscle development and chest-expanding. His passion for knives began when he was still at school and he attended health and strength classes to give him more arm power for knife throwing. He combined this hobby with a passion for cycling and always carried knives in his saddlebag so that he could practise throwing at trees. He became something of a Tarzan, using his powerful arms and legs to swing from branch to branch.

When he first started wearing gloves to protect his 'valuable hands' at work, his fellow labourers on building sites were quick to ridicule him. He silenced them by demonstrating his strength and skill—carrying double the normal load of bricks as he ran up and down the ladders and invariably hitting the target when he flung knives at small pieces of cardboard pinned to trees.

Ironically, it was the unusual care he took of his hands that helped the police to catch up with him. At least two of his victims had noted the incongruity of good leather gloves worn as an accessory to workmen's denims, and detectives of two counties were looking for a cyclist who always wore gloves whatever the weather.

7

Multiple Murders

To the average member of the general public whose knowledge of crime and criminals stems only from newspaper reports, the term 'sex killer' has broadly one meaning. It describes a man who kills a woman or girl-child during or after rape, either because his victim resists his advances or because violence is a necessary part of his sexual gratification. When the words 'sex maniac' feature in the headlines, the implication is that this particular murderer has killed, or is likely to kill, more than once and that the violation is of an unusually sadistic or otherwise perverted nature.

In fact, as any police officer or newspaperman knows, these over-simplified phrases cover a diversity of crimes in which, although the tragic final result is always the same, the methods and motives are as manifold as in any other type of criminal activity. There have been murders in which the rape of the victim was incidental to the main object of robbery and, conversely, murders apparently for material gain in which the initial motivation was sexual. Just as there are many rapists who would never kill, so there are sex murders without rape. Sometimes the motives are so confused that it is impossible to pinpoint with any certainty the primary urge behind the crime.

This was the situation facing the Scottish police in the two years from January 1956 to January 1958. During that period there were nine murders, all committed within an area of roughly six miles by four miles in semi-suburban districts to the east of Glasgow. In the same location and within the same two years there was also a number of housebreakings in which, although a good deal of senseless damage was done, little of value was stolen.

There seemed no real reason to connect the murders, many of which appeared to be without motive, and even slighter grounds for supposing that they were linked to the robberies, but gradually the investigating officers came to believe that all the crimes were the work of one man. The material links were tiny, but they were there.

Yet what kind of man could have committed such a variety of crimes? Was he primarily a thief? A 'sex maniac'? A psychopath whose main need was to bask in the limelight of notoriety? A creature who killed simply because he had a lust for killing? Or a homicidal maniac?

It says a great deal for the perspicacity of the Scottish police that, faced with this plethora of crimes and possible motives, they tracked down one man who was eventually to stand trial on eight charges of murder and five of housebreaking. It is perhaps as well that they were not able to foresee the future when, on 3rd January 1956, they were called to the golf course at Capelrig Plantation, East Kilbride, Lanarkshire, nine miles from the centre of Glasgow . . .

A forty-year-old labourer named George Gribbon had been walking on the golf course that afternoon, looking for lost golf balls. He pushed his way through some bushy undergrowth towards a clump of trees near the fifth tee and there, lying in a hollow, saw the body of a young girl. Her skull had been smashed, her clothes ruffled up as though she had been dragged along the ground, and a few yards away was an area of flattened grass heavily saturated with blood.

Police Sergeant William Woods found the girl's shoes some distance apart, embedded in the mud on either side of a deep ditch and judging by prints made by the shoes, it appeared that they had been sucked from her feet as she ran from her attacker. Her coat, head-scarf, wrist-watch and one earring were all recovered from different parts of the golf course, but her knickers and one stocking were missing and were never recovered.

The 'sex killing' newspaper reports were inevitable. Everything pointed that way, but the subsequent post-mortem examination revealed the rather surprising fact that there had been no attempt at any kind of sexual assault. It was apparently a murder without motive.

The victim, Anne Kneilands, was seventeen. An attractive blonde, unusually tall (five feet ten), she had lived with her parents, John and Martha Kneilands, in converted stables on the Calderwood Estate, about a mile and a half from the golf course. On Friday 30th December 1955 she and her sister, twenty-year-old Alice, had attended a dance at East Kilbride Town Hall, where they met two young men. One of these men, an ambulance driver named Andrew Murnin, escorted Anne home and made a date to meet her again on Monday 2nd January. The girl arrived at the appointed place at six o'clock as arranged, but Andrew failed to turn up (it was subsequently discovered that he had become involved in a New Year party and had forgotten all about his previous plan), so after waiting for twenty minutes Anne called in on some friends living nearby. She stayed only about half an hour and then left to catch a bus to East Kilbride. The conductress saw her alight at the Willow Café. Nobody knows for certain where she went or what she did after about seven o'clock.

Mr and Mrs Kneilands visited friends in Glasgow that evening and did not arrive home until nearly midnight. As Anne was not there they assumed that she had missed the last bus and was staying overnight with friends. The following day they reported her missing and the police were investigating her disappearance when her body was found.

Anyone who might have known anything relevant to the police enquiry was interviewed, but little of value was uncovered. There was some hopeful interest when PC J. Marr, on his way to talk to the man who had discovered Anne's body, noticed that one of a gang of Gas Board workmen in the area had what appeared to be recent scratches on his face. As a matter of routine this man, twenty-eight-year-old Peter Manuel, was asked to explain his injuries. He replied that he had been involved in a New Year fight. It seemed likely enough and there was no other reason to suspect him. He lived with his parents, Samuel and Bridget Manuel, in a council house at Fourth Street, Birkenshaw, more than eight miles away from the golf course. The Gas Board, for which he worked as an assistant mains layer, had halted operations in that area at noon on Saturday 31st December, and had not resumed work until 4th January—two days after Anne Kneilands was killed and a day after the discovery of her body.

Nevertheless the police took the precaution of visiting Manuel's home, from which they removed some of his clothing for examination. Nothing incriminating was discovered and little further thought was given to the young man with the scratched face.

Some of the public indignation and fear engendered by the Kneilands murder was, in any event, soon diverted to another part of Glasgow. On Wednesday 11th January, while the hunt for Anne Kneilands' killer was still being vigorously pursued, a fifty-five-year-old spinster was battered to death in her fifth-floor flat in Aberfoyle Street, Dennistoun. The victim, Anne Steele, was a quiet, intelligent woman who worked as a clerk and deputy buyer for the Glasgow paint firm of Montgomerie, Stobo and Company. She usually visited a friend, Mrs Louisa Pettigrew, on Wednesday evenings, but that week had decided to stay at home, and the police theory was that she surprised a burglar who had expected to find the flat unoccupied.

Neighbours hearing her screaming soon after eight o'clock rushed to her front door. As the screams became moans they heard the heavy footsteps of a man running from one room to another. He had evidently entered the flat by the front door and then, trapped by the rapidly growing crowd of people outside, was at first unable to find an escape route. By the time the police arrived, in response to a belated 999 call, he had disappeared—having shinned down a drainpipe outside the bathroom window to the yard fifty feet below.

Miss Steele was lying face down in a pool of blood on the kitchen floor. There was no sign of a struggle. The poker which had been used to kill the unfortunate woman was on a window sill.

At the end of January, when the police seemed no nearer a solution to either of the two murders, a group of Glasgow businessmen offered rewards totalling £900 for information that would lead to the arrest of Anne Kneilands' killer or the brutal attacker of Anne Steele.

There was not a scrap of evidence to link the two crimes and the police continued to search for two murderers, but as the weeks and then months passed and no arrests were made the general public began to forget the tragedies of the New Year.

There was no more than the usual quota of crime in the Glasgow area during that spring and summer of 1956, but events in September shocked the whole of Scotland into remembering the disquieting fact that there had already been two unsolved murders that year.

Early in the morning of 17th September, Mrs Helen Collison, a fifty-seven-year-old 'daily-help', arrived as usual at the home of Mr and Mrs William Watt, 5 Fennsbank Avenue, High Burnside. She knew that Mr Watt was away from home on a fishing holiday, but expected other members of the household to be up and about and was very surprised to find the back door of the bungalow bolted from the inside. She looked through the window of the bedroom occupied by sixteen-year-old Vivienne Watt and saw the girl apparently sound asleep in bed—a puzzling situation because Vivienne, a student at Skerry's College, Glasgow, was normally out of the house before Mrs Collison arrived.

By now worried, the woman walked round to the front door and saw that a pane of glass had been broken. As she was calling through the empty panel, postman Peter Collier arrived and opened the door by putting his hand through the panel and turning the Yale lock.

Together they went first to the main bedroom. Lying in bed, with the bedclothes pulled neatly up to their necks, were Mrs Marion Watt, aged forty-five, the semi-invalid wife of master-baker William Watt, and her sister, forty-two-year-old Mrs Margaret Brown. Both had been shot through the head at very close range and Mrs Collison could see that both were undoubtedly dead. There was no disorder in the room. The two women were lying quite naturally and it looked as if they had been shot while sleeping. Neither had been sexually assaulted, but Mrs Brown's pyjama trousers had been ripped from the waistband.

Vivienne, wearing a wrist-watch which had stopped at 2.52, was still alive when Mrs Collison found her, but she died before the ambulance arrived. She, too, had been shot through the head. There was some bruising on her thighs and body, but no sign of sexual assault.

When Superintendent Andrew McClure arrived it was clear to him that the girl, unlike the two older women, had put up a terrific struggle. She was lying in an unnatural position with her right arm behind her back, a table-lamp had been smashed and the room was strewn with buttons and pieces of torn clothing. Her pyjama trousers, ripped to shreds, were lying on the counterpane, and she was wearing a pyjama jacket and a cardigan, both without buttons. Among the clothing scattered about the floor was a brassière with its back fastening intact but torn down the front. The shoulder straps were broken, indicating that it had been wrenched from her body.

The only thing missing from the bungalow was Mrs Watt's wrist-watch. Robbery seemed the most likely motive when later the same day it was discovered that another house in Fennsbank Avenue had been forcibly entered. In this case the occupants, the Misses Mary and Margaret Martin, were away on holiday. A woman who noticed a broken pane of glass in the front-door—the same method of entry as that used at the Watt bungalow—alerted detectives already investigating the murder only a few doors away.

The police found a scene of curious disorder at No. 18, the Martins' house. There were dirty footmarks on the settee and a small burn on the carpet nearby, as if someone reclining on the sofa had stretched out a hand to stub a cigarette; there were also dirty footmarks on one of the beds; in the kitchen was an opened tin of spaghetti and the contents of a tin of tomato soup had been thrown over the floor; orange peel and pips were scattered all over other rooms.

The entire house had been ransacked and articles from wardrobes and chests flung haphazardly about the Martins' home. The only items missing were two gold rings, six shillings in silver and four pairs of nylon stockings. Other property of far greater value had been left untouched.

In terms of time and place there was an obvious link between this burglary and the Watt murders; in other respects there was a clear connection between events at the Martins' and a house-breaking discovered two days earlier at the home of Mr Henry Platt in Douglas Drive, Bothwell, a few miles distant.

On 12th September Mr and Mrs Platt and their son, sixteen-year-old Geoffrey, left for a holiday in the Lake District. Three days later the police were called to the house because a neighbour noticed that a window had been broken.

Here again a tin of soup had been opened and part of the contents spilt on the floor, though some had been poured into a jug and taken upstairs to a bedroom—where the intruder, with dirty shoes, had evidently been lying on the bedcover. In the kitchen was another empty can which had contained pears. The fruit had been tipped over the floor, but the juice had evidently been consumed. A mattress on one of the beds had a long split in it, presumably made by scissors which were lying on the floor, and there were holes in a quilt and a blanket. As in the Martin sisters' home, many valuable articles had been ignored by the thief, who had been content to take a pair of cufflinks, a wrist-watch, an electric razor, some tools, and £2 in cash.

The missing watch was later found in odd circumstances. Mrs Platt repaired the slit in the mattress soon after the burglary, but nearly a year later was obliged to unpick her handiwork to investigate an uncomfortable lump which had developed. There, inside the filling, was the watch she thought had been stolen. A second lump which necessitated further investigation of the mattress three months later, just before Christmas 1957, yielded something of far greater interest to the police—a bullet from a ·38 revolver, which ballistic examination proved to have been fired from the gun which had later been used to kill Mrs Watt, her sister and daughter.

But before Mrs Platt uncovered these significant finds another act of the drama had been played . . .

On 27th September 1956, ten days after the triple killing, William Watt was arrested and charged with the murder of his wife, daughter and sister-in-law. On 9th September the fifty-two-year-old bakery boss had arrived at the Cairnbahn Hotel, Lochgilphead, Argyll, for a fortnight's fishing holiday, and news of the tragedy had been broken to him by Mrs Ruby Leitch, owner of the hotel, at about noon on 17th September. He immediately left the hotel in his own car, intending to drive the eighty-five miles to Glasgow, but was too distraught to continue. He went into the police station at Lochgilphead and was provided with a police driver.

The reason for the arrest of Watt is obscure. He had an apparently sound alibi and there was ample evidence that he and his wife were happily married. The unfortunate man endured the agony of sixty-seven days in Barlinnie Prison while further enquiries were made and he was then released without standing trial.

It was during the period of Watt's stay in prison that a quite bizarre series of events took place.

Mr Lawrence Dowdall, a Glasgow solicitor who had been retained by the baker, received a letter from Peter Manuel, offering information 'concerning a recently acquired client of yours'. Manuel was the young man who, it will be recalled, had been interviewed after the murder of Anne Kneilands. He was at that time also in Barlinnie Prison, having been sentenced on 2nd October to eighteen months for housebreaking at Hamilton, Lanarkshire. He was seen by Mr Dowdall, to whom he told an extraordinary story.

He said that on the night before the Watts were murdered a man with a revolver had approached him and asked him to join in a housebreaking expedition to High Burnside. He, Manuel, had refused to go. The following night this man told him that he had broken into a bungalow at Fennsbank Avenue and had shot three women. Manuel gave an accurate description of the bungalow and details of the manner in which the women were shot, but refused to name the man who had given him this information. He added that the man had asked him to get rid of the gun and also two rings which he had stolen from another house in Fennsbank Avenue. Manuel described Mr Watt as 'a party who was, to my certain knowledge, doubly unfortunate'.

This was an extraordinary move on Manuel's part because it could only serve to implicate him in a crime of which he had not until then been suspected. Mr Dowdall advised him to tell his story to the police, but Manuel refused, so Dowdall himself passed on the information. Again Manuel's home was searched, but no gun was found, nor any rings, neither was there anything incriminating about clothing removed from the house for forensic examination. There was undoubtedly at that stage a very strong suspicion of Manuel, but no evidence apart from his own statement to link him with any of the crimes.

He was released from prison on 30th November 1957, and almost immediately drew further attention to himself by asking Mr Dowdall to arrange for him to meet Mr Watt—who was still in the invidious position of being unable to prove himself innocent of the murders for which he had been arrested but not tried.

The two men met at the Whitehall Restaurant, Glasgow, and Manuel told Watt that the entry into his house had been 'all a mistake'. Manuel said that three people were involved and that they had planned to break into a neighbouring house where there was supposed to be a safe containing between £5,000 and £10,000. They had picked the wrong house.

The conversation continued in Jackson's Bar in Crown Street, where Manuel said that the same three people had also broken into a house at Rothwell and fired a bullet into the bed.

'If that bullet is found and it matches the gun used at Burnside, it will prove conclusively that you had nothing whatever to do with the murders, having been on holiday at the time,' Manuel assured Watt.

Again, Manuel's object in telling this story to Watt is obscure. He did not ask for money and was not offered any. The only result of their meeting was to reawaken suspicion of Manuel's involvement, but the police may perhaps be forgiven for not treating the matter too seriously in view of the fact that Manuel was already well known as a man who was prepared to go to any lengths in order to draw attention to himself.

In September 1954 he had 'confessed' to taking part in a £40,000 bullion raid at London Airport and had claimed to be the mastermind behind a £55,000 Glasgow bank robbery the following year. He had even professed inside knowledge relating to the defection of spies Burgess and Maclean in 1951, and had in fact for years made a nuisance of himself by claiming to be involved in all sorts of criminal enterprises with which he had not the remotest connection.

Looking back on the whole picture of these Scottish murders and housebreakings during the 1956–8 period, it is clear that a significant factor was the gap in the pattern between early October 1956 and the end of November 1957—when Peter Thomas Anthony Manuel was safely under lock and key in Barlinnie Prison. There was nothing unusual in that situation because Manuel had been in and out of approved schools, borstals and prisons since he was twelve years old—and no one could foresee events that were to take place after he had served his sentence for the latest in his long list of assorted crimes.

Chapter two of the terrible story opened on the 8th December 1957—not in Scotland, but over the border in County Durham, where a taxi-driver named Sidney Dunn was found dead in his cab on bleak and deserted moorland at Edmundbyers. He had been shot through the back of the head and then his throat had been cut. Dunn had last been seen alive in the early hours of that morning when he had been hired sixteen miles away at Newcastle upon Tyne. The English police, who had a good description of the man who hired the cab, plus several useful clues, were still working on the case when their Scottish colleagues found themselves faced with another spate of murders and robberies in the Glasgow area.

This began, comparatively quietly, on Christmas Day. The Reverend Alexander Macrae Houston and his wife left their home at 66 Wester Road, North Mount Vernon, to spend the day with friends. When they returned that evening they found a window broken and both front and back doors wide open. A camera, £2 from a missionary collecting box and a new pair of gloves were missing.

Within a few days there was a further alarm in the neighbourhood. On 28th December Isabelle Cooke, a plump, dark-haired schoolgirl of seventeen, failed to return to her home at Carrick Drive, Mount Vernon, after leaving for a dance. She had arranged to meet her escort, classmate Douglas Bryden, at a bus stop in Uddingston. The young man waited for nearly an hour, but there was no sight of Isabelle. He tried to telephone her home, but the line was out of order. Assuming that their daughter had kept this appointment, Mr and Mrs William Cooke did not begin to worry until midnight. Then, as the hours passed, they went out on foot to look for her, and eventually Mr Cooke drove his car along the route they thought she would have taken on her way home. They hoped that Isabelle had decided to stay the night with friends and would arrive early in the morning, but by ten o'clock, after making enquiries among friends, they reported her disappearance to the police.

Later that day Isabelle's cosmetic bag, which she normally carried in her handbag, was found under a railway bridge in Mount Vernon Avenue. A full-scale police search was mounted, rivers were dragged, woods and open spaces scoured, and railway goods yards in many parts of Scotland were searched in case the girl's body had been thrown over a bridge on to a passing freight truck. A week after her disappearance hundreds of volunteers joined in the hunt following a pulpit appeal from the Reverend Mr Houston, the victim of the Christmas Day robbery. There was no trace of the missing girl.

While the search for Isabelle was being mounted, the

preliminaries to yet another tragedy were taking place only about three miles from the Cooke home.

At a pleasant bungalow in Sheepburn Road, Uddingston, the Smart family were happily discussing the alternative plans for their New Year holiday. Peter James Smart, aged forty-five, was office manager of W. and J. R. Watson Ltd, civil engineering contractors of Glasgow, but the offices were to be closed between 31st December and 6th January and Mr Smart thought it would be a good idea to take his wife Doris and ten-year-old son Michael away for a few days. Should they visit Mr Smart's parents near Jedburgh, Roxburghshire, or should they go to the Dumbuck Hotel, Dumbarton, whose proprietor, William McManus, was an old friend?

On 29th December Peter Smart discussed the possibilities with his brother Victor in a telephone conversation, and said he thought they would be going to Jedburgh on 2nd January. On 31st December Victor went to Jedburgh and stayed for a few days. He was not altogether surprised when his brother failed to arrive, because the weather was very bad and the trip there and back would have necessitated a drive of a hundred and seventy miles on icy roads. Upon returning to his own home in Edinburgh on the night of 2nd January, Victor Smart telephoned Uddingston but got no reply.

During the evening of 31st December the Smarts were visited by neighbours, Mr and Mrs Stanley Jackman, and told them it was almost certain that they would be going to Jedburgh. The Jackmans went off to a party. Returning home at about 2 a.m., they noticed lights still burning in the Smarts' bungalow. Later that morning—1st January—Mr Jackman saw that the Smart's garage doors were open and that their car had gone.

On the evening of 2nd January this car, which belonged to Mr Smart's employers, was found, apparently abandoned, in the Gorbals district of Glasgow. The police tried to report this discovery to W. and J. R. Watson Ltd, but were unable to do so because the offices were closed for the New Year holiday. When an officer made a second visit to the firm's premises on Monday 6th January he was told that Peter Smart, who had the use of the car and normally kept it in his garage, had failed to report for work that morning.

Alexander McBride, a foreman joiner employed by Watson's, went to the Smarts' house with Police Sergeant Frank Hogg. They found milk and newspapers outside the front door and the curtains drawn across the bedroom windows.

They entered a house of death. All the occupants—Mr and Mrs Smart and the boy Michael—had been shot through the head at close range as they slept in their beds. There was no sign of any struggle; not even the bedclothes had been disturbed. The three victims had been dead for some days.

On 31st December Mr Smart had received his usual monthly pay cheque, which he paid into the Parkhead Cross branch of the Commercial Bank of Scotland, at the same time drawing out £35 in new pound notes. This money was missing from the house, as well as Mrs Smart's purse containing 18s and a pair of women's gloves.

This second triple murder rekindled the public alarm which had followed the Watt killing fifteen months previously and a state of real terror descended on the neighbourhood. Women refused to go out alone after dark and within a week of the tragedy ironmongers had sold all their stocks of door bolts. At one small shop alone nearly a hundred door chains—for which there was normally almost no demand—were snapped up in a day.

At first it seemed that there was to be no more success in the solving of the Smart murders than there had been in any of the other crimes—until, a week after the killing, the name of Peter Manuel again came to the attention of the police.

It was learned that on New Year's Eve Manuel had been very short of cash and had borrowed £1 from his father in a public house. On New Year's Day, however, Manuel called at the house of a friend and gave two shillings to each of his friend's children. He was then seen to buy several rounds of drinks in a nearby hotel. Later that day Manuel went to a party given by his aunt, Mrs Devina Greenan, to celebrate her daughter's engagement. He took with him a dozen cans of lager, gave Mrs Greenan a pound for her young children and handed over another pound note to pay for a taxi to take his mother home. On the same evening he went into the Woodend Hotel, Fallside, and bought drinks and cigarettes costing £8 17s 6d, for which he paid in new pound notes. After the party he went with some friends to the house of Mary McCanley in Douglas Street, Viewpark, and offered a bottle of whisky to Miss McCanley's mother. He rounded off the evening by going to a dance at Tannochside—paying for the tickets for himself and two friends.

On 3rd January Manuel met a friend, Joseph Brennan, and paid for beer and whisky at the Woodend Hotel. He bought some steak, which they took to Brennan's house to eat, and later they visited two more public houses. At the Old Mail Coach, Manuel treated two barmaids to drinks and also bought a bottle of brandy.

On 13th January 1958 the third search of Manuel's home took place—this time by nine police officers led by Detective Superintendent Brown, of Glasgow CID, who with Detective Inspector Goodall was assisting Detective Inspector Robert McNeil (Lanarkshire CID) with enquiries into all the murders and the disappearance of Isabelle Cooke. On this occasion their efforts were rewarded. A number of items connected with the housebreakings were found at the Manuels' house and Peter Manuel was taken to Bellshill police station for questioning. Later, at Hamilton police station, Manuel was identified by several witnesses and was charged with the murder of Peter, Doris and Michael Smart, with stealing from their house and the theft of a car from their garage, and further with breaking into the Reverend Alexander Houston's house and stealing certain articles.

The following day Manuel said that he wanted to see Inspector McNeil 'concerning unsolved crimes in Lanarkshire'. He then wrote a detailed, factual and quite unemotional confession to the murders of Anne Kneilands, Mrs Marion Watt, Vivienne Watt, Mrs Margaret Brown, Peter Smart, Mrs Doris Smart and Michael Smart. He said that he had also killed Isabelle Cooke, adding 'I'll take you to where she is buried.'

Inspector McNeil and other officers went with Manuel to fields near Burntbroom Farm, behind Carrick Drive, Mount Vernon, where the Cooke family lived. About twenty yards from a ditch Manuel pointed to the ground and said, 'I think she's in there. I think I am standing on her.'

The girl had been buried several feet deep. She was wearing only a cardigan, a suspender belt and nylon stockings—both badly torn. Her brassière was tied tightly round her neck and a head scarf was tied round her face with the knot pushed into the mouth. She had died from suffocation and had not been sexually assaulted. Her shoes had been buried at different places in the field but there was no sign of her knickers or the rest of her clothing.

By the time Peter Manuel stood his trial at the High Court of Glasgow in May 1958, he had been charged with the eight murders to which he had confessed, plus housebreaking at the homes of the Watt family, the Smarts, Henry Platt, Margaret and Mary Martin and the Reverend Alexander Houston. But by that time, too, he had retracted his confession, claiming that the police had extorted it under threats involving action against his parents. As he faced the judge, Lord Cameron, he replied firmly to each charge, 'Not Guilty.'

The seventeen-day trial, before a jury of nine men and six women, was full of surprises.

Not content with leaving the burden of proof of his guilt on the prosecution, Manuel entered a 'special defence' plea in relation to two of the charges, claiming that William Watt had killed his own family and that a man then in prison and a Motherwell woman had been responsible for one of the burglaries. He put forward an alibi for the time at which the Smart murders were believed to have been committed, insisting that he was at home with his parents, his brother James, sister Theresa, and a US Army soldier, Ronald Flaubert.

This alibi, although supported by his relatives, was less convincing than it might have been because the Manuels' house was only about half a mile from the Smarts' bungalow. The jury must have realised that it would have been a simple matter for Manuel to have absented himself from the house while the rest of his family were sleeping—probably heavily—after the Hogmanay celebrations.

Halfway through the trial there was a further sensation when Manuel decided to do without counsel and undertook his own defence, cross-examining witnesses with a considerable degree of skill and eventually making an eloquent three-hour speech to the jury. The main plank of his defence was that the confession had been extracted from him under threats made by the police against his family.

'The thing I had in my head at that time was the diabolical threat by Superintendent Brown to put my father in prison on a charge of being involved in the Smart murders,' he said. 'At that time, situated as I was, I had no doubt in my mind that this man would have carried out his threat. He was a savage and determined man and he knew he had to produce some kind of case. He threatened to arrest my mother and my sister . . .

'I can assure you I have never been the confessing type and have never been considered by the police to be the confessing type. I have never in my life been in a position where I have supplied a statement to the police—yet here we have a situation where they say that without pressure I just confessed of my own free will. You must realise that when I was in the hands of the police there must have been some powerful reason for me to write these statements. They don't produce the reason. I do.'

Lord Cameron, in his summing up, told the jury that the catalogue of crimes was so formidable, with so many curious features, that it might be easy to infer that the person who committed them was not responsible for his actions, but no special defence plea of insanity had been intimated and therefore could not be considered.

He added: 'A man may be very bad without being mad.'

The judge directed that a formal verdict of Not Guilty be

given on the charge relating to Anne Kneilands because there was not sufficient evidence which went beyond suspicion and could be regarded as positive incriminating evidence from an independent source.

The jury took two and a half hours to decide that Peter Manuel was guilty of the other seven murders with which he was charged, as well as of housebreaking and stealing a car from Peter Smart's garage. The charge of housebreaking at Wester Road, Mount Vernon, was found not proven.

Had he been acquitted on the Scottish murder charges Manuel would immediately have been rearrested by two detectives from over the border. They had been sitting in the Glasgow court throughout the trial, ready with a warrant to arrest him on a charge of murdering the Newcastle taxi-driver, Sidney Dunn. While the accused man was in prison awaiting trial some fragments of glass and traces of earth in his trouser turnups were matched with glass from the broken taxi headlamps and soil from the scene of the moorland killing. The Dunn murder was not included in the indictment because it took place in England and the Scottish courts had no jurisdiction.

Peter Manuel, swarthily handsome with his thick mop of dark hair and deep brown eyes, was thirty-one years old when he reached the end of the road of crime on which he embarked at the age of twelve.

His Roman Catholic parents had emigrated from Scotland to America in 1922 and five years later Peter Thomas Anthony was born in Manhattan. The family moved to Detroit for a while, Samuel Manuel and his wife working mainly in hotels, but in 1932 they decided to return to Scotland. After five years in Oakfield Place, Motherwell, twelve miles from Glasgow, they moved south to Coventry, Warwickshire, and it was there that young Peter had his first brush with the law. He was caught breaking into a cycle dealer's shop and was put on probation for a year, but within five weeks he was back before the same juvenile court on a housebreaking charge and this time he was sent to an approved school.

In the next few years he came before courts in Coventry,

Cambridge, Manchester and Darlington, all for petty offences, and had six spells in approved schools. He escaped several times and during one period of freedom was found guilty of assault with a hammer in the furtherance of theft. Just before Christmas 1942, again during a spell on the run from an approved school, he robbed and indecently assaulted the wife of a school employee. The fifteen-year-old boy hid in the school chapel—behind a Nativity tableau—for more than a week before he was caught, emerging only at night to steal food. This time he was sent to Borstal.

When he was released in 1945 he rejoined his family, who had returned to Scotland after being bombed out of their home in Coventry in 1941. In 1946 he was in trouble again. He was sent to prison for a year on fifteen charges of housebreaking, and he had served only a few weeks of this sentence when he was brought from prison to answer charges of assault and rape. He was found guilty of these offences—committed before he was sentenced for housebreaking—and was sentenced to eight years' jail.

Not long after he came out of prison he began courting an attractive young girl from Carluke, Lanarkshire, and bought her an expensive engagement ring. He then boasted to friends of how he had taken the ring back to the jeweller, on the pretext that the stones were loose, and exchanged it for a much cheaper one. He was mightily proud of having saved money and fooled his fiancée without losing prestige in her eyes.

The wedding, planned for the summer of 1955, did not take place. The girl broke off the engagement after receiving a letter giving all the facts—with a few fictitious additions—of Manuel's criminal past. There was more than a hint of suspicion that Manuel had written the letter himself. He could not, in any event, have married on the appointed day because he was otherwise engaged at Airdrie (Lanarkshire) Sheriff Court—successfully defending himself on a charge of indecent assault.

This recital of crimes gives a picture of one side of Manuel's character. But there were other aspects of his personality so different that many people of his acquaintance found it almost impossible to believe that the Peter Manuel they knew was the Peter Manuel found guilty of multiple murder.

At the convent schools he attended he was friendly, popular and bright, with a particular aptitude for English. Although his many jobs were menial in nature, he was hard-working, conscientious and ambitious. During one spell as a dustman he used to arrive an hour early for work each day so that he could learn to drive the dustcarts and get a better job.

He was a voracious reader and to a great extent educated himself from books. As a child in Coventry he spent most evenings in the reference library and when still in his teens could recite long passages from Shakespeare and knew most of Burns by heart. He is said to have read the whole of Gibbon's *Decline and Fall of the Roman Empire* by the time he was fourteen.

His many talents made him popular with workmates and friends. He was keen on sport and at one time played for a works football team. He was quite an accomplished painter and sketcher, had a good singing voice and was always ready to play the piano—with a preference for the classics. But his greatest social asset was undoubtedly his brilliance as a story-teller and witty talker.

Tributes to his eloquence came from two vastly different sources during his trial. One of his pub cronies, asked if he had been drinking heavily on a certain occasion, replied, 'No. Peter is quite a good conversationalist and when Peter is in conversation you don't drink.' And Lord Cameron, in his final address to the jury, remarked, 'There is little doubt that the accused has presented his own defence with a skill that is quite remarkable.'

Manuel appealed against conviction on all charges, but the appeal was dismissed and he was hanged at Barlinnie Jail on Friday 11th July 1958.

But it was not quite the end of the story . . .

Before he took his last walk to the scaffold, Manuel is said to have confessed to three other murders and the police announced that they regarded those cases as closed.

The victims were:

Prostitute Ellen Carlin, known as 'Red Helen', who was strangled with a nylon stocking in a rooming-house in Lillington Street, Pimlico, in September 1954. The twenty-eight-year-old Irish girl was said to have been with a man with an American accent shortly before her death and a number of US servicemen were closely questioned. Manuel is known to have been in London for a short spell at about that time—with the object, it is believed, of working his way into the city's criminal underworld—and, probably because of his early years in the States, often affected a convincing American accent; the Glasgow woman Anne Steele, battered with a poker in her flat on 11th January 1956; Mrs Ellen Petrie, aged fifty, known as 'English Nellie', who was found dead with head injuries outside a bakery in West George Lane, Glasgow, on 15th June 1956. She had been sexually assaulted and one of her stockings was missing.

Manuel also admitted that he had killed Anne Kneilands—the one murder of which he had been acquitted at his trial.

Eighteen days after Manuel was hanged came the final postscript. An inquest jury at Shotley Bridge, Co. Durham, returned a verdict that Sidney Dunn, the murdered taxi-driver, had also been killed by Peter Manuel—bringing the total number of his known victims to twelve.

Had Manuel's counsel originally pleaded that the killer was suffering from diminished responsibility during the period he committed his horrific murders it is extremely doubtful whether the jury would have accepted the plea.

Manuel was not insane. His disturbance was connected with an attack upon the 'life-link'. He had within him an enormous fear of his own death and 'externalised' this fear by acting it out on other people—by severing *their* life-links.

The sexual factors involved in his crimes were quite inconstant, thus making the actual taking of lives far more significant than any sexual motivation.

Manuel's making a confession and then withdrawing it and alleging that he had made it only because of police threats, conforms to a known pattern among killers of his type.

8

Lesbian Lovers

In the pre-permissive fifties, when 'homosexuality' was a word rarely spelt out in the mass media and lesbianism was coyly hidden under the euphemism 'unnatural friendship', the world was shocked to read of a murder committed by—in the words of the trial prosecutor—'two dirty-minded little girls'.

Although the sexual obsession which provided the driving force would now be viewed with intelligent understanding and some measure of sympathy, the basic facts of the killing were in themselves so shocking that it is easy to appreciate the public revulsion against the perpetrators of the crime.

The girls, aged fifteen and sixteen, were intelligent, well educated, attractive in appearance, the daughters of kindly parents and in no sense deprived of material blessings. Their victim was the mother of one of them—a woman whose only crime was to show anxiety about the developing unhealthy relationship between her daughter and the other girl. She was killed—brutally, bloodily and with premeditation, because she thought it would be best to separate the friends. They planned the murder with joyful anticipation—'It's very exciting, like the night before Christmas,' wrote one girl in her diary. At no time did either show a vestige of remorse for their crime.

The younger girl, Juliet Marion Hulme, was the daughter of Dr Henry Rainsford Hulme, a Cambridge graduate who was Britain's Director of Operational Research at the Admiralty during the Second World War and who later became a lecturer at Liverpool University. According to Juliet's mother, Mrs Hilda Hulme, the child had suffered bomb shock during the air raids on Britain and had always been rather frail. She attended school in Liverpool until she was fourteen, when her father was appointed Rector of Canterbury University College in Christchurch, New Zealand, and the family began a new life in this rather staid, English-type city in 1953.

Juliet was a highly intelligent girl and had no difficulty in adapting to her new high school in Christchurch, but because of her health—she had once spent four months in a tuberculosis sanatorium—she was not able to take part in sports and organised games and had to spend a lot of time resting in bed.

Her parents were pleased when she struck up a school friendship with another girl who had spent some time in hospital and was also debarred from the usual teenage physical activities. This youngster, Pauline Yvonne Parker, a few months older than Juliet, had a less conventional background. Her mother was Mrs Honora Mary Parker, then aged forty-five, and her father was company manager Herbert Reiper; the couple had lived together for twenty-three years. Mrs Parker was known as Mrs Reiper, however, and there was no evidence that the family life was other than a normally happy one.

Pauline's parents, like the Hulmes, at first approved of the friendship and were happy for their daughter to spend most of her free time—often staying overnight and for weekends and holidays—at the Hulmes' pleasant home in Christchurch. They were both pretty girls, Juliet tall and slim with long fair hair, and Pauline petite and dark with flashing brown eyes. They seemed happy enough in a schoolgirlish fashion as they went for walks and to the cinema together, exchanging books and helping each other with their homework.

Gradually, however, the intensity of their friendship began to worry their parents. The girls resented any separation and developed such an obsession about each other that they became withdrawn from their families and all other friends. Pauline and Juliet showed open dislike of their mothers and there were quarrels in both homes.

There were anxious consultations between the parents. Then a natural solution presented itself when Dr Hulme accepted a new appointment in England and decided that on his way back to his home country he would take Juliet to a school in

South Africa. Pauline begged to be allowed to go too, but her parents were adamant in their refusal.

The date fixed for departure was 3rd July 1954.

Rightly or wrongly, the girls decided that the main stumbling block to their plans to remain together—eventually, they hoped to go to America—was Mrs Parker. So they decided quite simply to kill her.

They persuaded her to take them on a farewell picnic to beautiful Victoria Park, Cashmere Hills, Christchurch. The girls took with them an unusual pink stone and a brick wrapped in a stocking. They behaved well, seeming sad but resigned to their imminent separation, and the unfortunate Mrs Parker must have been relieved at the turn events appeared to be taking.

Then, by prearrangement, Juliet left the beaten track and wandered ahead of the other two. In a secluded glade she dropped the pink stone on the ground and walked on. 'Oh look at that pretty stone,' cried Pauline, as she and her mother reached the appointed spot. Mrs Parker, as the girls had foreseen, bent down to pick up the stone. Pauline snatched the brick from her shoulder bag and brought it down heavily on her mother's head.

It was at that point that their plans began to break down. The girls thought that one blow would kill Mrs Parker and their story was to be that she had slipped and banged her head on a brick as she fell. They overestimated Pauline's strength and underestimated her mother's resistance. When several more blows failed even to render the victim unconscious, Juliet ran back to help her friend. In turn they smashed the brick on to the woman's head while the other held her down. Screaming, shouting and pleading, Honora Parker continued to fight for her life—until, after twenty-four separate blows to the head and more than twenty other injuries had been inflicted, the beaten and exhausted woman died of shock.

Although they must have known that no one would believe their story, Pauline and Juliet put the rest of their scheme into action. They returned to a tea shop in the park which they had visited with Mrs Parker earlier that afternoon and Pauline sobbed out a story of tragedy to the proprietress, Mrs Agnes Ritchie.

'Mummy's been hurt terribly,' she cried. 'I think she's dead.' Juliet supported the story that Mrs Parker had slipped on a plank and hit her head on a brick.

Both girls had blood on their clothes and their hands and Mrs Ritchie helped them to clean themselves. At first they were hysterical, but when they became calmer Pauline elaborated her story.

'Mummy's head kept bumping and banging as she fell,' she said. 'It seems like a dream . . . we shall wake up soon.'

It was clearly a case of murder and there was never any doubt about the identity of the killers. Within a few hours both girls had admitted their guilt, though Pauline at first tried to shield her friend by saying that she had attacked her mother while Juliet was absent. She thought Juliet might have guessed what had happened, but hoped she would believe that Mrs Parker had fallen.

Juliet told detectives that she left home with the brick wrapped in a newspaper. She gave the brick to Pauline, who put it in a stocking. She was expecting Mrs Reiper (Parker) to be attacked while they were in the park.

'I heard noises behind me,' she said. 'It was a loud conversation and an angry one. I saw Mrs Reiper in a sort of squatting position . . . I saw Pauline hit her with the brick . . . I went back and took the stocking and hit her too. I thought one of them had to die and I wanted to help Pauline. It was terrible. Mrs Reiper moved convulsively. We both held her and she was still when we left her. The brick had come out of the stocking with the force of the blows.'

Juliet said that she and her friend had often discussed murder in connection with the plots of books they were writing.

The whole story of the relationship between the two girls and events leading up to the murder was revealed in a diary kept by Pauline, and in the evidence of psychiatrists at the Supreme Court trial at Christchurch in August 1954.

Extracts from the diary were read to the court both by

prosecuting counsel, Mr A. W. Brown, who described the book as 'a mirror of evil', and by medical witnesses called to support the defence case that the girls were insane.

Mr Brown said the diary revealed that the girls indulged in wild orgies which left them ecstatic but exhausted, and that together they had gone in for blackmail, attempted burglary and shoplifting.

Among extracts from Pauline's diary were the following:

14th February 1954: 'Why could not mother die? Dozens of thousands of people are dying, so why not mother? And father too? Life is hard.'

28th April: 'Anger against mother is boiling inside of me as she is the main obstacle in my path. Suddenly the means of ridding myself of the obstacle occur to me. If she was to die . . . I wish to make it accidental.'

15th June: 'We practically finished our books today and our main "ike" for the day was to murder mother. This notion is not a new one, but this time it is a definite plan which we intend to carry out. We have worked it out carefully and are both thrilled by the idea. Naturally we feel a trifle nervous, but the pleasure of anticipation is great.'

20th June: 'We discussed plans for "moidering" mother and made them a little clearer. Peculiarly enough I have no qualms of conscience.'

21st June: 'I rose early and helped mother vigorously this morning. Deborah [the name she used for Juliet Hulme] rang and we decided to use a rock in a stocking rather than a sandbag. We discussed it all fully. I feel very keyed up as though I were planning a surprise party. Mother has fallen in with everything beautifully and the happy event is to take place tomorrow afternoon. Next time I write mother will be dead. How odd, yet how pleasing.'

The entry for 22nd June was headed 'The Happy Event' and read: 'In the morning before the death I feel very excited. Last night I felt sort of "night-before-Christmassy" but I didn't have pleasant dreams.'

A diary entry dated 23rd April said that Juliet had surprised her mother in a bedroom with a man who was occupying a flat in the Hulmes' house. Juliet had given her account of this incident to Pauline, who wrote, 'They were in bed drinking tea. Juliet felt an hysterical tendency to giggle.' Pauline said that the man had given Juliet £100 at her request and that the two girls were saving the money to get to America to write novels and break into Hollywood.

Mrs Hulme, who was president of the Marriage Guidance Council in Christchurch, was subpoenaed to give evidence for the prosecution. She said that the incident was described in the diary in a very distorted and untruthful way. On the night in question she went to the man's room because she heard him call and found him in obvious pain. He had been taken ill. She made him a cup of tea and had a cup herself while sitting on the side of the bed. Juliet appeared and said something like, 'So the balloon has gone up. I had hoped to catch you out.'

Mrs Hulme added that she was in love with this man, Walter Perry, and that divorce was under discussion between herself and her husband.

Walter Perry said that Mrs Hulme's version of the incident was correct. He had not given any money to Juliet, but she had threatened to blackmail him. He had fallen in love with Mrs Hulme and there was no deception of Dr Hulme about the state of affairs.

An early diary entry spoke of 'friendship which became a bond' and recorded how Juliet and Pauline had ridden out into the country on bicycles and had wandered around 'getting ecstatic'. At night, when Pauline was staying with the Hulmes, the girls danced naked on the lawn beside a 'Temple of Minerva' which they had built in the grounds. They photographed each other in fancy dress (they frequently assumed bizarre identities, Pauline at one time saying that she was Lancelot Trelawney, a Cornish soldier of fortune, while Juliet was Deborah, mistress of the Emperor of Borovnia) and also had a collection of nude pictures of each other.

The girls shared a passionate interest in film stars and Pauline recorded that on one occasion they had enacted how they thought different Hollywood personalities—including Mario Lanza and Orson Welles—would make love.

'We only chose the first seven because it was by then 7.30 a.m. and we both felt exhausted,' she wrote.

At other times their eroticism took the form of acting out how each of the saints would express sexual love.

It was clear that they were anxious to make money in order to leave their homes and be together. They had gone on shop-lifting expeditions and Pauline had tried unsuccessfully to rob her father's business. One diary entry read: 'We worked out how much prostitutes could earn and how much we should make in this profession. "Should" has gradually changed to "shall" and we spent a wonderful day messing around and talking over how much fun we will have in our profession.'

Pauline had experienced sexual relations with a boy, her diary recording how she had stayed with him until the early hours of the morning and had been 'caught in the act' by her father. She was not happy in this relationship, but derived some pleasure in describing all the details to Juliet.

One woman in the packed public gallery of the court fainted after hearing a particularly explicit diary entry which ended, 'Nothing is now too disgusting or revolting for us.'

Further extracts from the diary were read by psychiatrist Dr Francis Bennett, giving evidence for the defence. He said he had been consulted some time previously by the parents of the girls about their association and had told Mrs Parker that he thought Pauline's loss of weight was due to an 'unnatural re-lationship' between the two girls.

'The girls formed a society of their own in which every act, thought and deed was approved and admired by the other,' he said. 'They lived in a world of illusion and ecstasy. They dis-posed of the lowlier world around them and took delight in secretly breaking the conventions. They did not hate other people. They despised them.'

Dr Bennett said that one entry from the diary read, 'We rose about ten and had some raspberries and cream and felt sick, after which we sat in the car and discussed who we would leave alive if we wiped out the rest of the world. We wrote out a list and had a wonderful time.'

As time went on entries described an increasing exaltation which was apparent in night-long verbal orgies. These were described in the diary as 'heavenly and glorious'.

Dr Bennett said that in an interview Juliet had told him of her ideas about heaven and paradise. She believed that she and Pauline would meet everyone they had known on earth. Asked if she expected to meet Pauline's mother with blood on her face, she replied, 'She would not arrive in that state. In any case she would be in heaven and we would be in paradise.' Questioned about regrets she might have about the murder of Mrs Parker, she said, 'No regrets whatever. Of course I do not want my family involved, but we have been terribly happy since it happened so it's all been a blessing in disguise.' Pauline, too, had told him she had no regrets.

In Dr Bennett's view the girls were not sane.

'To us—sane I hope—it was murder so bestial, treacherous and filthy that it was outside all kindly limits of sanity,' he said. 'It was a thousand miles from sanity.'

Another defence psychiatrist, Dr R. W. Medlicott, said that Pauline and Juliet lived in a fantastic world of their own making—with a religion, a god and a paradise they had created in their minds. They believed there were only twenty-five people who, like themselves, had a special part of the brain which enabled them to see the 'fourth world'. When Dr Medlicott asked them whether they thought they had been picked by God they replied, 'We don't think—we just know.'

'These girls exulted over their crime and showed no reasonable emotional appreciation of their situation,' he said. 'A reversal of the moral sense is apparent in both of them . . . they suffer from paranoia of an exalted type, in a setting of *folie à deux*, a term used to describe communicated insanity.'

Although he realised they were trying to prove themselves insane when he first met them, and consequently discounted statements they made, a study of their past and of the diary eventually convinced him that they were in fact insane.

'There is no proof that theirs was a physical relationship,' he added, 'but there is a lot of suggestion in the diary that a physical relationship occurred. Homosexuality is frequently allied to paranoia.'

Dr Medlicott was asked by Mr Brown how the girls acted when they were alone.

'There were love scenes,' he replied.

'Love is a mild word,' remarked Mr Brown.

Questioned about Pauline, Dr Medlicott said the fact that she had been intimate with a boy did not disprove the existence of 'unnatural' desires.

The psychiatrist agreed that day-dreaming and different ideas about God and the after-life were not evidence of insanity. The girls knew the law but did not recognise it. They considered their action in killing Mrs Parker morally right by their own standards.

Three other medical experts, however, all considered Pauline and Juliet to be sane.

Dr Kenneth Stallworthy, superintendent of Auckland Mental Hospital, said Pauline had told him, 'We knew what we were doing was wrong. We knew we would be punished if caught and did our best not to be caught. I would have been an absolute moron not to know that murder was against the law.'

'I saw no evidence of delusions,' he continued. 'Their conceit, common in adolescence, did not constitute a delusion of grandeur. The girls had some justification for their conceit. . . . Juliet in her interviews displayed the vocabulary, and shrewdness in answering difficult questions of a highly intelligent person of a much greater age.'

Dr J. D. Hunter, superintendent of Sunnyside Mental Hospital, Christchurch, also thought both girls to be unusually intelligent and quite sane. Dr James Saville, medical officer at the same hospital, said he had had five conversations with the girls, who at first were inclined to pretend they were insane but said later they wished to be regarded as sane.

'Juliet told me that if they were found insane they would probably be out of the mental hospital by the time they were eighteen or nineteen,' said Dr Saville. 'She said they could not see themselves getting out of prison as early as that if they were found sane and convicted.'

This witness added that he did not know of any crime committed by two insane people in combination.

The all-male jury took a little over two hours to reject the defence plea that Pauline and Juliet were insane when they killed Mrs Parker. They were sentenced to be detained during Her Majesty's pleasure and were sent to separate prisons four hundred miles apart.

The girls continued their education in prison and both passed their university entrance examinations. Juliet became an expert dressmaker, making her own designs rather than following the Vogue patterns sent to her by friends, and she confided to a fellow prisoner that she hoped to open her own dress shop when she was released. She designed and made her own 'going out' wardrobe, including a topcoat which was an adaptation of a German officer's greatcoat. According to this other prisoner, Juliet said that had she been a man—which she would have preferred to being a woman—she would liked to have been a German officer.

Juliet showed evidence of some literary skill and is said to have completed at least one novel during her period of imprisonment.

Both girls were released on licence in November, 1959. Juliet was stated to have left New Zealand a few weeks later to join her father in England. Her parents were divorced soon after the murder trial.

Pauline was converted to Roman Catholicism while she served her five years' jail sentence and expressed the wish to become a nun. It is believed that she either entered a convent or took up missionary work in the backward countries of Africa.

Juliet and Pauline seemed to idealise each other in a narcissistic way, which meant that they had really fallen in love with their own images. Somehow each identified all that was good with the partner, representing herself, and all that was bad with anyone who frustrated them in any way whatsoever. There was also a manic reversal of values, causing the murder of the mother to be likened to Christmas excitement.

Some normal feelings tried to break through in the unpleasant dreams of the night before the murder. It would seem that the reason the girls thought they would like to become prostitutes was that so they could remain aloof from men, from whom they would take money and who would become their 'subjects and slaves'. This despising of other people was typical of the attitude of the Moors killers Brady and Hindley. At a deep level there must have been a very destructive, death-orientated process in them, with which they could not cope. through the external acting-out of the terrible crime of matricide they were able to maintain some sort of psychic equilibrium, albeit on an entirely horrible and false basis.

Another lesbian love affair which ended in murder came into bloom, like that of the New Zealand teenagers, in an aura of physical sickness. As in the case of Pauline and Juliet, fear of separation was the match to the flame of violence—but there resemblance ended, because in this other case the victim was one of the lovers and her killer the woman who could not bear to let her go.

The pair met at Tehidy House, a sanatorium in Redruth, Cornwall—Bertha Mary Scorse, who had developed tuberculosis at the age of sixteen, and Joyce Mary Dunstan, a married woman six years her senior. Both were very ill, both were lonely and frightened of dying. A passionate friendship developed between them.

Bertha was eighteen when she was sent home to her mother at Newlyn, Cornwall, in the summer of 1950, and Joyce was discharged a few weeks later. During that period of separation Bertha wrote frequently to Joyce, begging her to break with her husband Frederick, who was looking forward to his wife's return to their home in North Road, Camborne, Cornwall.

One letter from Bertha read: 'I received your dear letter about ten minutes ago . . . I hate every single inch that separates us, darling. After you rang off last night I felt on top of the world for five minutes because I had heard your beloved voice. That didn't last long however. Before I got home I was swallowed up in unbelievable misery and loneliness. I went to bed about ten and lay awake for ages ... life is nothing without you, darling. Never forget that you have made my life worth while and so terribly happy—something that it never was before.'

In another letter to Joyce, Bertha mentioned that Frederick Dunstan had told her that Joyce would soon be home with him, and Bertha wrote: 'I feel as if the bottom of my world had dropped out. I am so fed up. I hate him. He's got to see once and for all that you are through. Please, Joyce darling, for my peace of mind and happiness, he's got to accept your word as final.'

Later Bertha wrote: 'I am crazy about you. I can only relax and feel contented when I am with you. After you have told Fred that you are leaving him it will be only natural for you to live at home or with a friend, so that side is all right ... I can't express the loneliness I feel.' In the same letter she spoke of 'memories—beautiful, wonderful, heavenly memories that I want to live over and over again, but can't without you'.

There is no doubt that this was a shared passion. Joyce Dunstan told her parents and friends that she wished to be known by her maiden name of Reynolds. The inscription on a photograph she sent to Bertha made it clear that she regarded herself as the other woman's 'wife'.

In an attempt to strengthen the pressures on her friend, Bertha wrote to Joyce's father, mineworker William Reynolds, who lived in the little hamlet of Pool, near Camborne.

'Joyce and I are desperately unhappy,' she told him. 'For some time Joyce had been considering leaving Fred, who she was unhappy with before her illness. No one can expect her to return to Fred, a man she now hates. It would only mean great misery and heartbreak, not only for her but for myself as well. She can stay here until her legal separation comes through and then we'll go away. Our whole future hangs on your helping us to find peace and happiness together ... happiness is the greatest thing in the world, for without it life is worthless. Life is so short and death so very long. We ask for so little, just to be together.'

In the second week of August 1950, Mrs Dunstan left the sanatorium and returned to her husband, who was employed as a catering supervisor. But she stayed only a few days and on the fourteenth of that month she packed her personal belongings and moved into the Scorses' home at Chywoone Crescent, Newlyn. She was received ecstatically by brown-eyed, crophaired Bertha and made quietly welcome by widowed Mrs Bertha Ann Scorse and her younger daughter, Elizabeth Maureen.

For some time Bertha and Joyce shared the same bed, but Joyce's health improved and Bertha's again deteriorated, and they were persuaded to occupy separate single beds in the same room.

For a few months they seemed happy in their new shared life, but passion began to wane and friendship to turn sour as Joyce grew stronger and Bertha became so ill that she was obliged to spend almost all her days in bed. Joyce was active enough to go out and Bertha was tortured by jealousy. She complained to her sister that Joyce no longer loved her and wanted to end the association. There was constant bickering, which culminated in a fierce quarrel on 12th January 1952. Two days later Mrs Dunstan walked out of the house and went to her parents' home at Higher Pumpfield Road, Pool.

Bertha was so upset that a doctor was called to calm her. He begged her to be reasonable and when she said she was going to follow her friend, told her she was too ill to get out of bed. Eventually her mother and sister tied her ankles together with a clothes line, but she managed to free herself and appeared at the top of the stairs dressed in trousers and a topcoat. When all efforts to dissuade her failed, Elizabeth called a taxi and accompanied Bertha on the fifteen-mile journey to Pool.

In response to a message sent to her, Joyce Dunstan came out to the taxi, but returned to the house within a few seconds because her mother called to her. Bertha ran after her, begging her to return with them to Newlyn, but Joyce refused.

From under her coat Bertha drew a dagger and stabbed her friend, thrusting the five-inch blade in up to the hilt.

Mrs Dunstan died in hospital four days later after making a deposition in which, emphasising that she wished her name to be given as Reynolds and not Dunstan, she said, 'We were lovers . . . she once said she would kill me if I ever left her, but I did not take her seriously. She had shown me the knife and said she would use it if anyone came between us.'

Bertha, charged with murder, told the police, 'Joyce said she would never come back to me and that her mother needed her more than I did. It was not premeditated and I didn't want to murder or hurt her. I only wanted her to come back.'

By the time Bertha Mary Scorse was brought to trial at Exeter Assizes at the end of February 1952, she was so ill that she had to be carried into court on a stretcher—tilted so that Mr Justice Pilcher could see her face.

Mr G. D. Roberts, QC, prosecuting, spoke of the 'abnormal and unnatural passion' which had grown up between the two women, and submitted that the case was one of premeditated, clear, cold-blooded and callous murder'. But Mr John Maude, QC, for the defence, maintained that Bertha Scorse was suffering from a disease of the mind to such an extent that she did not know the difference between right and wrong.

In a voice shaking with emotion, he told the jury, 'She is, in fact, dying. It may be quick—or it may be three years. She has had haemorrhage after haemorrhage, there are large cavities in one lung and she had been lying in bed for about sixteen months. Something got her out of bed, something so powerful that, despite the ghastly scene of her mother and sister tying her legs together, she got out of the house . . . being shut up with this illness, she had no hope of being loved by a man, but she wanted, as every person does, to be loved by somebody.'

A report showed that the girl had been difficult since early childhood and was irritable, selfish, callous and morose, and by the time she was fifteen it was clear that something was very wrong with her. According to one of the nurses at the sanatorium, Bertha wanted to be loved, but she made herself unpopular with patients and staff. She never reconciled herself to her physical illness and was afraid of dying. Quite unbalanced at times, she acted hysterically.

'Ordinarily, if an abnormal affection develops between normally healthy persons, it is a matter for horror,' continued Mr Maude. 'But when it comes to judging this girl, is it not possible to ask quite humbly, "Might that not have happened to me? Might I not at last have found a friend? Might it not have happened that we loved each other?" If the jury want to judge by moral standards they will say that the devil brought these two women together in their sickness and misery, but it is not the jury's function to do anything of the sort.'

Dr Roy Neville Craig, a mental specialist, said he considered that when Miss Scorse struck the blow she was not in a state to know the difference between right and wrong.

'In my opinion she is a psychopath, a person with very strong anti-social trends and abnormal traits,' he said. 'Punishment and treatment have no effect on such people. This woman suffers a gross perversion which is an extremely powerful driving force, not to be denied by anything. Her friendship with the other woman ran a typical course. Gradually it began to wane and she began to realise she was going to lose someone who meant everything to her in an otherwise empty life.'

The position, he said was that of a weak rope feeling an ever-increasing strain, with one strand after another giving way until there was just one strand left . . . a strand that broke when she was told she had lost the other woman. He could not agree that it was just a case of a woman scorned. There was a finality about her act which brought a good deal of mental relief.

This witness was asked by Mr Roberts, 'The perverted passion of a woman for a woman, or a man for a man, is no stronger than a normal natural passion?' Dr Craig replied, 'I could not disagree more. It is much stronger.'

Summing up, the judge said, 'It is clear that during their association these women formed for each other this perverted passion. You may feel disgust or sorrow that this sort of thing should be, but there is no doubt that this girl was passionately attached to the dead woman and it would seem it had been reciprocal.' The important thing for the jury to decide was whether or not during the material moments Bertha Scorse knew that what she was doing was wrong.

The jury of nine men and three women took just an hour to decide that she was sane at the time she killed her friend. The judge passed sentence of death and Bertha was carried on the stretcher to an ambulance waiting outside the court. Four days later she was reprieved—to await what she thought would be a speedy release by natural death from the commuted sentence of life imprisonment.

But Bertha Scorse did not die. She was transferred from Exeter jail to Holloway and from there taken to a hospital just outside London. One lung was removed. For many months she was desperately ill, but slowly she recovered, and by the time she was twenty-four she was working in the sewing shop at Holloway Prison.

In August 1959, released on licence, she returned to her home in Newlyn, but in an interview shortly afterwards she said, 'I would be better off in Holloway. I am supposed to have paid for my crime, but people are so unpleasant. Do they think I am going to murder again? I was a sick girl filled with drugs when I stabbed my friend.'

By March 1960 she was back in prison, the reason for recall being given as 'conduct giving grounds to fear further violence'. In November 1962 Bertha was again released on licence, but returned to Holloway in July 1963 because she had been found under the influence of drugs.

Nearly nine years later, at the end of October 1972 she was being prepared for parole, and as part of that preparation was allowed out of prison each day to do civilian work and to lunch occasionally with friends. But only a few weeks before the date provisionally fixed for her release she returned fighting drunk to the prison and assaulted a prison officer who had been deputed to strip and search her.

She was transferred to Styal Prison in Cheshire where, now aged forty-two and twenty-one years after the murder for which she was sentenced to death, she continues to serve her life sentence.

In this case the envy of the more attractive and healthy by the less attractive and ill was complicated by 'the death thing' in Bertha—the threat of death by a very invasive attack of pulmonary tuberculosis. This threat complicated matters so much that in her psyche, Bertha evacuated her fear of death in the form of a murderous attack upon her beloved victim, Joyce.

9

Homicidal Homosexuals

Gordon Lockhart, an attractive, blue-eyed, curly-haired lad of fifteen, left his home at Stephenson Road, Newcastle upon Tyne, at lunchtime on Monday 18th November 1957, to start a new job as a trainee cinema projectionist. During the afternoon tea-break he slipped out of the Pavilion Cinema in Westgate Road to collect some money owing to him from previous employment.

'I'll only be a few minutes,' he told his workmates. But he did not return to the cinema and he failed to arrive home for his evening meal.

His mother, Mrs Evelyn Lockhart, was worried and felt instinctively that something was wrong. She could not help recalling her son's odd behaviour the previous day when he had seemed agitated and frightened, shouting, 'Shut that door quickly', when anyone entered or left the house. Gordon had been reluctant to explain his fears, but she had the impression he was anxious not to be seen by a middle-aged man who had been staring at the house during the day. Mrs Lockhart remembered that the same man had been in Stephenson Road on a previous Sunday and that Gordon had spoken to him for a few minutes.

She reported her son's disappearance to the police, who at first treated the matter as a routine missing persons enquiry.

On Wednesday that week she received an unsigned letter-card which read: 'Gordon has gone to London as a woman is after him for money.'

By first post the next day came another card: 'Gordon is living with prostitutes and says he is making money like them. I am an old school pal of his aged seventeen. He borrowed £1 from me to go to London.'

Gordon's twenty-four-year-old sister Doris opened the door when the postman rang the bell the following morning. Recognising the printed writing on the package as matching that on the two cards, she ripped off the wrappings. Inside was a 1958 calendar with a tender picture of a mother and baby. Scrawled across it was a three-word message: GORDON IS DEAD.

On the same day the Chief Constable of Newcastle received an anonymous letter saying that the boy's body was in a sack in the River Tyne—a statement that was disproved within hours by a gruesome discovery at St James' Boxing Hall at Gallowgate, Newcastle. Police called to the hall discovered Gordon's body in a sump under the arena. It had been cut in half and disembowelled and the intestines packed in a suitcase. The boy had died from extensive brain damage, having suffered fifteen separate blows on the head. He had been sexually assaulted before death.

On the morning of Saturday 23rd November the national newspapers carried a description of a man the police wanted to see in connection with the murder. That afternoon a shabby, balding, middle-aged man walked into Glasgow Central police station and said to Probationer Constable John Neil: 'I am the man Newcastle police want to interview.'

He was bachelor Albert Edward Matheson, aged fifty-two, who worked as a handyman at the boxing hall and had been missing from his lodgings in Lovaine Place since Thursday of that week. He was taken back to Newcastle by Detective Chief Inspector J. Angus, to whom he made several statements.

Matheson made no attempt to deny his guilt. Speaking with a pronounced lisp, he first said that Gordon had demanded two pounds as the price of buggery and as he (Matheson) was willing to pay only one pound he had killed the boy. He had first smashed Gordon's head with a glass bottle, filled with water to make it heavier, and had then used a claw hammer to inflict further injuries.

In a later statement Matheson said he killed the lad because he knew he would have money on him and that he had taken thirty-five pounds in a registered envelope from Gordon's pocket.

These two statements resulted in some legal argument when Matheson appeared at Durham Assizes in January 1958, charged with capital murder in the course of or in furtherance of theft, for which the penalty at that time was death by hanging.

Mr Stanley Price, QC, for the Crown, said there was a good deal of evidence of some form of association between Matheson and the boy, but Matheson had said that the murder was committed in the course of theft. He told the jury they would have to consider if the accused man was lying about this, just as he had lied in the anonymous letter-cards.

'If you think other motives lay behind this killing, that would be a case of murder but not of capital murder,' he said.

Mr Justice Finnemore commented, 'This is entirely new. I don't know whether you have considered that point—if the theft was the motive or intention that led to the murder, or if the intention of the man was to murder and the theft just followed.'

Mr G. S. Waller, defending, told the jury that the facts of the killing were not contested, but submitted that Matheson suffered from an abnormality of mind which diminished his responsibility. He was therefore not liable to be convicted of murder but of manslaughter.

Outlining the killer's previous history, Dr Ian Pickering, senior medical officer at Durham Prison, said that Matheson had spent the best part of his life—since he was eighteen, in fact—in borstals or prisons. He had a psychopathic personality and had been a voluntary patient in a mental hospital as recently as September 1957. On first appearances he was a good conversationalist and gave the impression of intelligence actually higher than he possessed, his true mental age being less than that of a boy of ten. He was much given to self-injury and had undergone seven operations for the removal of razor blades, needles, pieces of wire and other things he had swallowed.

Dr Theodore Cuthbert, consultant psychiatrist to the Royal Victoria Infirmary, Newcastle, stated that the question of right and wrong hardly ever entered Matheson's head. He had no feeling of remorse for his crime and no serious feeling that he had done anything wrong.

Speaking of Matheson's anonymous letters to Mrs Lockhart as 'a refinement of cruelty', the judge pointed out that the accused man was known to be a sexual pervert.

'He formed a wicked, unnatural association with this boy,' he said. 'According to his first statement he wished to commit a foul crime on the lad. Sexual perversion, however, is not an abnormality of mind but an abnormality of morals.' If the jury thought that Matheson also suffered from a mental abnormality which substantially impaired his responsibility the only verdict they could return was one of manslaughter.

The jury took only an hour to bring in a verdict of capital murder and Matheson was sentenced to death, but the Court of Criminal Appeal later allowed his appeal against conviction and substituted a verdict of manslaughter and a sentence of twenty years' imprisonment.

Giving the court's reasons for allowing the appeal, Lord Chief Justice Goddard said they found Matheson was suffering from diminished responsibility.

'It is one of the most horrible cases I have come across,' continued His Lordship. 'The man is a monster—there is no other word for it. Having regard to what must have affected the minds of the jury or any other body of ordinary citizens, we would not care to say that their verdict was unreasonable, though we feel bound to say it is not supported by the evidence.'

Three medical men, all experienced in matters relating to mental health, had said that Matheson's mental development was that of a boy of ten and that his mind was so abnormal as substantially to impair his responsibility. The prosecution had not called any medical evidence in rebuttal.

Albert Matheson started his prison sentence with one mystery still unsolved.

When he walked into Glasgow police headquarters and confessed to the murder of Gordon Lockhart he told detectives that he had also killed another boy.

He said he had been on a cycling holiday in Scotland in 1948 when he met a sixteen-year-old Irish boy who had just arrived in Glasgow to look for farm work. They went to the seaside town of Largs, Ayrshire, where they had a quarrel about money. Matheson said he hit the lad with a brick and killed him, hiding his body in a cave.

Inspector Angus described how Matheson took him and other officers to the cave at Largs but they found no body—not surprising in view of the fact that ten years had passed and that the sea washed into the cave at high tide. Other points of Matheson's story—including an address at which he said he had stayed in Glasgow—had been checked and found to be accurate.

'We simply do not know if this tale of another murder is true or false,' said the inspector. 'If there was a body it has vanished.'

Within Matheson's psyche there was a great deal of destructive nastiness and cruelty which flared up when he was rejected by Gordon Lockhart.

At fifty-two he was an ageing queer and often such men find it more and more difficult to find sexual love objects.

Research has shown that homosexuals have an intensification of all the primitive destructive elements of sexuality which one sometimes finds in heterosexual crimes. The reason is thought to be attributable to the fact that love in which there is true regard and concern for the object of sexual desire is so much harder to achieve in homosexual relationships.

All the more primitive attitudes, the passions of envy and jealousy, anger and revenge at rejection and refusal—especially after initial teasing—are much more dangerous. At another level, the situation is complicated by the self-hatred of the homosexual, which is then projected or displaced onto another person, whom he then feels the need to harm.

It was early in the morning of 20th May 1962, and the motor vessel *Cornwall* had been berthed for five hours in Mount Stuart dry dock at Newport, Monmouthshire. Dockman Walter Powell was cleaning out the bottom of the dry dock when he was startled to see the body of a lad, wearing only a pyjama jacket, come flying through the air. The boy hit a steel plate, bounced off against a ledge, then landed almost at the feet of the horrified dockman.

The boy had clearly come over the side of the ship, from the deck, and had been killed in the sixty-foot drop. He was quickly identified as David John Fulton, a sixteen-year-old cabin boy, of Marlborough Road, Banbury, Oxfordshire, who had joined the crew of the 7,583-ton vessel only two weeks previously.

Detectives called to the ship were mystified. A nightwatchman had heard some laughter and then a scream coming from the direction of Fulton's cabin and had thought 'something was going on that shouldn't have been going on'. This witness, Frank Thuell, stayed near the cabin for twenty minutes but heard nothing more.

There was no sign of a struggle in the cabin and the boy's spectacles were on a table beside the bed. Fulton was very short-sighted and was never seen outside his cabin without his glasses. After two days of questioning the *Cornwall*'s crew of sixty-three, not one of whom admitted to seeing or hearing anything unusual, the investigating officers thought it possible that young Fulton had sleepwalked to his death.

Mr Glyn Evans, the deputy coroner for Newport, said he was satisfied that the scream and David Fulton's death were somehow linked.

'Everything was not as it ought to have been that night,' he added. 'The only inquest verdict I can record is an open verdict.'

The *Cornwall* continued her voyage and berthed in Liverpool's West Gladstone dock just a week after the death of the cabin boy. On 28th May the members of the crew were paid off and most of them had left the ship when it was discovered that one man, Seaman Patrick Kelly, had not collected his pay. He was last seen entering his cabin at 11 o'clock the previous night. Crew members who went to Kelly's cabin found the door locked. When they forced their way inside they saw him lying face downwards, naked, in bed. He was dead.

Kelly, a ship's greaser aged forty, whose home was at Holmfauldhead Drive, Glasgow, was a friend of Fulton and just before the inquest had said, 'I am number one suspect.' There was no question, however, of suicide, because a post-mortem examination showed that Kelly had died of suffocation and that there were bites and bruises on his face.

Detectives investigating the first death immediately left Newport for Liverpool. The ship was sealed off, loading stopped, and all crew members interviewed. Those who had already left the ship were traced and brought back.

One of the men questioned was David Owen Norman Wright, an eighteen-year-old galley boy, of Kingston Road, Romford, Essex, who was told he was believed to have spent the previous night with Kelly in his cabin. 'Yes,' replied Wright, 'I was with him for homosexual purposes.' He denied all knowledge of Kelly's injuries and said he knew nothing about his death.

The following day, however, he made a statement to Detective Inspector Muat, of Liverpool police, in which he said, 'I did not mean to kill Paddy. He was one of my best friends. I had no reason to kill him because he owed me two pounds and was going to pay me when he got paid off. He was dead and I was the only one there. I knew he was dead and I was frightened. He must have been suffocated as I was lying on top of him.'

Wright added that he covered Kelly with the bedclothes, locked the door of the cabin and threw the key over the side of the ship.

A few days later Wright was accused at court in Liverpool of the manslaughter of Kelly and of committing indecency with him. He was committed for trial on both charges to Monmouthshire Assizes.

But when he stood before Mr Justice Edmund Davies at the Assizes in July, however, it was to answer a charge of murdering David Fulton.

During his period of remand in custody, Wright had been closely questioned about the death of Fulton and had made a statement in which he said he had gone into the other lad's cabin for homosexual activities, to which Fulton had not objected.

'After a few minutes he started to cough, making funny noises like wheezing,' said Wright. 'The noise continued so I pulled his head off the pillow to see what was the matter. He had vomited and there was blood on the pillow. I panicked . . . I pulled him to the floor. Then I took him to the ship's rail and lifted him over. I watched him drop and his head hit one of the stays. It made quite a clunk . . . it all seemed like a dream, it did not seem real.' After dropping Fulton over the rail, Wright returned to his own cabin and went to sleep.

Three doctors called for the defence said that the accused man was a psychopathic personality. One of them, Dr Thomas Riordan, medical superintendent at Cefn Coed Hospital, Swansea, gave his opinion that Wright had a split personality and it was likely that a fractured skull suffered in a road accident had aggravated his condition. He had been treated at three mental hospitals.

'He told me of one incident while he was in hospital,' continued Dr Riordan. 'He said he was holding a budgerigar tightly to prevent it pecking him . . . he admitted choking the bird and subsequently cutting off its head with a knife.'

A prison medical officer, Dr Marshall Fenton, said, 'I think Wright is possessed of violent tendencies and is capable of grossly irresponsible conduct.'

The jury found Wright not guilty of murder but guilty of manslaughter on the grounds of criminal negligence.

Making an order for his detention at Broadmoor for an unlimited period, the judge told Wright, 'Even in the light of the medical evidence, you are clearly a public menace and in need of urgent mental treatment . . . I express the fervent hope that you will never be discharged unless the advisers to the Home Secretary are perfectly satisfied that to release you would in no way imperil the public. I want it to be clearly known that had I decided to imprison you instead of making a hospital order, I should in respect of the manslaughter conviction have sentenced you to imprisonment for at least twenty years.'

Mr Justice Davies ordered that the indictment relating to the manslaughter of Patrick Kelly should remain on the file.

Mr Justice Davies wisely underlined the dangers of Wright being released from detention too early.

He is a most disturbed individual, and the budgerigar incident clearly illustrates his complex fantasies. It appears that in his case, murderousness is uppermost in his psyche and homosexuality is second and set *within* the murderousness.

When a butler was found knifed and battered to death in an elegant three-storey house in London's fashionable Belgravia, it appeared at first to be a clear-cut case of murder in the course of robbery.

The victim was Julian Sesee, a tall, distinguished Belgian aged sixty-four, always correctly dressed in pin-striped trousers and black jacket. Neighbouring residents of Wilton Crescent, SW1, knew him as the perfect manservant and to Mr Geoffrey Bernerd, landlord of the nearby Grenadier public house, he was a quiet, respectful and respectable customer.

During the weekend of 18th–20th December 1970, Mr Sesee was alone in the house. His employer, Lord Bernstein, chairman of Granada TV, was holidaying with his family in Barbados, and other members of the household staff had been given a few days' leave. On Monday 21st December servants who returned to the house found cupboards open, drawers pulled out and further obvious signs of disturbance. The door of the bathroom in the butler's self-contained basement flat was locked. Police called to the house by Lord Bernstein's secretary, Miss Muriel Haselwood, forced this door and discovered Julian Sesee lying dead in the bath. There were numerous wounds to the head, and his throat and abdomen had been slashed, the body afterwards having been swathed in towels. A bloodstained meat cleaver and a kitchen knife were in the lavatory pan.

It seemed likely that the butler had disturbed intruders, but in the absence of Lord and Lady Bernstein it was impossible to establish whether or not anything had been stolen. When the family returned from their Christmas holiday in the West Indies, in time to attend Mr Sesee's funeral service at St Mary's Catholic Church, Chelsea, they discovered that eighty pounds had been taken from a drawer in Lady Bernstein's bedroom.

By that time, however, detectives had decided that this was no straightforward murder for gain. In their search of the butler's flat they found the names and personal details of several young men, as well as letters from men which made it plain that Sesee had had a number of homosexual relationships. The disappearance from his flat of fifty pounds in cash, as well as some items of personal property, gave rise to a new theory that the butler was being blackmailed.

The inquest was formally opened and adjourned no fewer than eight times because, said the Westminster coroner, Mr Gavin Thurston, 'enquiries are still proceeding'. In fact, the Scotland Yard team led by Detective Chief Superintendent John Hensley, one of the Yard's most brilliant and most popular detectives, was virtually certain of the identity of the killer. They knew, too, where he was living. A warrant for his arrest was issued only ten days after the murder but it had not been possible to serve it because the man had flown to Morocco, a country which has no extradition treaty with Britain.

Nearly ten months after the butler's death his killer was named as Mustapha Bassaine, the twenty-seven-year-old son of a Moroccan Government official. After being warned by the coroner that they might be required to name a person in connection with Mr Sesee's death, the eight-man jury at the resumed inquest on 1st October 1971 returned a verdict that Sesee had been murdered by Bassaine.

Chief Superintendent Hensley was put on to the track of the Moroccan by a girl with whom Bassaine had been living at a flat in Anson Road, Tufnell Park, N7. Irishborn Jean Fitzgerald, aged twenty-three, a nightclub hostess, said that Bassaine had worked as a nurse and in an insurance company's canteen, but was sometimes unemployed.

'We paid the rent of the flat between us,' she told detectives. 'He used to get money from some place else when he was unemployed. Sometimes he gave me money but I don't know where it came from. He said something about going with "queers", drinking with them and getting money from them. He showed me a picture of Mr Sesee and told me that the butler often gave him money.'

On the night of 19th December Bassaine had said he was going to see a friend. He did not return to Anson Road that night, but the following evening he telephoned Miss Fitzgerald and asked her to go to Sesee's flat in Wilton Crescent.

'I thought it was funny he wanted me to go there,' she said. 'He said he wanted me to have a drink there and was angry when I refused to go. I was frightened of Bassaine because sometimes he was very vicious and I was afraid he would beat me up as he had done before.'

Later that night Bassaine returned home. He seemed drunk and was crying. He told her he had had an argument with his friend. Miss Fitzgerald noticed that he was wearing a pullover and trousers too big for him—not the clothes he was wearing earlier—and she realised that they belonged to Sesee. There was blood on his shoes and scratch marks on his hands.

'He was carrying a bag full of drink and fruit and he showed me a watch, a camera and a ring which he said Julian had given to him as Christmas presents,' she continued. 'On 22nd December he threw some clothes and papers into the dustbin and told me he would have to visit his home in Morocco immediately because his mother was sick. He bought a single air ticket for Morocco and I saw him off on the plane. He had no difficulty in paying cash for the air fare, although he had had no money when he left for Julian's flat at the weekend.'

When they had seen the newspaper reports of the murder, Bassaine had commented that he could not understand anyone doing such a thing to his friend because Julian was such a nice man. He asked Jean Fitzgerald to send him cuttings of any further reports on the case and gave her an address in Morocco. After days and nights of worrying about Bassaine's possible implication in the murder, Miss Fitzgerald went to the police and told her story. They were able to identify fingerprints found in Sesee's flat with Bassaine's fingerprints in the Anson

Road flat. Bassaine's trousers were in the washing machine at Wilton Crescent and more bloodstained clothing was recovered from the other flat.

This substantial evidence came too late for the police to arrest the suspect. Bassaine—an educated, cultured man, son of a good family—was safely in Morocco before they were made aware of his identity. Secure in the knowledge of his country's extradition laws, he probably thought he could escape justice so long as he kept out of England.

But he reckoned without the determination of the British police. Within days of his flight Scotland Yard, through Interpol, asked the police of all European countries to watch out for him. Superintendent Hensley and Detective Sergeant Bernard Davis continued to take a close interest in Bassaine's movements and after eighteen months of patient waiting, were tipped off that the Moroccan was planning a trip to Germany and Holland.

They contacted police in all major cities in those countries and on 28th June 1972 Bassaine was taken into custody by the Dutch police as he stepped off a plane at Rotterdam. By 10th July, after extradition proceedings had been completed, he was on a London plane with Hensley and Davis.

At the Old Bailey in February 1973, more than two years after the killing of Julian Sesee, Bassaine pleaded Not Guilty to the murder and to the theft of eighty pounds from the Bernsteins' house.

He tried to put the blame on Jean Fitzgerald, saying that she was jealous of Sesee and had threatened to injure 'the old bastard'. He told the jury that the butler was alive and unhurt when he (Bassaine) left the flat after spending the night there while the Bernsteins were away. That same day Jean Fitzgerald had gone out and he did not see her again until the evening. She was trembling and told him she was ill.

The jury did not believe his story and found him guilty of murder and theft. Sentencing him to life imprisonment, Mr Justice Forbes told him, 'This was a brutal murder and you have been convicted on the clearest possible evidence. Your attempt to shift some of the blame on to Miss Fitzgerald has received the treatment it deserved.'

There was one common factor in the three foregoing cases. The victims were all apparently willing partners in casual acts of sexual deviation, and it might be argued that a man or boy who indulges in promiscuous homosexuality—either for pleasure or profit—is at almost as much risk as a female prostitute. A homosexual murder of quite a different nature was committed in Wales at the end of 1960, when the unfortunate victim was an entirely innocent lad, killed because he rejected an aggressor's homosexual advances.

It was nearing dusk on the afternoon of 29th December when Mrs Aline Bonnick was called into the front garden of her home in the tiny seaside hamlet of Gileston, near Barry, Glamorganshire. There she saw a young man with blood on his clothing, face and hands. He seemed agitated and Mrs Bonnick thought he had been involved in a fight until he told her, 'I've found a boy in a shelter down there pretty badly knocked about, with blood all over his face.'

Mrs Bonnick accompanied the young man to the beach and they were nearing a concrete pillbox—one of several erected during the war—when they met the woman's husband, Albert Bonnick, who was collecting driftwood. It was Mr Bonnick who went into the pillbox indicated by the stranger, and there saw a boy who was so badly injured about the face and head that he was quite unrecognisable. It was not until Mr Bonnick looked at the lad's clothing that the full sickening realisation of his discovery hit him. The boy was his own son.

Andrew Bonnick, aged fourteen, the only son in a family of four children, had left home shortly after lunch that day to go for a walk on the beach. At about 2.30 he was joined by two friends, Brian Dunn and Geoffrey Willmott, who both lived in nearby St Athan, and the three of them played around at the edge of the sea. Half an hour later Andrew left the other boys. They saw him walking towards one of the pillboxes and also noticed a young man strolling in the same direction.

Andrew was not seen again until he was found, already dying, in the pillbox. As Mr Bonnick and the stranger carried the boy on to the beach the father noticed that Andrew's trousers had been pulled down and that his stomach and buttocks were exposed, although his trousers belt was still in position round his waist. The boy was taken to hospital where he died at 8.30 that night from shock and hæmorrhage following multiple injuries. He had evidently been beaten with the branch of a tree which was covered in blood and showed traces of his hair.

One of many people interviewed was the man who had first reported the finding of the lad. He was Malcolm Keith Williams, aged twenty, a fitter's mate living at Llwynpia and employed at the power station at Aberthaw—one mile from Gileston.

Williams was first seen at 9.10 that night when he agreed to go to Ton Pentre police station to make a statement. He was to be interviewed by Detective Chief Superintendent Tom Williams, the local CID chief, but this officer was delayed by the post mortem on the dead boy and was not able to talk to the man until five o'clock the next morning. Malcolm Williams, who was accompanied by his father, Edmund Williams, also a power station worker, was given several cups of tea and slept at the police station until his statement was taken.

Malcolm's story was that he had worked as usual on 29th December, lunching in the works canteen at 12.45. He went to the beach at 1.30, returned to the power station a quarter of an hour later and was again in the canteen between 3 o'clock and 3.40. He made a second visit to the beach to collect some wood which he intended to store in the pillbox and found Andrew Bonnick. He reported the discovery.

Most of this statement was quickly disproved.

Mrs Edna Buffett, a waitress at the Stratford Café, St Athan, said Malcolm Williams was in the café between 1 and 2 p.m. and his father and another power station labourer were both certain that he was not in the canteen at lunchtime. A schoolgirl, Sandra Crick, identified him as a man who had spoken to her as she was sitting on a seat on the road between St Athan and Gileston soon after two o'clock. The story of this encounter was confirmed by two other girls. Shop assistant Christine Adamson saw Williams walking towards the beach after talking to Sandra Crick.

Forensic examination of Malcolm Williams' clothing showed heavy bloodstaining on his donkey jacket and one trouser leg. Additionally there were a number of blood spots at the bottom of each trouser leg and on the jacket, such as would have been caused if the garments had been in the path of a spray of blood. Scrapings from the fingernails of the murdered boy yielded blue and purple fibres matching the cloth of Williams' jacket.

Two days after Andrew Bonnick's death Superintendent Williams was taken ill and investigations were continued by two officers from Scotland Yard—Detective Chief Superintendent (later Deputy Assistant Commissioner) John Du Rose and Detective Sergeant (later Detective Chief Inspector) John Fyall. Superintendent Du Rose told Williams that his story of his movements on 29th December did not stand up and asked if he had anything more to say.

'I haven't slept well,' said Williams. 'I panicked and there was a struggle. It would not have happened otherwise . . . he would not take his jeans off and I punched him in the front of his neck.'

In reply to other questions by Du Rose, Williams said he had had a homosexual weakness since he was nine years old and that he was specially interested in young boys. He said he 'had a funny feeling twice a day'.

Told that anything he said would be written down, the young man replied, 'You can write if you like. I did not intend to kill him. I will tell you what happened.'

In a written statement Williams said, 'I had the feeling and I went to the beach looking for a boy to masturbate me . . . I looked at several boys on the beach and I seen this Andrew. I did not know him before . . . I told him a boy had an accident in the pillbox and asked him to come and help. He went inside first and said, "There's nobody here." I told him to drop his trousers and he said he would not.'

Williams went on to describe how he held Andrew against the wall and got his trousers halfway down. The lad said he would tell his parents. Williams hit him in the eye and then beat him with a notched stick. He thought the lad was dead when he saw the blood, and put his jacket under Andrew's head. He then ran for help.

'After I realised what I had done I tried to do what I could for him,' he continued. 'It was an accident. I did not intend to kill him.'

None of this evidence heard by Superintendent Du Rose was heard by the jury when Malcolm Williams was tried for murder at Glamorganshire Assizes, Cardiff, in March 1961. Mr Justice Ashworth ruled that Williams' verbal admission of guilt to Superintendent Du Rose, and his subsequent statement, were both inadmissible. The Scotland Yard man was criticised for interviewing Williams without first cautioning him and it was suggested that the local CID had kept Williams at the police station and left it until five o'clock in the morning before taking his first statement as a deliberate 'softening up' measure.

Pleading not guilty to the charge of murder, the accused man suggested that Andrew could have been killed by his own father or that the other boys on the beach might have been involved. There was not a scrap of evidence to support these allegations and the jury took less than an hour to find Williams guilty. He was sentenced to life imprisonment and later refused leave to appeal.

Malcolm Williams lived with his parents in not very satisfactory home conditions. Of a family of nine children only six had survived. Two of them left home and a third—a younger daughter—had been classified as being beyond the control of her parents since the age of eight and was under the care of Glamorgan County Council. Malcolm, too, had been committed to care when he was twelve years old because his parents were not exercising proper control and guardianship. He was sent to a children's home, but absconded several times. After a conviction for factory-breaking and theft he spent some time at an approved school.

None of these measures improved his character. He had a string of convictions—for school-breaking, for stealing a wallet and driving licence, stealing a bicycle, obtaining a few shillings by false pretences, stealing cash from gas and electricity meters. He had twice been sent to borstal and had returned to his parents' home only a few weeks before the murder.

There were no convictions for sexual offences, but it was discovered that he had indulged in homosexual practices with other boys at an approved school. He told the police that he had attempted sodomy with one of his brothers, who was at that time twelve years of age, and the brother confirmed this admission.

Without doubt Andrew Bonnick's rejection of Williams led Williams to kill. Having no criminal history of violence, it is unlikely that Williams himself was aware that he was capable of such brutality.

His attempt to implicate Andrew's father reflects a particularly nasty aspect of his psyche. In such cases therapy will never improve a murderer of this type until he accepts full responsibility for the crime committed.

10

Panic in Paradise

The Atlantic Ocean island of Bermuda, often lyrically described as 'Paradise Isle', the 'millionaires' playground' or the 'island of flowers', lost its holiday magic in the spring and summer of 1959 and became instead for a few months an island of terror.

Three women were murdered, and a number more sadistically attacked, within an area of one square mile at Warwick, on the southern coast of the island.

The first victim to die was a widow of seventy-two, British-born Mrs Gertrude Robinson, who lived alone in a cottage overlooking the pink sands and coral rock of Southlands beach. Just after seven o'clock in the morning of 7th March she was found lying on the edge of a banana patch. It was believed she had lain there, terribly injured and unconscious, since being attacked when she went outside the cottage to call her cat some time the previous evening. She died within a few hours, without regaining consciousness.

Two months later, on 9th May, police officers called at another cliffside cottage in the same area after being alerted that the occupant, again a woman living alone, had not been seen for several days. They found Mrs Dorothy Pearce, a 59-year-old divorcee from Harrogate, Yorkshire, lying dead on her bed.

Both women had been raped and their injuries were similar. Their faces had been battered almost beyond recognition, apparently by a man's fists, and their bodies bore bite marks and clawing scratches. The island coroner, Mr S. S. Toddings, said that Mrs Robinson had been 'ravished from head to foot', and that there was clearly a sex maniac at large.

These murders marked the culmination of a series of attacks

on women dating back to the previous summer. Some had been raped, others seriously injured, a few no more than unpleasantly molested.

Bermuda's Colonial Secretary, Mr J. W. Sykes, cabled Sir Joseph Simpson, then Commissioner of the Metropolitan Police, asking for help. Two Scotland Yard officers, Detective Superintendent William Baker and Detective Sergeant John O'Connell, were flown to the island. Working with Bermuda's CID chief, Detective Superintendent James Lodge—himself a former Yard man—they organised an intensive hunt for the killer. They decreed that all males between the ages of eighteen and fifty living in the south shore locality should be fingerprinted, hundreds of people were asked to fill in questionnaires, and close enquiries were made among American servicemen at an Air Force base and a Naval operating station. No one was allowed to leave the island without police approval—a ruling which resulted in extended honeymoons for dozens of couples from Britain and the United States.

None of these measures yielded anything useful and after six weeks the two Yard men returned to England.

For a while there were no further alarms and the islanders began to relax, hoping either that the killer had been a visitor who had left Bermuda or that he had been frightened into inactivity by the visit of the Yard men.

Until early in July . . .

Then, just about two months after the murder of Mrs Pearce, came a report of an attack on a middle-aged Englishwoman, Mrs Rosaleen Kenny, who also lived within the murder mile. She was in bed in her flat when an intruder broke in and tried to rape her, but she resisted so fiercely that he flung her back on the bed and ran away. She told detectives that he was a dark-skinned man and was carrying what looked like a hoe. Mrs Kenny's life may well have been saved because, unlike the two earlier victims in their lonely cottages, she had neighbours close enough to be alerted by her cries for help.

Fear again gripped the island. Holiday bookings were cancelled and some visitors hastily packed and left before the end of their vacations. Residents formed parties to swim and sun-bathe on the beautiful sandy beaches, while in the remoter parts of the island the roads and plantations were deserted. Yachts belonging to wealthy playboys still anchored off the coast, but most of their women guests preferred to stay on board. Few members of these yachting parties ventured ashore after dark and the usually gay night spots were unprofitably quiet.

After the murder of Mrs Robinson, coroner Mr Toddings issued a statement in which he said that the sex maniac responsible must be caught quickly. He appealed to every member of the public to act as a policeman. After the second murder Mr Toddings said, 'If the culprit is not caught there is little doubt that he will strike yet again.'

The July attack proved him right, yet so short is public memory that less than three months later the life of Bermuda had returned almost to normal and a young Englishwoman went alone to a quiet beach . . .

Her name was Dorothy Barbara Rawlinson. She was a 29-year-old secretary who until May 1959, had lived with her parents, Mr and Mrs H. E. Rawlinson, and her brother John at Boston Vale, Hanwell, London, W7. She was a quiet girl, fond of reading and playing the piano, and since leaving school had worked in the London area. Then, 'in search of adventure' as she put it, she took a job with an import firm in Bermuda and found a home with a fellow employee and his wife, Tom and Anne Sayers. Although in letters to England she admitted to being a little homesick, she loved the sunshine and the opportunities for swimming, and was settling happily into her new life.

Barbara, as she was usually called, had no men friends either in London or Bermuda, but she soon found girl companions on the island and it was customary for her to go swimming and sunbathing with some of these friends at the weekends.

On Sunday 28th September she tried hard to persuade two of these girls to accompany her to the beach, but the water was too rough for swimming because of an approaching hurricane and her friends refused. Barbara, with her blonde-streaked, curly brown hair blowing in the breeze, set off alone on her motorised bicycle, wearing her swimsuit under her shorts and shirt and carrying a towelling robe to spread on the sand while she soaked up the sun.

She cycled to Southlands, a secluded private beach owned by a retired commanding officer of the Bermuda garrison, Brigadier H. Dunbar Maconochie, who had given her permission to bathe there because she had occasionally typed letters for him. She told her friends that she had no intention of entering the rough sea and at different times during the afternoon was seen by two schoolgirls as she lay on the sands in her swimsuit reading Vicki Baum's *Mortgage on Life*.

She had arranged with Mr and Mrs Sayers that she would be home to tea as usual, and as she was a considerate girl who would not have changed her plans without telling them, they began to worry when she failed to return on time. By 6.30 p.m. they were so concerned that they reported her missing.

An immediate police hunt of the area was started but there was no sign of the missing girl, and it was feared that she had decided to brave the rough seas and had been swept out to the rocks by the heavy breakers.

Sidney Hart, manager of Brigadier Maconochie's estate, saw Miss Rawlinson's autocycle on Southlands beach on Sunday evening. Next day, after hearing that the girl was missing, he went again to the beach and found the Vicki Baum book—borrowed from the public library—and a blue swimsuit half-buried in the sand. Both were bloodstained and the suit was torn in such a way as to suggest that it had been ripped from her body.

Police officers detailed to go over the rest of the beach—within a mile of the scenes of the first two murders—found a number of small rocks heavily stained with blood. Buried in the sand nearby were the girl's green linen shorts, white shirt and sandals. There was no trace of the towelling beach robe, nor of the thick-lensed spectacles she usually wore.

Throughout the hot, late-summer day the digging continued and the officers had just returned to their task next morning when Frederick Astwood, hunting for rockfish, found the remains of a body on a coral reef two miles away. It was undoubtedly Dorothy Rawlinson, but after thirty-six hours in the water the body had been so savaged by sharks that little more than a skeleton remained and it was impossible to determine the cause of death. Had it not been for the blood on the buried clothing it might well have been recorded as a drowning accident.

Fear which had been lying dormant erupted into something approaching panic.

The previous murders and all the other attacks had taken place after dark, but Miss Rawlinson had been killed in the afternoon, in brilliant sunshine, on a beach clearly visible from the road above. It was felt that no woman, of any age, was safe anywhere in the island at any time of day or night. Among the 42,000 residents of Bermuda was a large proportion of spinsters, widows and retired women living alone, many of whom had been attracted to the island by the climate and by low taxation which enabled them to live comfortably on restricted means. These advantages paled into insignificance beside fears for their personal safety, and within days of the Rawlinson murder property agents were being approached by numbers of women who had decided to sell their homes and leave the island.

Many others grouped together for emergency communal living, moving about in pairs during the day and sleeping five or six to a house each night, guarded always by one or two dogs. Men who worked at night or had to leave the island on business advertised for companions for their wives. In spite of the humid heat, windows and doors were kept closed and barred from dusk to dawn each day.

There were reports that people living in the murder mile were planning to launch their own 'catch the killer' fund and wanted to hire a private criminologist from the United States, but the Colonial Secretary gave his assurance that the government fully intended to carry out its duty to protect its citizens.

'There is no question of money or the lack of it standing in the way,' he said. 'We have given the Police Commissioner carte blanche to ask for what he wants.'

Pressure continued for outside help to be called in, however. The writer of a long letter published in the local newspaper, the *Royal Gazette*, advised the police to offer a reward of £5,000 for information, and to call in Scotland Yard or the United States Federal Bureau of Investigation. In fact the Yard received an appeal for help just a week after the murder and on 6th October 1959 Detective Superintendent (later Commander) Richard Lewis and Detective Sergeant William Taylor flew from London to Hamilton to work in collaboration with Detective Superintendent Lodge.

Hampered by the lack of evidence relating to the cause of death—post-mortem examinations showed only that no bones of the victim's body were broken—the detectives could do no more than build up a presumed sequence of events. They thought it likely that the killer had approached the girl as she lay sunning herself on the beach, attacked and probably raped her, and had then carried her body into the sea in the hope that it would never be recovered.

An immediate alarm call went out when it was learned that a man in wet clothes who appeared rather agitated had called at a bicycle shop near the beach—one of many such shops which did a brisk trade in the hire of cycles to tourists and servicemen—about an hour after the presumed time of the murder. His description tallied with that of a man who was seen walking up the beach from the direction of the sea by one of the schoolgirls who had earlier noticed Miss Rawlinson.

He was identified as Wendell Willis Lightbourne, a nineteen-year-old negro golf caddie, who was taken for questioning to Hamilton police station.

After an interview lasting two and a half hours, Lightbourne suddenly burst into tears and told Superintendent Lewis, 'The girl on the beach. . . . I done it, sir. I bashed her.'

He said he saw the girl sitting on a rock on the beach and started talking to her. He grabbed at her bathing costume and she said, 'You rascal, you,' and tried to hit him.

159

'I hit her head,' continued Lightbourne. 'She made funny noises. I didn't like those noises. I didn't have intercourse with her. I just ran away. The girl wasn't dead when I left her. She was a long way from the water and I didn't put her in the water. I want to get it off my mind. I can't go to Heaven now.'

After being charged with the murder of Dorothy Rawlinson, the accused man was asked if he knew anything about the murders of Mrs Robinson and Mrs Pearce. He replied that he knew where the women had lived. Showing Superintendent Lewis scars on his knuckles, he said, 'These are where I beat up women, but I don't know where. Sometimes after a drink I want to do something. I get nasty. I go all over the place. I go along the beach sometimes at night. I may have gone into someone's house.' Asked whether he had been in Mrs Robinson's house. Lightbourne said he did not know, but he might have been.

He was also questioned about assaults on Mrs Kenny, a Mrs Plant and a Miss Lucy Brown, and was told he would be further charged with the attempted murder of Mrs Evelyn Flood, wife of a taxi-driver, at Warwick in July 1958.

'I know nothing about that,' replied Lightbourne.

Because of the smallness of Bermuda and the possibility that prospective jury members might be prejudiced by newspaper reports, the Magistrates' Court proceedings—at which Lightbourne was charged on both counts—were heard in camera. When he stood before the Supreme Court at Hamilton in December 1959, he was accused only of the murder of Miss Rawlinson.

He pleaded not guilty and said detectives had told him that if he admitted certain things he would be sent to a school where he would be taught to read and write.

'I can't read and it makes me mad,' he added.

He told the court that it was Miss Rawlinson who made the first approaches on the beach, asking him to help her take off her bathing costume and then inviting him to have sexual intercourse with her. Afterwards she became upset when he jokingly threatened to tear up her costume. She slapped him and he slapped her. She fell against a rock. He went to help her but saw she was bleeding from the head.

'I don't like blood,' he said. 'It makes me feel funny, so I walked away and left her.'

He denied telling a prison warder that he had killed the girl in retaliation for twelve lashes he received unjustly the previous year, nor did he say, 'Get the rope ready.'

His negro counsel, Miss Lois Browne, who was Bermuda's only woman barrister, questioned Superintendent Lewis about his methods of interviewing Lightbourne and asked if the accused man had been threatened.

'No,' replied the superintendent. 'I asked Lightbourne, in the presence of a doctor, if anyone had been roughing him up since he arrived at the police station or if anyone had asked him to make any statement he did not want to make. He replied "No" to both questions.'

Lightbourne had said that after Miss Rawlinson's body was found he tried to hang himself but lacked the courage, and then tried to shoot himself but could not pull the trigger.

The Chief Justice, Sir Newnham Worley, told the jury of seven white and five coloured members that they had to rid their minds of other murders and crimes that had occurred during the year. It was for them to decide whether Lightbourne was insane.

It was nearly midnight on the sixth day of the trial when the jury, after a retirement of two hours, gave their verdict of Guilty with a recommendation to mercy.

Lightbourne was sentenced to death, but the execution was postponed only a few hours before he was due to be hanged to enable the Queen's advisers to consider two petitions—one, signed by 600 people, asking that clemency be not exercised, and the other, praying for clemency, with 3,000 signatures.

At the end of January 1960, three leading psychiatrists from London flew to Bermuda to examine the condemned man. A few days later it was announced that, following their report regarding Lightbourne's mental state, the sentence of death would be commuted to one of life imprisonment.

Lightbourne was brought to Britain and is serving his sentence at a prison in this country.

Lightbourne was a man in whom a savage aggressive part of himself was linked with a devouring destructive sexuality, clearly related to revenge upon the white 'haves'. Feeling underprivileged and unable to read or write, he regarded himself as what Freud called one of the 'exceptions'; having been wronged, he was entitled to do whatever he liked to whoever affronted, rebuffed or stimulated him.

His job as a caddy put him into daily touch with the 'haves' so that his feelings of inferiority were roused, and his envy of the idle rich stimulated.

He also hated the sight of damage that he had done (blood) because he felt reproached by it. This made him more rather than less destructive. He felt he had to attack further the person whose injuries, inflicted by him, had disturbed his conscience.

11

The Window Peeper

It was the day before Christmas Eve, 1959. By six o'clock in the evening many of the fifty girls living at Eden Croft, the YWCA hostel in Wheeleys Road, Edgbaston, Birmingham, had already departed to spend the holiday with families or friends. Others were on their way to parties in the city and the few girls remaining in the rambling Georgian-style house were absorbed in their own last-minute personal preparations.

One of them was a pretty 21-year-old Scots girl, Margaret McDonald Brown, an interior decorator who was looking forward to spending Christmas with her fiancé and his family at Sutton Coldfield. Margaret was ironing in the hostel laundry when she heard the door open behind her. At first she took no notice, assuming that one of the other girls was coming to join her, but she swung round as the lights were switched off —just in time to glimpse a man, one arm raised, before he struck her a vicious blow on the head. Fortunately, Margaret was wearing her long, thick fair hair in a bun at the back, and this softened the impact and saved her from serious injury.

As she screamed in terror, her attacker was swiftly absorbed by the darkness of the walled grounds. By the time the police arrived in response to a 999 call he had disappeared in the busy streets around the hostel, leaving behind the weapon he had used—a heavy stone wrapped in a brassière snatched from the laundry line.

As police officers searched every corner of the several buildings comprising the hostel, they found that room No. 4 of the ground-floor Queen's Wing was locked from the inside. One policeman went outside, peered through a chink in the curtain and saw a pair of naked human legs. Officers broke down the door and were confronted by a sight which resulted in one of them being off duty, sick with shock, for several weeks afterwards.

The girl in the room had been decapitated and her headless body mutilated in a way that could only be likened to the crimes of Jack the Ripper—and it is perhaps significant that a film based on the murders of this 1880's sex maniac had recently been shown at a Birmingham cinema. An ordinary table knife was found in two pieces, the handle on the floor and the bloodstained blade wrapped in some of the girl's underclothing. A scribbled note, 'This was what I thought would never happen,' had been placed near the naked body.

The victim of this sickening crime was a young woman of twenty-nine, Sidney Stephanie Baird, elder daughter of a Scottish father and a Welsh mother. She was an unusually attractive girl, with crisply curling dark hair, tip-tilted nose and warm, smiling mouth, but was said to be shy and quiet, with a limited circle of friends. Her home was at Bishop's Cleeve, near Cheltenham, Gloucestershire, and she had taken a secretarial course after completing her education at Pate's Grammar School for Girls in Cheltenham. For a while she worked in her home town, but had been deeply distressed by the death of her father and had moved to Birmingham shortly after her mother's remarriage.

Chief Superintendent James Haughton, then head of Birmingham CID and later to become Chief Constable of Liverpool, led the hunt for Stephanie's killer. His only lead was Margaret Brown's inevitably sketchy description of the attacker she had glimpsed and the task was made more difficult by the seasonal shift of population. Christmas Day fell on a Friday, making it a four-day holiday for many people, so that a number of residents left the district on Christmas Eve and did not return until the following Monday or Tuesday. Conversely, there were a lot of visitors to the city at that time, people who might or might not have been there on the night of the murder.

An unfortunate coincidence resulted in an immediate false start. At just about the time of the murder a dishevelled young man with blood on his hands, face and clothing was seen by Mrs Evelyn Peake, wife of the landlord of the Welcome Inn in Wheeleys Road. He was slumped against a wall in a road near the hostel and Mrs Peake thought he was drunk. So did another passer-by, who asked the young man if he was hurt.

'I've had a fall . . . I'll be all right when I can get on a bus,' was the reply.

He *did* get on a bus—a No. 8—where he sat on the top deck four rows from the front. Although the bus was full, no one would sit next to the young man because of his bloody condition. His description roughly tallied with that of the killer given by Margaret Brown and it seemed at least possible that he was the wanted man. Boxing Day appeals were made by the police at the city's football grounds and on cinema and TV screens. They asked all the bus passengers to come forward, hoping that some at least would have noticed where the blood-stained passenger alighted. Not one person responded to this appeal and after four days only the driver, conductor and one lower-deck passenger had been traced.

It later transpired that this young man had nothing to do with the murder—the killer, in fact, had not boarded a bus but had walked to his lodgings only about 400 yards from the hostel —but his appearance at that particular time, in that place and in that condition, certainly complicated the police investigation.

Haughton decided that every man who had been within a three-mile radius of the YWCA on the night of 23rd December would have to be traced and questioned. It was a gigantic undertaking, comparable only to the Cannock Chase murder enquiry eight years later, in which fifty thousand men were interviewed before the killer of seven-year-old Christine Darby was caught and sent to prison for life. Haughton was undeterred by the magnitude of his task and a team of police officers, armed with questionnaire leaflets, began the weary slog from house to house and into offices, shops and factories.

Dr Frederick Griffiths, a Home Office pathologist, found that the cause of Stephanie's death was manual strangulation. The skull had been fractured and there were many wounds and abrasions on the body. There was no evidence of recent sexual intercourse.

The late Dr Francis Camps, another pathologist helping on the case, said that the mutilation of the girl's body could have been done by a man who was experienced in cutting flesh—so 4,000 butchers and their assistants and 700 medical students were interviewed. So was every man with a record of violence living within fifty miles of Birmingham. Every mental patient in the British Isles was checked. No fewer than twenty men who had been bloodstained on the murder night were traced and questioned. The note which had been found by Stephanie's body was compared to 4,000 specimens of handwriting.

Two thousand houses had been visited and 50,000 statements taken when detectives who called at a lodging-house kept by Mrs May Jeanes in Islington Avenue, Birmingham, were told that one of the boarders had left the house just before Christmas and had not returned.

This man, 28-year-old Irish labourer Patrick Joseph Byrne, was only one of three thousand who had failed to return to their work or lodgings in Birmingham after the Christmas holiday. There was no reason to suspect that he might be the killer, but on 9th February 1960 a routine call was made at his mother's home in Birchall Street, Warrington, Lancashire. Mrs Elizabeth Byrne said that her son had visited her for Christmas and had decided to stay when he got a building job in the town. He was not at home at the time the police called and a message was left for him to attend Warrington police station.

Later the same day Byrne walked into the station and sat down opposite Detective Sergeant George Welborn. The fresh-faced, wavy-haired young Irishman gave ready replies to the questionnaire, but Welborn had an intuitive feeling that something was being held back.

At the conclusion of the interview Byrne rose to his feet and turned towards the door. His hand was on the handle when Welborn put one final question.

'Is there anything else you would like to say about your stay in Birmingham?' he asked quietly.

For a few seconds there was silence, then Byrne swung round to face the detective. 'Yes . . . there is . . . yes,' he blurted. 'I want to tell you about the YWCA. I had something to do with that.'

There are always a few twisted types ready to confess to a murder they have not committed—in this case there had already been three such 'confessions'—and Byrne might well have been another perverted hoaxer, but it soon became clear to Welborn that the horrifying story which came tumbling out could have been told only by the man who had butchered Stephanie Baird.

An urgent message was sent to Chief Superintendent Haughton. He hurried to Warrington. With Detective Superintendent Gerry Baumber he listened as Byrne relived the scene of carnage in the YWCA. Like Welborn, they were satisfied that the Irishman *must* be the killer because some of the details he gave, too horrible to publish in the Press, had been known only to the pathologists and a few police officers.

On the day of the murder Byrne had been working on a building site in Birmingham. He had taken a very extended lunch break and when he returned to work was so drunk that his foreman thought it unsafe for him to remain on the scaffolding. At 3.30 p.m. he was ordered down to the ground and at 4.30 p.m. he left the site. He was not seen again until he returned to his lodgings at 7.50 p.m., still wearing his working clothes.

In a long statement, Byrne said that he remembered finishing work and some time later decided to have a peep through the windows of the YWCA.

'I have done this before a few times,' he continued. 'I was once caught on the stairs in the main building by two girls late at night about twelve months ago. Another time I went into a girl's room in the block of cubicles in the garden and switched on the light. I sat on the bed talking to the girl and my main intention was to get into bed with her, but she spoke friendly and when she asked me to go I went.'

On the night of the murder he went into the hostel grounds

167

and peeped through a window where he saw a girl combing her hair. He decided to have a better look, so got in through a corridor window, then stood on a chair outside the girl's room and looked through the pane of glass above the door. The girl was wearing a red pullover and underskirt. He got 'browned off' when she did not remove any more of her clothing and had decided to leave when the girl opened the door.

'She came face to face with me and asked what I was doing. I told her I was looking for somebody and she said "Let me get the warden." We were standing quite close together . . . I kissed her and she tried to shove me away and for a second I got her round the waist. She screamed and then I put my hands round her neck. She went backwards inside the room with me squeezing her throat and then fell backwards. Her head bounced on the floor and I was lying on top of her, kissing her and squeezing her neck at the one time. I heard a couple of small noises in her throat, but kept on kissing her. After a while I knelt up and I had a strong urge to have a good look at her. I was fully sure she was dead then because I had the whole power of my back squeezing her throat.'

Byrne's statement went on to say that he did various things after undressing the girl and then bolted the door. He saw a table knife in a cupboard. He scored the body round the chest with the knife and then cut lower down the body and down the back. Finally he cut off the head, later holding the head up to the mirror to look at it.

Referring to the note left on the dressing-table, Byrne said, 'I can't remember the words I used, but I wanted everybody to see my life in one little note. The other times I had been definitely satisfied with peeping, but this time was different somehow. What I meant when I wrote the note was that I thought I might be had for rape but not murder.'

When he left the room he saw another lighted window. The girl inside the room did not appeal to him, but then he saw a girl in another room who attracted him.

'I was very excited and thinking that I ought to terrorise all the women,' continued Byrne. 'I wanted to get my own back on them for causing me nervous tension through sex . . . I felt I only wanted to kill beautiful women . . . I watched this other girl for a while and stood close to the window. I only looked at her face and the urge to kill her was tremendously strong. I thought I would take her quietly and quickly and picked up a big stone from the garden . . . I struck at her with the stone, but she screamed and the stone swung out of my hand.'

Byrne then ran back to his lodgings and washed himself. He wrote a note to his landlady and the other men lodging in the house, saying he was very sorry they should have to receive 'such a horrible letter' and that he thought he had two personalities—one very bad and the other 'the real me'.

The statement continued: 'I put the note in my pocket and went into the bathroom. I stood by the mirror talking to myself and searching my face for signs of a madman, but I could see none. I felt I ought to commit suicide . . . then I thought of my mother and Christmas. I didn't want to upset nobody for Christmas so I thought I would put it off until afterwards.' He tore up the note the same night and scattered it in the street.

Patrick Byrne's belief in his dual personality was supported by the evidence of his mother and of friends who thought they knew him well. John McCabe, one of his fellow lodgers, who knew Byrne by his nickname of 'Acky', thought he was a quiet chap, easy to get along with but 'shy with women'. This assessment of his character was shared by other men living in the boarding-house, although at least one must have been aware of the Irishman's Peeping Tom activities because scrawled on a wall near the house were the chalked words, 'Acky Byrne, the window peeper.'

One man who thought he knew Byrne very well was Robert McCleary, a Scotsman who had been his friend for several years and was one of the few people to visit him in prison after his arrest for murder. Paddy Byrne had been a regular visitor to McCleary's home and sometimes, when his friend was out on business, spent the evening there with Mrs McCleary and the couple's seven children.

'He was good with kids,' recalled the Scot. 'They liked him and called him Acky just like we did.' McCleary found it almost impossible to believe that this unobtrusive, kindly, thoughtful man was the maniacal killer of Stephanie Baird.

There is no record that Byrne ever had a steady girl, but in the months before the murder he had become friendly with eighteen-year-old Jean Grant, to whom he was introduced by a mutual friend at a social evening at the Birmingham Mint where she worked. He was clearly attracted to her because he began to make regular weekly visits to the social club, but he was too shy to join in the dancing and seemed to prefer the Housey-Housey games. One night he asked Jean if he could walk her home to Paxton Road, Key Hill. She agreed and in subsequent weeks it became an understood thing that he would accompany her and carry the record player she took to the club for the dancing.

Jean Grant, like Byrne's other friends, found it hard to believe the truth about him.

'He was such a nice fellow,' she said. 'I always thought he was shy of women. At the club I often had to drag him out of his corner to join in the fun. He never put his arms round me or kissed me goodnight. He was always worrying about missing the bus to his lodgings and I used to tell him I would walk home alone, but he said somebody might jump out and attack me. I was very fond of Acky, but I did think it strange the way he was always talking about girls being attacked. I just cannot understand how he did all those terrible things . . .'

Someone who did see another side to Patrick Byrne's character was Michael Murphy, a fellow Irishman with whom he became friendly when he returned to his home in Warrington after the murder. One night the two men walked into the Vine Hotel, near Warrington market, where the landlord, Len Bradbury, refused to serve Byrne because he had obviously had enough to drink already.

'Give us the drinks or I'll knife you', shouted Byrne, who continued to hurl abuse at the landlord in spite of Murphy's efforts to calm him. Three other customers forced him out of the public house, although he was gripping the bar so tightly that they had to prise his hands free finger by finger.

'The demon was certainly in him that night,' said Murphy, 'but that was the only time in our acquaintance that he failed to behave like a perfect gentleman. All the time I was with him I never saw him look at a girl and he never talked of sex. Usually he was a quiet, shy chap.'

In fact, this was not Byrne's first aggressive outburst triggered by alcohol. In January 1958 he had been sentenced to two months' imprisonment at Birmingham for being drunk and disorderly and assaulting a policeman.

There was no indication in his childhood or boyhood of the violence latent in him. Born in Dublin, he was the second son of a large, happy family and was devoted particularly to his mother. He left school at the age of fourteen and got a job in a factory. For the next four years, until he came to England, he weekly handed his unopened wage packet to his mother, and continued to send her money all the time he thought she needed it. He was always regarded as a steady worker and had a good service record during his two years in the Royal Army Ordnance Corps.

According to Mrs Byrne, who moved her family from Dublin to Warrington only a few months before her son's arrest for murder, Patrick had been injured in an accident when he was eight years old. Part of a wall had fallen on him while he was playing. One leg was broken and he was unconscious for three days as the result of head injuries.

Byrne himself believed that his sexual troubles started when he was seventeen years of age. He told a friend who visited him in prison that he had been seduced by a middle-aged widow in Dublin.

'She started it all,' he said. 'I was never the same after I escaped from her. She seemed to hold me in her spell and made girls of my own age seem silly and stupid. It got so bad that I began to hate all women, yet I badly wanted a steady girlfriend.'

According to one psychiatrist, however, Byrne had displayed sexual abnormalities when he was still a child. Dr Clifford

Tetlow said he believed Byrne when he told him that he had thought policemen and members of the public were in the YWCA hostel room with him while he was killing and mutilating his victim. He thought, too, that Byrne genuinely believed himself innocent of crime.

Dr Percy Coats, senior medical officer at Birmingham Prison, came to the conclusion that Byrne was a sexual psychopath who obtained satisfaction by perverted activities and that his condition was brought about by sexual immaturity.

Byrne told another medical examiner, Dr J. J. O'Reilly, lecturer in psychological medicine, that he had had dreams and thoughts about sexual things which had even frightened himself. His fantasies had included one of cutting a woman in half with a circular saw.

The facts of the killing of Stephanie Baird were not disputed when Byrne stood in the dock before Mr Justice Stable at Birmingham Assizes in March 1960. The issue to be decided by the jury was the condition of the mind of the killer at the time he committed the crime.

Byrne's counsel, Mr R. K. Brown, QC, maintained that it was as clear a case of abnormality of mind as there could be. Requesting the jury to bring in a verdict of manslaughter on the grounds of diminished responsibility, he asked:

'Now that you have heard some of these horrifying and shocking details, is not your reaction that of a man saying to himself "No responsible person could have behaved like this"?'

The medical witnesses were closely questioned by the judge, who asked Dr Coats, 'Would it be fair to say that where you get such a marked degree of depravity, the individual cannot be guilty of murder?'

Dr Coats replied 'No.'

'Are you saying that there was nothing wrong with his mind except these depraved desires to which he surrendered?'

'Yes.'

'You are saying that when a man behaves like this he is completely outside the category of normal human beings?'

'Yes.'

Dr Tetlow, in reply to questions from the judge, said that in his opinion Byrne was partially insane and was suffering from some disease of the mind.

Mr Justice Stable: 'You are telling us that according to him [Byrne] he thought the place was full of policemen and other people while he was doing this. What does that indicate in your opinion?'

'That he was abnormally sexually excited.'

'That we have grasped, but if it be true the man was in such a state that he went on doing these dreadful things thinking there were crowds of policemen there, does not that mean he has brought himself within the Macnaghten Rules?'

'I do not think so. I think this fantasy was part of his sexual excitement, but it goes further back . . . he had this feeling that women did not want him and he wanted to get his revenge in these fantasies.'

Summing up, the judge said the jury had to consider whether it was murder or whether it could be called by a milder name. The enquiry involved some consideration of 'that awful and mysterious thing, the mind of man'.

The all-male jury took forty-five minutes to find Patrick Byrne guilty of murder and he was sentenced to life imprisonment. In July 1960 three judges in the Court of Criminal Appeal quashed the murder conviction and substituted a verdict of guilty of manslaughter. The life sentence, however, remained unaltered, Lord Parker (the Lord Chief Justice) commenting that it was the only possible sentence having regard to Byrne's tendencies.

Lord Parker said: 'The evidence of the revolting circumstances of the killing and the subsequent mutilations, as of the previous sexual history of the accused man, pointed, we think plainly, to the conclusion that he was what would be described in ordinary language as on the borderline of insanity.'

Byrne has undergone extensive psychiatric examination since he began his life sentence and he will continue to receive treatment. It is unlikely that any doctors will ever have the courage to recommend his parole.

He is the perfect example of the apparently harmless Peeping Tom, the underwear thief or the bottom pincher whose sexual fetish suddenly escalates to the act of murder.

Byrne's own view of the duality of his character is not far from the truth. There was a profound split between the shy young man and the ruthless sexual killer.

Alcohol enabled the ruthless killer part to take control of the whole personality, and then he projected his conscience into imagined or hallucinated police who were with him, according to his story, when he murdered his victim.

His history of seduction by a mother figure at the age of seventeen made him unable to respect and value women who were also sexual—his mother presumably not being viewed by him as sexual.

The voyeuristic perversion involves intrusiveness. When the eye intrusion does not suffice rape follows, and then murderous intrusion with a knife.

The psychiatric study of Byrne is of tremendous social importance because it is hoped that research into the mind of such a murderer will produce some clues to indicate at what point the ruthless killer part of his mind took control.

Although alcohol provided the impetus for the 'takeover', there could have been other events in his life—although they could, in a normal person, have been trivial—that in Byrne's mind further strengthened the murderousness over a long period.

Only when the personality of a man like Byrne is probed month after month and year after year, can psychiatrists pinpoint danger signals that could provide valuable aids during the analysis of other, lesser, sexual offenders. Early steps could then be taken to prevent these offenders' activities from escalating in the same disastrous manner as Byrne.

12

A Gruesome Parcel

My colleague Tom Tullett, chief of the *Daily Mirror* Crime Bureau, was in his office at 10.30 a.m. on Monday, 11th September 1961, when he received a call from the reception desk. A man named Edwin Sims, who came from Gravesend, Kent, wanted to see him on 'confidential' business.

'Send him up,' said Tom, and after a few minutes he strolled along to meet his visitor in room 392 on the third floor. Seated in a red leather armchair was a man who looked about thirty, of medium height, with curly, gingery hair. He was wearing big mud-stained boots, a light brown raincoat, khaki trousers which looked as if they had been washed many times, and a shirt open to reveal on his chest a huge tattoo of an eagle in flight. He looked like a labourer.

'Good morning,' said Tom, 'and what can I do for you?'

The man wiped his forehead, which was gleaming with sweat, and looked hard at Tom through horn-rimmed spectacles.

'I want to confess to a double murder,' he said.

It is not unusual for newspapermen, like policemen, to be the recipients of fake confessions made by mentally unbalanced people or by egomaniacs anxious to share in the publicity when a killer is being hunted. Moreover, there was no murder in the headlines at that time and Tom was not impressed.

'Oh yes,' he said. 'Who have you killed?'

'A man and a woman in the marshes at Gravesend . . . teenagers I think,' came the quiet reply. At the same time he stood up and took from the pockets of his raincoat a beige handbag, a red and blue plastic wallet, and two watches—one a woman's and the other a man's.

Tom's scepticism began to evaporate. He opened the door of the interview room as photographer Edward 'Dixie' Dean was passing and called him to keep guard. It took only seconds for Tom to alert Roland Watkins, then the News Editor (and now Assistant Editor). A call to the police was organised. As Tom re-entered the room he asked Sims why he had chosen to make his confession at the *Mirror* office.

'I wanted to get it off my chest . . . I wanted to tell someone.'

Sims pointed to a newspaper-covered parcel on the table in which Tom thought his visitor might have wrapped his sandwiches. 'That parcel contains parts of their bodies,' said Sims.

He was still telling his story, with Tom making notes when Detective Inspector Clifford Lloyd, of the London City police, walked into the room and unwrapped the parcel. A pair of breasts were revealed. . . .

At just about the time this grisly drama was being enacted in the *Mirror* office in Holborn, a fifteen-year-old lad who was setting out for a day's eel fishing found the naked, mutilated body of a young girl in a dyke on Denton Marshes, two miles from Gravesend. Police and frogmen dragged the waters of the dyke—near the Ship and Lobster public house, a favourite rendezvous of Thames Estuary seamen and fishermen. They discovered a girl's suede jacket, then a pink cardigan, a summer dress, a lace-trimmed yellow slip, a white belt, a black shoe and two stockings . . .

The pathetic trail of clothing was found along the grassy banks of the dyke as forty policemen, assisted by cadets from a training college and soldiers with mine detectors, continued the search for a second victim after being alerted by the City police. Late that afternoon frogmen dragged the body of a youth from the dyke, about a hundred yards from where the girl had been found. Both had been strangled by cords round their necks and had their hands tied behind their backs.

The girl was Lilian Edmeades, sixteen-year-old daughter of Mr Ernest Edmeades and his wife Rose, of Peppercroft Street, Gravesend, and the youth was Malcolm Johnson, also sixteen son of William and Lilian Johnson, of Abbey Road, Gravesend.

Lilian Edmeades, a slim, sweet-faced girl with long fair hair, had left school less than a year before and had worked as an assistant in a local grocery shop. Malcolm had just started work in the laboratory of a Gravesend paper mill. They had met at a youth club and for several months had been walking out together, with the full approval of their parents.

Unlike many of their contemporaries, the young couple preferred church to all-night coffee bars and were more likely to be seen setting off on country walks than sneaking into X-certificate film shows or trying to persuade publicans that they had reached the permitted age for alcohol. Lilian, one of a large church-going family, was a member of Emmanuel Baptist Church and a leader in the Girls' Life Brigade. Malcolm, a keen member of the Boys' Brigade, belonged to the Methodist Church in Milton Road. Both were deeply religious and always attended Sunday service together, sometimes at the Baptist church and sometimes with the Methodists.

On that fateful Sunday, 10th September, the Baptist pastor, the Reverend William Cobley, saw them sitting in the front of his church when the service started at 6.30 p.m. An hour later they were noticed standing in the porch for a while, chatting to other young people. They were still enjoying a happy day which had been spent mostly at Lilian's home, where Malcolm had taken a picture of his pretty sweetheart as she sat in the sunny garden.

They were last seen alive as they walked from the church, arm in arm, for a stroll along the sea-wall near the marshes. It was unusual for them to be out after ten o'clock in the evening and by midnight their anxious parents had reported them missing.

Because they were known to be very fond of one another and to have spoken of marriage when they were older, it was at first suspected that they might have eloped. But the caller at the *Mirror* and the marshland search organised by Detective Chief Superintendent James Jenner, of Kent CID, together revealed the terrible truth.

The late Dr Francis Camps, pathologist, confirmed that death in each case was due to strangulation by ligature. There was no evidence of sexual assault on the girl in spite of the mutilation after death.

The double killing aroused strong local feeling. When Edwin Sims, charged with the murders, made his first court appearance at Gravesend he had to be hustled out of a side door to dodge the angry crowd in front of the building. Even so, dozens of shouting, booing women broke through a police cordon and banged on the side of the van as he was driven away.

There were more emotional scenes at the double funeral on 18th September. Hundreds of people lined the streets of Gravesend, and women wept as the two coffins passed by en route for the cemetery, where Lilian and Malcolm were buried in the same grave. Two heart-shaped wreaths, linked by the inscription 'Sweethearts', stood in the porch of the Methodist church during the funeral service, which was attended not only by relatives, neighbours and friends but by dozens of curious sightseers.

For the full story of what happened on the marshes during that September night we have only the killer's own story, partially told to Tom Tullett and later in full to police officers.

Edwin David Sims, a carpenter aged twenty-eight, who lived with his mother, a married sister and the sister's husband at Hampton Crescent, Gravesend, made no attempt to deny anything when the police arrived at the *Mirror* office. He said to Detective Inspector Lloyd, 'I killed them on impulse, and impulse is a funny thing, you know.'

Sims was seen in the Ship and Lobster public house at 7.15 p.m. on 10th September. It was known that he arrived home at 10.45 p.m. and that he washed his face and hands before going to his bedroom. During the intervening three and a half hours he spoke to no one except the couple he killed.

He said he left home at seven o'clock, taking with him a ·410 sawn-off shotgun, seven cartridges, two knives, a pair of rubber gloves and some nails. In one statement he said his intention had been to throw the gun and cartridges into the river, but that on his way to the ferry he changed his mind and went for a walk round the town. He told Tom: 'I have had the idea of murder for some time and I walked round thinking about it. I have had the gun for about four years now.'

He saw a couple in front of him as he was walking along the towpath and pulled out the gun with the intention of frightening them.

'I had no other thoughts in mind,' he said. 'I drew up behind them and told them to keep quiet and not move. I made them lie face downwards on the towpath and tied their hands behind them. Then I pulled them to their feet and made them walk along the towpath. We came to a plank across a ditch and the boy said if I would let them go they would not tell anybody. I told them they would be free in a couple of hours.'

Sims later elaborated on this part of his statement when he was talking to Dr James Brown, medical officer at Maidstone Prison. He told the doctor that each of the youngsters had said to him, 'Do what you like with me, but let the other one go.'

The three of them continued to walk across the marshes and when they came to a barbed-wire fence Sims told Lilian and Malcolm to lie down.

'I separated them by about fifteen yards, tied their feet together and gagged them,' went on Sims. 'I stood there smoking a cigarette when I heard a noise from the boy, and thought his gag had slipped. I took a cord and went over to the boy, intending to gag him more securely. As I put the cord around his face it slipped down to his neck and I pulled it tight. It seemed a few seconds and he was still. I felt him by the wrist and he was dead.'

Asked what the girl was doing while he strangled the boy, Sims replied, 'She was just lying there. She could not do anything. She was bound and gagged.'

He then slipped a cord round the girl's neck and pulled it tight. After a brief struggle she became still. He removed all her clothing and threw it into the dyke and then cut her body with the knives 'for some reason I do not know'.

He took the girl's handbag and the boy's wallet and their watches, then toppled both bodies into the dyke.

The statements continued: 'I didn't hold up the couple for monetary gain or any other reason except to frighten them. Events followed so quickly on top of one another. I didn't seem to have control of myself. I just can't understand how it happened . . . I was frightened the gun might go off. I suppose I was just as frightened as the pair of them. I wish to say I am sorry for what I have done and all the sorrow I have caused their parents.'

Sims went home but could not sleep when he got to bed.

'My mother saw I was worried next morning,' he continued. 'I went to work, taking the parcel and the handbag, but I could not work so I went off sick.'

He took ten shillings from Lilian's handbag and the same amount from Malcolm's wallet to pay the expenses of his journey to London to see Tom Tullett.

After Sims was taken from the *Mirror* office and driven back to Gravesend, he went with Detective Sergeant Thomas Bush to the scene of the murders. There Sims pointed out where he had thrown the shotgun, cartridges, knives and pieces of cord.

Mr Tristram Beresford, QC, appearing for the Crown when Edwin David Sims stood in the dock at Kent Assizes, Maidstone, in November 1961, said, 'This was almost the perfect murder. Unless he had told somebody about it, unless he had given himself up, it was unlikely that he would ever have been found because he had taken such great pains to conceal all traces of the crime. If he had said nothing about it, no suspicion would ever have arisen against him.'

When the trial opened the only two women on the jury were challenged and replaced by men. Mr Beresford said he had made the challenge because the facts were so horrible that he thought the women should be spared the details.

Sims, who pleaded Not Guilty, was said by Dr Francis Brisby, principal medical officer at Brixton Prison, to be a grossly perverted sexual psychopath.

'The abnormality of his mind existed at the time of the two killings,' said Dr Brisby. 'It was due to his inherent defects and what he did was almost an end product of the insidious degeneration of his perverted instincts. His abnormality developed over the course of years from morbid fantasy into pathological obsession. His condition would substantially impair his mental responsibility.'

The jury accepted this assessment of Sims and found him not guilty of murder but guilty of manslaughter on grounds of diminished responsibility.

Sentencing him to twenty-one years' jail, Mr Justice Finnemore said, 'This was a very wicked, cruel, ruthless killing of two innocent young people—as dreadful a crime as it has been my misfortune to have to try. The jury has found, on the evidence, that your responsibility is not the full, normal responsibility, but it is of course still very considerable.'

Sims, who was later sent to Broadmoor Criminal Lunatic Asylum, was already in some trouble before he walked out to the marshes to commit his ultimate crime. He had run away to France for three weeks after fiddling union funds and was awaiting a probation officer's report on his behaviour. Like both his victims, Sims came from a respectable home and for some time when he was younger had attended church regularly. Psychiatrists who examined him found him of above average intelligence, but he had been expelled from two schools and had never kept a job for long. He served for a while in the Merchant Navy but was dismissed for the theft of a pair of cufflinks.

There was no record of violence, sexual or otherwise, against him, but after his conviction for manslaughter a former girlfriend told her how their friendship ended after Sims had twice attacked her.

The girl, Mary, had started going out with Sims while they were both still at school. The teenage romance continued until they were in their late teens, in spite of opposition from Mary's parents after Sims was thrown out of the Merchant Navy.

The couple often walked together along the riverside at Denton Marshes and it was there one evening that Sims pleaded with her to allow sexual intercourse. She refused and they were still arguing about it as they walked homewards along the towpath.

Suddenly he shouted, 'For two pins I'd push you in the river and drown you!' In fact he did push her and she fell in the river, but fortunately the tide was halfway out and the water came only up to her waist. Mary screamed and Sims seemed to come to his senses. He pulled her out and apologised, saying he did not realise how hard he had pushed her.

Next day he repeated his apology to Mary's mother. He was forgiven and the couple continued to meet.

Then, some weeks later, an argument on the same subject started as they were crossing a field on their way home from a cinema. As Mary once more said 'No' to his suggestions, Sims whipped out a flick knife and cut off her two long plaits of hair. Mary, thoroughly frightened, started to run away, but he caught her and threw her to the ground.

She fought furiously as he ripped off her dress and slip, but once again he seemed suddenly to realise what he was doing. As he relaxed his grip the girl broke away and ran without stopping until she reached home.

Her parents, shocked and angry, at first decided to go straight to the police. Compassion held them back because they knew that Edwin's father was seriously ill and they felt that Mrs Sims had enough trouble without the added burden of policemen calling at the house to arrest her son. In fact Mr Sims, a railway worker, died shortly afterwards.

Mary was of course forbidden to see Sims again, but he did not give up easily. Night after night he walked up and down outside the girl's house, always singing or whistling 'Come Back To Sorrento'. Even her engagement to another man did not deter him and he was at the church when she married about a year later.

Mary's husband warned Sims several times not to pester her, but if ever he saw her in the street he would invite her to the cinema or ask her to go for a walk with him. Once she asked him why he didn't marry and settle down. He replied, 'I'm waiting for you.'

Not until Mary and her husband moved to the North of England did Sims apparently give up hope. She did not tell him she was going and heard no more of her childhood sweet-heart until ten years later when she read of his arrest on the double murder charge.

Murderousness had long brooded in Sims' mind. It was a tendency which had been satisfied by murderous fantasies until it could no longer be subdued.

The experience with Mary, ten years before the crime, showed that when some love was set against the murderously violent part of him, there was only a narrow victory for the non-murderous part. When confronted by the sight of two young lovers, he was almost certainly reminded of Mary, whom he had lost to another man. Suddenly he became impelled to hurt, damage and frighten the young couple because he was both jealous and envious of them.

He then proceeded to absorb them into his perverse fantasy system, and once he got them into his power, he could not resist the temptation to act out the double murder in line with his fantasy of killing. The relatively healthy part of him was shocked and burdened by his horrible crime so that he had to tell someone. His confession to Tom Tullett was evidence of his wish to be caught, his exhibitionism and his need to evacuate his guilty secret. The mutilation of the girl was attributable to his envy of womenkind.

13

The Mystery 'V'

Robbery, sex—or voodoo?

This was the initial problem which faced detectives investigating the savage killing of a London prostitute in December 1958. The first of the three possible reasons was quickly ruled out because nothing had been taken from the girl's room or the rest of the house at Charteris Road, Kilburn, NW6. The ferocity of the attack indicated sex as a likely motive, but a curious and seemingly deliberate scar design on the mutilated body did not fit in with the usual pattern of sexual murder, and engendered the suspicion that witchcraft might be involved and that killing was part of a sacrificial ritual.

The victim was a pretty brunette, Irish-born Veronica Murray, aged thirty, who was well known in the Soho area and had been lodging at Charteris Road for about six months. A girl friend of hers became worried when Veronica disappeared from her usual West End haunts and tried unsuccessfully to contact her. Eventually she telephoned the Yugoslav landlord of the house, Mr Ratonir Tasic, on 19th December. Mr Tasic took one look into Veronica's room and immediately dialled 999.

A police team led by Divisional Detective Superintendent Evan Davies found the room in a state of chaos. Furniture had been smashed, torn clothing scattered around the floor, there were pools of blood on the carpet and widespread splashes of blood on the wallpaper.

The woman, lying on the bed naked except for a brown pullover partly covering her head, had been battered to death. Twenty-four bones in her body had been broken. Apparently the weapon used was a pink-painted metal dumbbell—one of a pair Miss Murray had used for 'keep fit' exercises.

A puzzling feature of the injuries was a V pattern repeated on several parts of her body, each V being made up of a number of small circular abrasions. Pathologist Dr Donald Teare said that these minor wounds had been inflicted after death and could have been caused by any manufactured object with a small flat end. Because it was felt that some special significance must be attached to such a deliberate pattern of mutilation, the police consulted a London University professor who was a voodoo expert. He was unable to help—except to say that the marks did not correspond with any known voodoo sign and were not significant of ritual killing.

With that possibility eliminated, it was clear to the murder team that they were looking for a perverted sadist who might well kill again. They had a vague description of a man seen visiting Miss Murray's room, plus a set of fingerprints which probably belonged to the murderer. For months the hunt went on to find an unknown man to fit that description and those prints. It seemed an impossible task—until the same set of prints was found at the scene of a burglary in the West End of London.

From that point onwards any prints found in any case of housebreaking were compared to the vital prints—a pains-taking task which brought useful results. The suite occupied by the film star George Sanders at London's Westbury Hotel was broken into. Several articles were stolen and the thief left his fingerprints on a bottle of whisky when he helped himself to several drinks. The same significant prints were found at fifteen houses in the Chelsea area, and in a nurses' home in Holborn; a nurse who saw the intruder managed to lock him in a bath-room, but he succeeded in making his escape before the police arrived.

Most of the things stolen were of small value, but the thief always helped himself to drink and it was clear that he chain-smoked during his marauding activities.

Gradually the police built up a picture of the man they wanted. He was known in the West End bars and clubs as Mick, was thought to be either a flautist or a drummer in a band, had a long scar on his nose, and was a heavy drinker and smoker. From ten o'clock at night till six the next morning, special police squads sealed off sections of the West End in a number of sporadic operations and questioned all men passing through the area. One night thirty-six men were questioned and all agreed to be fingerprinted. None matched those of the wanted man, and their prints were destroyed.

Then, ten months after the murder of Veronica Murray, another woman was attacked.

Mrs Mabel Hill, the mother of three children, living apart from her husband, had been celebrating her thirty-first birthday on 10th October 1959 with a woman friend at Streatham. On her way home to Ismalia Road, Fulham, she changed trains at Leicester Square and while she was on the platform was approached by a tousle-haired, pleasant-faced young man who asked her for a light for his cigarette.

The man got into the train with her and insisted on walking beside her when she got off at Fulham. He told her his name was Mick and that he was working with a band. When they reached Mrs Hill's house he asked if she would give him some coffee. After some hesitation she agreed because he had clearly been drinking and she thought it would help to sober him.

Mrs Hill sat at a table as her visitor drank the coffee and smoked a cigarette. Then suddenly he removed his pullover and shirt. Mrs Hill told him sharply to dress himself and go.

'I remember nothing else,' she said. 'The next thing I knew was that I was in hospital.'

She was taken to St Stephen's Hospital, Fulham, in the early hours of 11th October after her thirteen-year-old son Alan had found her lying unconscious in the kitchen. Two nylon stockings had been tied round her neck so tightly that a crucifix and chain she wore had been forced into the flesh of her throat. Her entire face and the upper half of her neck were covered in small hæmorrhages, her lips and tongue were swollen and bruised and there were pinpoint hæmorrhages all over her scalp.

On her chest, face, neck and left foot was a series of perfectly circular markings made with some object with a serrated edge. Each set of twelve one-inch-diameter circles formed a larger circle.

This mysterious scar pattern sparked off something in the memory of Detective Inspector Peter Vibart (later Detective Chief Superintendent), head of Walham Green CID, who joined Detective Chief Inspector Basil Acott (later Deputy Commander) in the hunt for Mrs Hill's attacker. Vibart recalled the markings found on the body of Veronica Murray and, although in one case the small circles formed a V and in the other were joined to make a larger ring, he thought it probable that one man was responsible for both crimes.

A comparison of the fingerprints found in the murdered woman's flat with those on the coffee cup handled by Mrs Hill's assailant proved his surmise correct. They had both been made by the same man—the man who had also by this time burgled at least twenty-five houses in the West End and Chelsea.

As Mabel Hill slowly recovered from her injuries and one hundred detectives formed a team to track down the elusive 'Mick', two more sets of his prints were found.

The first was in a house at Skinner Place, Pimlico, where Mrs Annie Belcher, a widow of seventy-one, was beaten about the head with a poker by an intruder she disturbed in her bedroom. Then, at the end of November 1959, he broke into the home of Mr and Mrs William Sloane in Markham Street, Chelsea, while they were out at a party. His prints were found on bottles of gin and Italian vermouth to which he had helped himself. When he left the house he took with him some jewellery, a small amount of cash and a quite distinctive cigarette lighter. At the request of the police, national newspapers published a picture of an exact replica of this lighter, which was presented to Mr Sloane by the Texas Golf Sulphur Company and was engraved with the company's name and crest, the matching lighter used in the pictures having been given to Mrs Sloane at the same time. Anyone who saw a man using such a lighter was asked to dial 999 immediately.

Policewomen chosen for their attractive looks were drafted

in to join male detectives in their hunt for the wanted man. They walked around the West End at night, mingled with the crowds in cafés, bars and clubs, and were instructed to contact the special detective squad if they saw anyone answering the description of scar-faced Mick.

The break for which the police had been hoping came soon after the lighter picture appeared in the press. A telephone call from an officer at the Welsh Guards camp at Pirbright, Surrey, sent Basil Acott and Peter Vibart hurrying to Woking police station to interview a guardsman who had been taken from the camp by Surrey police.

This man, Michael Douglas Dowdall, aged nineteen, had been seen by a fellow soldier using the stolen lighter. He was taken to Chelsea police station and charged with breaking out of the house in Markham Street after stealing the lighter and other articles. He was shown a number of items removed from his quarters at Pirbright and, pointing to a tube of toothpaste, he said, 'I like the taste of that. It belonged to the actor George Sanders. I was going to send their bracelet back but I threw it in the river.'

Chief Inspector Acott told Dowdall that in addition to the housebreaking with which he was charged the police were investigating a number of serious offences he was believed to have committed.

'Everybody is against me,' replied the young guardsman. 'It is when I get drinking I do these things. I'm all right when I am sober. It has been worrying me for a long time and I have wanted to go to a doctor. I'm glad it's all over. I'll tell you what I can remember.'

In a long statement Dowdall said, 'I want to tell you now about something I think is serious. Just before Christmas 1958 I had been drinking in the West End and I got very drunk. I picked up a prostitute in Trafalgar Square. She called a taxi and gave an address in Kilburn . . . at her house I had sex with her and went to sleep. When she woke me up we had a row over something and she called me a filthy little Welshman. I threw a vase at her and I believe it smashed.'

Dowdall went on to describe how the woman hit him with something and scratched his nose. He rushed at her, knocked her down and hit her on the head.

'I pulled her on the bed and I remember chucking some clothes over her. I took a bottle of whisky and then I left the place. I went back to the Union Jack Club and went to sleep. When I woke up I found blood on my hands and on my shirt and suit. I tried to wash the shirt but could not get rid of the blood, so I chucked it away in a dustbin at the camp. I sent the suit to the cleaners. A day or two afterwards I read in the newspapers that a prostitute had been found murdered at Kilburn and I knew then that I had killed the woman.'

Referring to his drinking habits, Dowdall said that once he started heavy drinking bouts he found he liked it and kept it up, sometimes getting 'paralytic' on spirits.

'When I was drunk, very drunk, I would try anything . . . my mates think I am a queer. I have tried to show them they are wrong.'

At the Old Bailey in January 1960 Michael Dowdall's plea of not guilty to the murder of Veronica Murray, on grounds of diminished responsibility, was supported by medical evidence.

Dr F. Brisby, principal medical officer at Brixton Prison, said he was a psychopath. Although he had talked freely about the facts of the case he was unable to throw any light on the circular marks found on the body of Miss Murray and on Mrs Hill.

'I believe this amnesia about certain facts is genuine,' said Dr Brisby. Dowdall was an untruthful type who thought people laughed at him and disparaged him. This was typical of the personality of a psychopath. If he had not drunk at all he would still have had an abnormality of mind that would substantially impair responsibility for his actions.

Support for these findings came from Dr A. D. Leigh, a psychiatrist at Bethlem Hospital, who said the characteristics of a psychopath were aggressiveness, impulsiveness, lying, sexual perversion and often alcoholism, with no remorse or sense of guilt for harm done to others.

Replying to a question put by Mr Desmond Trenner,

defending, the doctor said, 'I have no doubt he is a sexual pervert.'

Dowdall was found guilty of manslaughter and sentenced to life imprisonment. Mr Justice Donovan told him, 'It would be clearly unsafe to impose upon you a sentence of a fixed term of years, at the end of which you would be set free. The sentence must be one which will enable the authorities to detain you until they are satisfied that you can safely mingle with your fellow creatures once again.'

The boy who committed murder three days after his eighteenth birthday had been a problem child from his early days.

He was two years old when his father, an Army captain, died on active service in 1942. When his mother died six years later Michael, his elder sister and younger brother left their home in Uckfield, Sussex, and went to live with an aunt, Mrs Alice Jenkins, in the Monmouthshire mining village of Llanhilleth. Even before that big change in his life he had been described by his schoolmistress as 'quite uncontrollable' and at the age of six and a half years his situation had been discussed as a problem case at a school conference. On one occasion he had tied up a cat with string and thrown it down the stairs. Twice he had been before juvenile courts—once for stealing railway property and another time for breaking into a school and causing damage. For a short period he had been committed to a council home.

When he left school he took a job as a baker's vanboy, but had always been keen to follow his father's career as a soldier and at the age of fifteen enlisted as a drummer boy in the Welsh Guards.

Two of his uncles, who gave evidence for the defence at the trial, admitted to being heavy drinkers and to outbursts of violence under the influence of alcohol. Young Dowdall, too, began drinking at an early age. He told a prison medical officer that for some time before his arrest he had been going to London at weekends and drinking up to two bottles of spirits. He said he was glad the police had caught up with him because he thought that in six months he would have been an alcoholic 'on methylated spirits'.

He celebrated his eighteenth birthday with other guardsmen at an hotel in Guildford, Surrey, where he was said to have drunk four or five half-pints of gin in a beer tankard. He had to be carried out of the hotel and taken back to barracks in a taxi. He was not fit to go on parade the next morning because he was still partially drunk and was taken for a walk to restore him to sobriety.

Four times Dowdall had been in trouble for being absent without leave. While in detention he had tried to hang himself with a dressing-gown cord, saying that he did not want to face life any more.

Lt-Col John Mansell Miller, Commanding Officer, 1st Battalion Welsh Guards, told the trial court that he always knew Dowdall was 'odd'. It was a well-known fact and was reported to him when he took command of the battalion.

'I knew he was unusual,' the officer told the trial court. 'It was my impression that he liked showing off and had what can be described as delusions of grandeur. I think it is because he is small, weak and insignificant. He had a desire to impress people and pretend to be someone more important than he really was.'

Dowdall's consumption of half-pints of gin on his birthday had not been reported to his commanding officer. Asked by the judge if he would let a young recruit in the Welsh Guards drink to such excess without saying anything about it, Colonel Miller said he would not. He would have taken steps to curb it.

The judge: 'I should hope so.'

A Welsh Guards sergeant said he had always had trouble with Dowdall, who was sullen and difficult to handle and at times untruthful and deceptive. On one occasion Dowdall had tried to throttle him.

The young drummer boy only just measured up to the Welsh Guards' minimum height and was teased by his fellow soldiers about his frail, rather girlish appearance. They pulled his leg, too, because he spoke only to the married women on the camp and seemed to have no girlfriends.

In his favourite public house in Chelsea, where he always wore the latest fashions in civilian clothing, he invariably had plenty of money to spend and drank nothing but double gins or brandies. He was flamboyantly generous and sometimes insisted on treating everyone in the bar. Regular patrons dubbed him 'The College Boy'.

It was in this public house that he met the one girl who was sympathetic towards him. She was a student nurse who said after the trial that she would visit Dowdall in prison because he was kind and generous to her.

'He seemed to have a certain sadness which made me want to mother him,' she said. 'He boasted about his conquests with dozens of other women but I knew he was lying. He would shrink from me when we were alone together and used to blush when we kissed.

'He liked mixing with the Chelsea set because he could relax in their company. He told me he was a drummer and clarinet player with jazz bands in West End clubs. Sometimes he took me dancing in cellar clubs and often I stopped him from buying drinks for everyone in the place. I think he spent so lavishly because he wanted to impress people . . .'

Dowdall often got drunk during evenings out with his nurse girlfriend. She would then take him back to her flat to recover.

There, although they were frequently alone together, he behaved with the utmost propriety. This man who in his perverted passion savagely attacked at least three women (police believe he may have been responsible for other, officially unsolved, sexual assaults and murders) showed nothing but gentleness and shy respect for the girl who listened to him without laughing at him.

There was a distinct similarity in Dowdall leaving a 'signature' sign on his victim to the pair-of-lips impression left on the murder victims in the film *No Way To Treat a Lady*. In Dowdall's case the leaving of a sign was certainly an act of triumph, but also an attempt on behalf of a split-off part of him to get caught.

He clearly demonstrated what is becoming more and more apparent to psychiatrists, that individuals who have a split-off or encapsulated murderousness within them, drink large quantities of alcohol in order to commit the crime which is going on in their fantasy life all the time and plaguing them from within. The diminished state of responsibility and control brought about by alcohol enables them to enact the crime or the token crime in the external world and to relieve themselves of the impulses to murder although only for the time being. Unfortunately, the internal situation builds up again, so that there is almost always a tendency to repeat the crime.

It is often the person who is underprivileged, somewhat impotent, small or deformed, who finally becomes a killer.

It is quite likely that Dowdall's enlistment in the Welsh Guards constituted a vain attempt to get into a situation which provided adequate controls to keep him from acting out his murderous impulses.

14

Death of a Hitch-hiker

She was a girl who would never walk or board a bus if she could thumb a lift. Her parents had pleaded with her, and her boyfriend had warned of the hazards of hitch-hiking, but Diana Stephanie Kemp continued to wave a hopeful hand at the first likely looking car whenever she wanted to get from one place to another. She dismissed as 'fussing' the anxiety of family and friends, and was convinced there was no real danger for a decent girl who made it plain that she was interested only in a free ride. She thought she could look after herself.

Events were to prove her tragically wrong.

The evening of Thursday 16th October 1969 looked like being much like any other evening in the Kemps' semi-detached house in Elizabeth Avenue, Christchurch, Hampshire. Twenty-year-old Diana—an unusually attractive girl with a slim figure, long dark hair and classically beautiful features—had supper soon after arriving home from her job as secretary to a Bournemouth estate agent. At ten minutes to eight she borrowed a sixpenny piece from her father, Mr Bernard Kemp, and left the house to telephone from a nearby kiosk to her boyfriend, Richard Coomber, at Mudeford, on the outskirts of Christchurch.

The couple had arranged to meet the following night, but Diana asked if she could see Richard that evening, as she did not want to stay at home. Richard replied that he was going to have a bath and thought that by the time he was ready it would be too late to go out. He confirmed the appointment for 7.30 outside Christchurch Town Hall next evening.

Diana returned home and went upstairs to her room, but stayed only a few minutes and called 'Cheerio' to her parents as she went out again at 8.15. She did not say where she planned to go, and one of the minor mysteries of the sad affair is what in fact she intended to do when she left the house for the second time that evening.

Mr and Mrs Kemp settled down to watch television. At about 9.30 there was a knock on the front door which Mrs Angela Kemp answered. A young man was standing on the doorstep, holding Diana's shoulder bag. He said he had found it in the road at Mudeford. He had been able to return it because Diana's address was on a letter inside. Mrs Kemp thanked him and the young man departed without giving his name. The contents of the bag were intact and included three five-pound notes—money Diana was saving to buy a new dress.

Thinking that her daughter would be worrying about the loss of her bag, Mrs Kemp telephoned Richard Coomber and was slightly surprised to learn that he had not seen Diana that evening and was not expecting her. By midnight her parents were seriously concerned and checked with the police in case she had been involved in a road accident. The following morning she was officially listed 'missing from home'.

At that early stage in a missing persons enquiry there would not normally be any suspicion of foul play, but the return of the girl's shoulder bag gave a sinister aspect to the whole affair. Had Diana been planning to leave home—and there was not a shred of evidence to suggest this—she would surely have abandoned the idea after the loss of her bag, or at very least would have reported the matter to the police. Nothing was heard from her and she seemed to have disappeared without trace.

The young man who found the bag, Peter Deane, a doctor's son, went to the police after reading in a Sunday newspaper three days later that Diana was missing, but he was able to tell them no more than he told Mrs Kemp.

Six weeks later, on Sunday 30th November 1969, Mr Norman Young, of Poole in the adjoining county of Dorset, took his family for a morning drive, following the coast road towards Swanage. He parked just off the Studland–Swanage road at the hamlet of Ulwell and started to walk along a bridle path leading to the headland when he saw, protruding from a covering of bracken and leaves, a pair of bare feet and legs.

Officers from Swanage police station who were called to the scene uncovered the decomposing body of a girl with her raincoat and short blue dress pushed up around the upper part of her body. Her underwear, tights and shoes had vanished. A check on the list of missing girls indicated that she might be Diana Kemp and her identity was definitely established by the Bournemouth dentist, Mr Michael Wolfson, who had examined her teeth only a week before she disappeared.

The cause of death was strangulation and a full-scale murder hunt was launched under the leadership of Detective Chief Superintendent William Mayo, head of Dorset and Bournemouth CID. It was not an easy task, because the girl had been dead for several weeks and her body had been found forty-five miles from the point at which she disappeared. Sixty officers from Hampshire joined the one hundred and forty from Dorset, visiting more than three thousand houses along both the routes from Christchurch to Ulwell, taking countless statements, questioning motorists who might have been in the area at the time and checking and cross-checking every scrap of information that could turn out to be evidence.

Because of Diana's known habit of hitch-hiking, it was assumed that she had thumbed a lift from a man, who had assaulted her, and that she had perhaps thrown her shoulder bag from the car in an attempt to attract attention. The bag had been found not far from her boyfriend's home and it was thought likely that, in spite of the earlier telephone call, she had decided to call on him—or to visit a girlfriend who lived in the same area.

It was purely speculative—but it was all the police had to work on until they visited Diana's stricken parents on the day after the discovery of her body. Mrs Kemp identified the girl's clothing and a ring taken from her finger, and then, almost as an afterthought, she asked, 'But where's the watch she was wearing when she disappeared?'

Armed with a very clear description of Diana's gold-coloured Pontiac wrist-watch, thirty officers began the task of checking every shop at which it might have been offered for sale. One of them, Police Constable John Welch, of Poole, was walking along Ashley Road, Parkstone, when he paused outside a secondhand goods shop. There in the window was a lady's Pontiac watch. It was later identified by repairers' marks as Diana's.

The watch had been sold to the shopkeeper only a week before it was spotted by the constable and the transaction was fresh enough in the dealer's mind for him to give a full description of the young man who had sold it. He remembered the incident clearly because of some conversation about a tape recorder.

The man had asked the price of a recorder in the window and mentioned that a friend of his had owned one just like it. He even thought it possible that it was the very same tape recorder and that his friend had sold it to the dealer. Told that the price was £35, the seller of the watch said he could not raise that amount immediately but would return at the weekend to pay a deposit and would settle the balance within two or three weeks. The dealer had agreed to this arrangement, but the customer had not returned to the shop.

By a stroke of good fortune, the dealer had taken the name and address of the vendor of the tape recorder. This young man, when traced after a camping holiday, volunteered the information that a man named Ian Troup had for a time worked with him in the projection room at the Regent Cinema, Christchurch, and for a few weeks had lodged at his (the informant's) home. Troup had shown a great interest in the other man's tape recorder and said he would like to buy one if he could afford it. The mother of the young man recalled having seen a lady's wrist-watch—very like the Pontiac shown her by a detective—in Troup's room. Troup had told her it belonged to his wife, from whom he had been separated for three years.

A check with Criminal Records Office revealed that Ian George Troup, aged twenty-nine, was wanted on warrant for failure to surrender to bail at Greenwich Magistrates' Court, on 22nd August 1969, on a charge of indecent exposure. He already had two convictions for indecent exposure and others for false pretences, theft and garage-breaking.

After leaving the home of the friend with the tape recorder, Troup had moved to a flatlet house at Westbourne, near Bournemouth, on 23rd October 1969, but had left for London 'in rather a hurry' on 2nd December. It was here that the police had their second stroke of luck. Troup had bought a white Hillman from the landlord of the flatlet house and had sold his old black Standard to another of the tenants. Although Troup had gone, the car he had owned at the time of Diana Kemp's murder was still on the premises. Under the passenger seat of this car detectives found a button which matched those on Diana's blue dress, while long dark hairs identical with those from the head of the murdered girl were extracted from the carpet and upholstery of the car.

Troup, a painter and decorator, was traced to Eastmearn Road, Dulwich, London SE21, and taken back to Bournemouth. At first he said he had found the girl's watch at Boscombe and had sold it because he was short of cash, but after further questioning blurted out, 'It was sex. I haven't had it for a year.'

In a long statement Troup said he saw the girl thumbing a lift and picked her up in his car near her home. He stopped at Mudeford, near the place at which the handbag was found.

'She told me she was visiting a friend. I tried to tell her how lonely I was and how my marriage had broken down. I asked her if she would drive round with me and just talk, but she said no. I tried to kiss her and she slapped my face . . . her being in the car in that dress, the miniskirt, started to build up the sex impulse . . . I put my hands behind her neck and she began to struggle. Something just built up inside me and I wanted her to be unconscious. The sex urge was very great and when she stopped struggling I drove to a cul-de-sac and had sex with her.'

Troup pleaded Not Guilty to murder but Guilty to manslaughter when he stood trial at Hampshire Assizes in Winchester in March 1970. He said he only wanted to make the girl unconscious and waited for two hours for her to 'come round' after he had intercourse with her. When he felt her go cold he knew she was dead. Because he did not want to acknowledge that he caused her death he dumped her body in the ditch at Swanage where he thought it would not readily be found.

He agreed with Mr Raymond Stock, QC, for the Crown, that he was anxious to have sexual relations with the girl, regardless of what sort of condition she was in at the time.

'Conscious or unconscious?'

'Yes.'

'Alive or dead?'

'Yes.'

Troup reiterated that he did not mean to kill Diana and did not want to kill her.

'I am now deeply sorry and ashamed of myself,' he added.

Asking for a manslaughter verdict, Sir Joseph Molony, QC, for the defence, said, 'It was not a planned murder. It was done on impulse under sexual urges.'

The jury took only fifteen minutes to find Ian Troup guilty of murder and he was sentenced to life imprisonment.

Like so many killers, he was a man of contradictions. Described as a pleasant, quiet man, a good worker, reserved, polite and even-tempered, his hobby was the construction of model ships. Although separated from his wife, he seems to have had few girlfriends. One fifteen-year-old girl who was invited to spend an evening with him was surprised because he did not even kiss her goodnight. He took her for a country drive, then for a walk. After supper in a café they sat in the car and looked at the sea and she was driven back to her home at ten o'clock.

'He never made any passes,' she said. 'He was just a quiet, ordinary boy. . . .'

But Troup was certainly not 'ordinary'. His record of indecent exposure reflected a sexual inadequacy. He mentioned in his statement to the police that he had not experienced sexual intercourse for more than a year, and there would appear to be no reason to doubt that declaration.

The key to Troup's attitude to sexual deprivation during that year will be found only during psychoanalysis in prison.

It may well emerge that he was sexually inhibited, as are many offenders found guilty of exposure, and a man who found it difficult to satisfy a woman or receive satisfaction himself.

The fact that he did not mind whether or not Diana Kemp was conscious or unconscious suggests that in his sex life he was not bothered about the response of his female partner.

Such an attitude may have arisen over a period, when he discovered that he could not satisfy a woman. In these circumstances he would have become concerned solely with obtaining satisfaction for himself and he had, of course, reached a point where his sexual urge became overpowering.

15

Double Murder

Early in the morning of Monday 7th February 1972, a 999 caller reported smoke pouring from a third-floor window of a block of council flats in Finchdale Road, Abbey Wood, in south-east London. Firemen raced to the scene and had to smash the front door to get into flat No. 30. Through the acrid-smelling smoke they ran to the bathroom—the obvious source of the fire—and there faced a sight that none of them is ever likely to forget.

In the bath were the mutilated bodies of a young woman and a little boy, wrapped in still smouldering, paraffin-soaked blankets. One of the first police officers to arrive at the flat fainted as he went into the bathroom, and a detective said the scene was comparable only to the ritual killing of actress Sharon Tate and four friends by the Charles Manson hippie group in Hollywood three years previously.

The child had been badly beaten before being strangled and stabbed several times in the chest and abdomen. The woman, too, had died from stab wounds, those in her chest having penetrated to her lungs and heart. The murderer had cut off one of her breasts, gouged out an eye and severed a section of her nose. These parts of her body, together with one of her hands, on which were two rings, were discovered in different parts of the flat.

Two nine-inch knives, believed to be the murder weapons, were found in the flat by detectives, one of whom commented: 'Only a maniac could have inflicted those injuries. He was either out of his mind—completely berserk—or he was so drugged that he was unable to stop himself. It was one of the most sickening sights I have encountered in many years of police work.'

Both bodies were so badly burned that positive identification of the woman was possible only from her dental records. These established that she was, in fact, the occupant of flat No. 30— Mrs Margaret Richmond, estranged wife of Peter Richmond, a twenty-one-year-old window dresser in a chain of tailors. The child was their son, Justin, aged two years.

Margaret Richmond, aged twenty-four, was a tall, slim, very attractive girl with long dark hair. She had met Peter Richmond on her twenty-first birthday and they married a few months later at Ashford, Middlesex. The couple separated, however, in the autumn of 1971, and the husband returned to his parents' home at Alabama Street, Plumstead, a few miles away. He was staying with relatives in Hertfordshire when police officers called to tell him of the death of his wife and child.

In an attempt to build a new life for herself, Mrs Richmond had become a representative for Avon Cosmetics, visiting house-wives in the area to show them the products and take their orders—a job she was able to combine with the care of little Justin.

Her killer had first tried to burn the bodies by pouring over them the contents of perfume bottles, part of her sales stock, which had evidently failed to ignite. He had then saturated his victims in paraffin.

Detectives trying to build up a diary of the murdered woman's last hours established that she had spoken on the telephone to her husband on the previous Friday and had seemed perfectly normal. On Saturday afternoon she went shopping, telling a friend that she was going to bake some cakes because she was expecting a few people to visit her. In fact she went out to a party on Saturday evening and returned to her own flat with a group of people afterwards.

What happened on the fateful Sunday of 6th February remained a mystery, but interviews with the sixty-four other tenants of the block of flats made it clear to detectives that the murders had taken place in the early hours of Monday morn-ing—and that the screams of the victims had been heard clearly by some of their neighbours.

There was later some criticism of people's apparent callousness. Mr Michael Worsley, prosecuting for the Crown at the subsequent Old Bailey trial of the double killer, said that neighbours and passers-by had heard screams, a child crying, dull thuds and cries of a woman. 'They were heard for about thirty minutes, but apparently nobody intervened,' he said. 'Not only that, nobody made the slightest effort to call any help, as far as is known.'

Neighbours felt such criticism to be unjust, explaining that most of them were unaware that Mr Richmond was no longer living in the flat and thought it was a case of husband and wife quarrelling. There had been a number of rowdy parties during the year in which the Richmonds were tenants of No. 30. Only four weeks after they had moved in the Greater London Council sent them a warning letter following complaints from neighbours about the noise.

Widow Mrs Mary Rushton, a pensioner living in the flat below the Richmonds, said that she had heard a banging noise at about three o'clock in the morning of the day the murders were discovered. She got up because she thought there was something wrong with her television, but after checking the set she went back to bed.

'I couldn't sleep because of the noise,' she said. 'Mrs Richmond was an attractive girl, but there were always strange, long-haired people visiting the place for parties she used to throw. I shared a telephone line with her but couldn't use it over the weekend because her receiver had been taken off the hook.'

Mrs Harriet Coombes, aged seventy-three, said she heard screams but did not do anything about it. 'I might have done something if I had been a bit younger,' she said, 'but when you're my age you don't go poking your nose into other people's business. I was going to send my daughter down to see what it was all about but suddenly the screams stopped.'

Another neighbour who heard screaming 'for quite a long while' was Mrs Irene Saunders.

'Living in a place like this you get used to people screaming,' she commented. 'It gets to such a point you say to yourself "What the hell—it's nothing to do with me". If I had gone down there I might have been attacked as well.'

A seventy-year-old woman living in an old people's bungalow opposite the flats said, 'So many bad things are done that you get to a stage where it doesn't pay to help your neighbour. If you interfere in this area you find people ganging up against you. If you have a disagreement with anybody in this street they send their kids round to pour paint over your car, ruin your garden and throw stones at your windows.'

Mrs Lynn Bell, also resident in the flats, said that she and her husband had heard a disturbance in the Richmonds' flat about two months before the murders.

'You just have to try not to listen when you live in flats, she said. 'You hear shouting and banging but you just have to let people get on with it. It's not a case of being un-neighbourly. It's best to let people sort out their own troubles. Who's to know someone is being murdered?'

Other people living nearby spoke of hippies who visited Mrs Richmond and suggested that she held drug-taking parties, but Peter Richmond was emphatic that such an idea was ridiculous.

'I used to take drugs,' he said. 'I was on amphetamines for a long time and that was partly what led to the break-up of our marriage, so if drugs could cause a split like that it is hardly likely that my wife would get involved with a load of junkies. The long-haired people neighbours saw going into our flat would have been my friends. I used to see a lot of them when Margaret and I were together and when we split up they continued to be friendly with my wife.'

He added that he and his wife had remained on good terms. He frequently visited the flat and used to have Justin at his parents' home most weekends. There had been discussions about a possible reconciliation.

Margaret Richmond's father, Mr John Rashid, of Ashford, Middlesex, was also indignant at the stories circulating about his daughter.

'All this stuff about her being a hippie is complete lies,' he declared. 'She would not have had wild parties in her flat because of the baby. She loved him too much for that. She was a wonderful mother. She was a very trusting girl who was always helping people.'

The hippie angle, however, was about the only lead the police had to work on, and within twenty-four hours two long-haired male hitch-hikers had been picked up in the West Country and taken to the murder headquarters in Plumstead. They were not suspects, but it was thought they could give information about Mrs Richmond's friends.

In the meantime police with dogs scoured nearby woods and a helicopter was used to search Plumstead Marshes in case the killer was trying to hide in the locality.

Interviews with a number of youths enabled detectives to build up a picture of a possible sequence of events, and on 10th February two officers travelled to Salisbury, Wiltshire, where they caught up with another hitch-hiker—Jonathon Richmond, eighteen-year-old brother of Peter. He was taken to Plumstead and charged with the murder of his sister-in-law and her child.

German-born Jonathon, one of five brothers, had been unemployed for some time and had no settled address. He made no attempt to deny the charges and pleaded Guilty when he stood before the Recorder of London, Sir Carl Aarvold, at the Old Bailey in June 1972.

Mr Michael Worsley, outlining the case, said that Richmond had visited his sister-in-law.

'It seems that he tried to rape her. She screamed and, in his own words, he tried to keep her quiet. While that was going on the poor young child came into the room where it was happening, crying . . . he must have had the most appalling beating in addition to the stabbing and strangulation.'

Richmond had made a full confession to the police and said in a statement, 'I wanted sex and she would not let me.' He also told detectives that he bought some tablets of ephedrine in a public house before the murders, but Mr Worsley said it seemed unlikely they were ephedrine—a common treatment for

205

asthma—which did not give rise to hallucinations or aggression.

Sentencing him to life imprisonment, the Recorder said to Richmond, 'It is open to me to make such recommendation as to the period of time which you should be detained as I think proper. In this case I shall make no recommendation. The horror of the facts of this case will always be before the minds of those who may in due course have the responsibility of allowing you your freedom.'

Sir Carl added that the defendant was very young and immature and that was something which those in authority in many years to come would take into account.

After the trial Peter Richmond said that he and his wife had done a lot for Jonathon, who was often without a job or a roof over his head. They had taken him in and found work for him, but he was a good-for-nothing who already had a number of convictions.

'Now I wash my hands of him as a brother,' he said. 'I can never forgive him. I never want to see him again in my life.'

There is no doubt that Richmond is a psychopath. Being of German origin, it is also quite likely that he had identified himself at some stage in his life with Nazi brutality.

The most alarming feature of the gruesome double murder is the effect that the drugs had on Jonathon Richmond. It is certain that the tablets diminished his sense of reality and his control of his perverse impulses.

The extreme danger which arises when drugs and alcohol are taken by a person with disturbed 'inner worlds' has been repeatedly proven in murder trials.

16

The Doctor's Mistress

When Dr John King was called to a seaside bungalow at Vine Close, Hemsby, Norfolk, on the morning of Sunday 2nd July 1972, he found a beautiful girl lying dead in bed. The man who had telephoned him was wandering from room to room listening to the Jim Reeves record 'My Last Affair', and he was still playing the same sad tune when the village constable, summoned by Dr King, arrived on the scene. He said he had selected the record for sentimental reasons because he liked it and 'she liked it'—and now she had killed herself.

The girl, blonde and shapely Carole Califano, aged twenty-eight, had been working as a receptionist at the group surgery where Dr King was one of the partners. The man in the bungalow was another member of the same practice, Dr Peter Drinkwater, with whom Mrs Califano had been living since leaving her husband and child some months previously. English-born, she was the wife of an Italian hairdresser.

The girl's body was taken away for post-mortem examination and Detective Inspector Roy Hipperson went to the bungalow, called San Remo, to talk to thirty-seven-year-old Dr Drinkwater.

'We had an argument over my ex-wife and Carole was frightened I would leave her,' said the doctor. 'She thought life was unbearable and that she had nothing to live for. I tried to calm her.' He added that Mrs Califano was also distressed by the separation from her child and her own marital affairs. As an employee at the group surgery she had access to drugs and had evidently helped herself to provide the means to end her life.

Pathologists found that Mrs Califano had in fact died as a

result of drugs. She had been injected with five substances, four of them in combination to form 'a cocktail of death'. A contributory cause of respiratory failure could have been 'postural asphyxia'.

Dr Drinkwater was later interviewed by Detective Chief Superintendent Reginald Lester, to whom he made a second statement. This time he said that after the argument he filled a syringe with a more than fatal dose of drugs and told Carole, 'If you want to do yourself in, have a go with this lot.' Questioned more closely about this, he replied, 'Yes, she wanted to end it all. I supplied the means. I feel awfully guilty about it now.'

It seemed at first to be a fairly straightforward case of suicide by a girl who was worried by the circumstances of her life and was in a position to end it, but a search of the bungalow revealed evidence which began to throw a more sinister light on the affair . . .

Detectives found five black and white Polaroid photographs and one colour print wrapped between two shirts which had been tucked into the foot of the bed. Seven more colour photographs were in the doctor's medical bag. All the pictures showed Carole Califano in positions described later in court as 'lewd and bizarre'. In some Dr Drinkwater was committing obscene acts with his mistress and in others her naked body was depicted with wine bottles and a cucumber.

After the discovery of these photographs the doctor was again questioned by Superintendent Lester and he made a third statement, admitting that he had injected the drugs. He said he did this at the request of Mrs Califano 'to fulfil her sexual desires'. She had asked him to make her unconscious before taking the pictures.

'She liked that sort of thing,' he said. 'I was a bit disgusted by it all. I know I was very confused and acting illogically. We seemed to have sunk so low. I thought Carole would feel better if she got a really long sleep.'

Dr Drinkwater gave a fuller version of his story at St Albans Crown Court in December 1972, when he pleaded not guilty to murdering Mrs Califano. He said that until May of that year their sexual relationship had been quite normal, very full and mutually satisfying. They had intended to get married as soon as it was legally possible and he had bought her an eighteen-carat gold wedding ring with which she was 'absolutely thrilled'.

Carole, however, had become anxious and depressed because of her matrimonial problems and her desire to gain custody of her eight-year-old daughter, Bridgetta, who had been sent to one of her husband's relatives in Italy. She did not sleep well and often had nightmares, so he gave her mild oral sedatives to help her relax.

She then started to worry about his relationship with his ex-wife and on one occasion became hysterical because he had telephoned his former wife about their son of nine and their five-year-old daughter.

'She thought I did not love her and that I preferred my ex-wife. She threatened to leave me.'

On 14th June he bought a Polaroid camera, as he was very keen on photography and on the night of 30th June Mrs Califano asked him to take some erotic pictures. He gave her an injection of Pentathol to put her to sleep and attempted to take some photographs, but he had taken several doses of amphetamine tablets during the day and was not able to work the flash action on the camera. Next morning he told Mrs Califano that the pictures had not come out and she was rather upset.

During that day, when he saw thirty to forty patients, he took some more tablets. In the evening he went to a public house and had two large gin-and-tonics, which combined with the amphetamines, made him feel 'somewhat euphoric, light-headed and happy-go-lucky'. He took a bottle of red wine back to the bungalow and both he and Carole had quite a lot to drink—she taking Pernod as well as some wine.

'I sat down and started to write a final letter to my ex-wife,' he continued. 'Carole came in and I told her about the letter. This upset her. She asked me if we could go back to the activities of the previous night.'

Mr Justice Thesiger asked him: 'Can you tell us the words she used?'

'She said she would like me to take erotic-type photographs with me involved and this would bring us closer together. She wanted erotic pictures with phallic objects.'

'Did she use the words erotic and phallic?' 'Yes.'

Questioned by his defending counsel, Mr William Howard, about his reaction to this request, Dr Drinkwater replied, 'I didn't want to do it, basically. I said I didn't think it was a normal, decent sort of thing for people to do. She wanted me to do these things and take photographs so that she could look at them for erotic reasons. She persisted. I gave in to her request because the drugs and the alcohol had released my inhibitions, lowered my normal moral standards. I had some fear that if I did not comply with her request she would think I didn't love her.'

The doctor said that Mrs Califano suggested he use Pentathol, as on the previous night. She wanted him to start taking pictures with her partly clothed and then some pictures in which she would be naked and he would be involved. She removed some of her clothing and he injected her while she was lying on the settee in the sitting-room. He took some photographs he thought would please her and he then removed the rest of her clothing and carried her into the bedroom. There he gave her another injection because he wanted her to stay asleep.

Continuing his story to judge and jury, Dr Drinkwater said when he awoke the following morning Carole was lying face down in bed beside him. She was tucked beneath the sheets and seemed to be asleep. He did not think there was anything wrong with her and he went back to sleep. Some time later he went into the kitchen to make a cup of tea.

'In the sink I saw the syringes and two open packets of the drug Pentathol,' he said. 'I then recalled the events of the previous night . . . I was absolutely panic-stricken about how Carole would be. I rushed into the bedroom and pulled back the bedclothes. She was lying with her face on the left side and I noticed that her face was swollen and there was a mark on her upper lip. I didn't or couldn't believe that she might be dead. I felt her pulse and waited but I couldn't feel one. I felt her heart but I couldn't feel anything. I then gave her extra-cardiac stimulation for a few moments, but there was no response.'

Dr Drinkwater said he filled a syringe with a respiratory drug and tried to inject Mrs Califano in a vein. When this failed, he injected the drug directly into the heart.

'All the time I was saying, "Oh God no, please don't be dead, I love you darling" and things like that. When everything failed and I knew she was dead I sat on the bed and wept. I sobbed. I loved her so much. I had lost the only girl I loved.'

He was emphatic that when he gave the injections as a preliminary to the photographic sessions he had no intention of endangering Carole's life.

'I didn't think any harm would come to her,' he declared. 'I loved her dearly. I never once ceased to love her, and I still do.' He had been in a state of panic and confusion when he decided to make up the story that Mrs Califano had committed suicide. He had tidied up the house and put the girl's body back into position before telephoning Dr King.

'I thought she must have suffocated,' he said. 'I wanted to keep the perverted sex acts of the night before a secret.'

During the trial the dummy of a woman of approximately Mrs Califano's build was brought into court to demonstrate the positions in which she had been photographed. Each one of the thirteen pictures was handed to the jury of eleven men and one woman after being described by Mr Rodney Bax, prosecuting counsel.

'The circumstances of the woman's death were strange in the extreme,' commented Mr Bax, who suggested that the lewd positions, 'required to satisfy the doctor's perverted instinct,' had brought pressure on Mrs Califano's windpipe and that the drug mixture was calculated to kill by asphyxia.

'She was quite unconscious when these pictures were taken,' he said. 'If he had not filled her with this lethal mixture of drugs, she would not have allowed herself to get into these positions . . . things between the doctor and his mistress had not been entirely happy and it would appear that she had thoughts of leaving him . . . if those obscene photographs had not emerged this case would have been written off as suicide and the course of justice would have been averted.'

Later in the trial Mr Bax said that Dr Drinkwater was a man 'who you may think will lie and then change his lies and then lie again to suit the purpose at any given time'. The jury might think that the man, by his attitude to drugs either in relation to himself or to the woman he professed to love, had proved himself to be wholly irresponsible and very dangerous.

Mr Howard asked the jury for their 'intelligent understanding' and suggested that the case should be approached without prejudice.

'It may be that some of the matters brought to your attention disgust or revolt or shock you, but we can't have room in this court for those emotions. People do things sometimes which to others of us are odd. The real issue in this case is the state of mind of Dr Drinkwater when he gave the injections and did the acts he undoubtedly did. It is the state of mind of a man who was undoubtedly suffering from the effects of drink or drugs or a combination of both.'

Showing the jury some colour photographs of Dr Drinkwater and Mrs Califano together, Mr Howard said, 'These pictures tell a story all their own of a couple who are happy together. Do you think it is plausible that he was plotting her death? If a doctor plans murder he has many ways at his command of executing it, and he does not do it in the state that he was in. The offence is not to be excused because he took drink and drugs, but the right verdict is one of manslaughter.'

Mr Justice Thesiger, in his summing-up, said, 'It is murder as the prosecution allege if the person causing the death intended at the time to put her to sleep for ever or even did what he foresaw was going to do serious bodily harm.' Reminding the jury of the alternative verdict of manslaughter, he added, 'If a man is doing a series of acts, starting by rendering a woman unconscious and behaving in an erotic way with the body, he is guilty of murder even if death occurs in an unexpected way during the transaction.'

The jury was out for more than five and a half hours before finding Peter Drinkwater not guilty of murder but guilty of manslaughter, by a majority of ten to two. Passing sentence of twelve years' imprisonment, the judge said, 'I don't believe for one moment that that woman would have suggested these practices, inviting him to put her under so that they could take place.' He told Drinkwater, 'I think you are a dangerous man and your conduct was dreadful, negligent and reckless . . . it is impossible to imagine more reckless conduct for a man who had already had two serious warnings about consuming drugs.'

Mr Justice Thesiger was referring to a warning given to Drinkwater by the Director of Medical Services during a period of Army service and to another, when he had set up in private practice, by the Home Office Drugs Branch. After qualifying at St Bartholomew's Hospital, London, in 1959, the doctor had joined the Army for five years, and as a captain in the Royal Army Medical Corps was posted first to Germany and then to British Guyana. He began to drink heavily and to take drinamyl and amphetamine tablets at the same time. After an incident when he put a pistol to his head and threatened to kill himself if no one listened to him he was reprimanded and sent home. His conduct was reported to the Home Office and he was sent an official warning about his future behaviour.

These warnings seemed to have been ineffective, because a medical report from Norwich Prison, where the doctor had been on remand before his trial, said that over the past two years he had drunk to excess and taken both drinamyl and amphetamines.

His career began brightly enough. Son of a doctor practising near Yarmouth, Norfolk, the young Peter went to Gresham's, a Norfolk public school, and then to Magdalene College, Cambridge, where he gained a hockey blue and a Trial cap for the England side. He seemed all set for success until he started experimenting with mixtures of drink and drugs.

After leaving the Army, Drinkwater joined a practice in Reading, Berkshire—where he first met Carole Califano. He was soon in trouble with the police and was fined first for careless driving and then for dangerous driving. Eventually he lost his licence for three years after a conviction for causing death by dangerous driving. He overtook a line of cars and hit an elderly male cyclist, who was dragged for forty yards before the doctor stopped his car. He walked back to feel the victim's pulse and told witnesses, 'He's dead.' He then drove away and did not call the police until thirty minutes later. When an officer called at his home Drinkwater said, 'I knew he had died—and I am only interested in the living, not the dead.'

In May 1971 Peter Drinkwater was divorced by his wife, Christine, who had left him after twelve years of marriage, taking their two children with her. The decree was granted on grounds of cruelty.

'His drinking got worse and when he came home he would be in foul moods,' she said in an interview after his conviction for the manslaughter of Mrs Califano. 'There were rows and he would take it out on me. He beat me until eventually I left him. I understand now he must have been under great stresses, but he would never share them with me.'

Christine Drinkwater was shocked by the evidence given at her ex-husband's trial.

'It was like hearing about a complete stranger,' she said. 'Peter was never like that in the years we were married. We had a very normal sex life . . . he is a handsome man and I know many of his woman patients must have fancied him, but he had no need to yield to their temptations. . . . The evidence which came out about the photographs was a great shock—it didn't seem possible it was the same man that I had been married to.'

Carole Califano had been one of Drinkwater's patients since 1965 but it was not until 1970, after the break-up of his marriage, that they began to be closely involved. At that time she was living happily with her husband, Gerard, at their home in St Peter's Road, Reading, and helping him to run his chain of hairdressing salons—three under the name 'Gerard of Rome' and one called 'Moderne Ladies' Hairdressers'.

Dr Drinkwater was called to the house to attend their daughter, Bridgetta, who was suffering from tonsillitis, and became friendly with both husband and wife.

Mr Califano said after the trial, 'I thought he was an English gentleman and, like every other doctor I have ever known, a man of integrity and honour . . . he had been banned from driving after the accident and was looking for another job because his medical partnership in Reading could no longer employ him without a driving licence . . . his marriage had broken . . . he was really down on his uppers and like a fool I helped him.'

Both the Califanos assisted the doctor by driving him round to visit his patients—until the hairdresser began to notice changes in his wife.

'Carole became remote and moody,' he said. 'She started slimming and said Dr Drinkwater was giving her drugs to help her lose weight. She also said he gave her drugs for migraine. Before she ran off with Dr Drinkwater in August 1971 she was like a woman in a dream. I just couldn't get through to her. Nobody could, except the doctor. She was totally under his control and obeyed him like a slave.'

Gerard Califano was so worried that he told the police that Dr Drinkwater was dominating his wife with drugs, but they said they could not interfere between doctor and patient.

Carole's mother and step-father, Edna and Colin Pearce, of Stoke Row Road, Peppard, Oxfordshire, were also deeply concerned about their daughter's association with the doctor.

'A year ago I asked the police to investigate the activities of this man,' said Mr Pearce. 'We knew what was going on but were powerless to stop it. He had Carole on drugs and she rapidly went downhill.'

Mrs Pearce said that sometimes the doctor would telephone her daughter in the early hours of the morning. He would often get drunk in the Califanos' home and Gerard would drive him to his own home or surgery.

'The first thing he would say to me was: "Barmaid, get the bar open," she said. 'He would grab a bottle of gin and pour some down his throat. He was so bad he couldn't wait for a glass.'

Yorkshirewoman Mrs Pearce added that her suspicions about the association between her daughter and Dr Drinkwater were confirmed when Gerard and Bridgetta went on a visit to Italy. She discovered that during their absence Carole and the doctor had stayed at a London hotel as man and wife. It was shortly afterwards that Drinkwater joined the Norfolk practice and Carole left her husband to go with him.

'I had lunch with her after she left Gerard and I hardly recognised her,' said Mrs Pearce. 'She was like a zombie, drinking large gins and smoking heavily. I warned her that if she stayed with Drinkwater she would end up on a mortuary slab.'

Both Gerard Califano and Edna Pearce were emphatic that Carole was a normal, happy girl until she became involved with the doctor.

'Not only did Dr Drinkwater rob me of a wonderful wife, but he tried to save his skin by branding Carole as the worst sort of sexual pervert,' he said. 'I remember her as she really was—a lovely girl without an evil thought in her body.'

To Mrs Pearce she was 'a wonderful daughter'.

'Her name has been ruined, but she was not the sort of girl people now think she was,' she said sadly.

In letters to his former wife, Christine, written while he was in jail awaiting trial, Drinkwater tried to give some explanation of the stresses that had driven him to drink and drugs.

In one he wrote: 'To give you a specific cause of my initially developing anxieties would be difficult and would take too long to write. Perhaps I will talk to you about it one day . . . basically it is to do with my childhood, adolescence and university success in all fields all the time; that became expected of me, and to fail or even feel I might not do well or make errors in medicine would be an admission of personal failure . . .'

In a later letter he wrote, 'If only I had sought advice a long time ago it would have been so easy and you would not have suffered.'

He said he was not a murderer. 'How I hate that word. The whole thing was a tragic accident, though I must accept my responsibility in the matter, I know, and am prepared for it.'

Mrs Drinkwater said that her ex-husband was a perfectionist and worked very hard. She did not blame him for being attracted to Carole.

'I had left him and he was lonely and she was a very attractive, long-legged blonde. It was only when I left him and took the children with me that he missed us, so at holiday times I allowed the children to stay with him and Carole. I firmly believe he was in love with her.'

From a psychiatric viewpoint, Drinkwater was a narcissistic man, rather like a Nazi. He was exceedingly perverse; one part of him could not leave women alone and another part despised them and did everything possible to lower them. That explains his photographing them in lewd positions and putting abnormal things such as bottles and cucumbers in their genitals.

Drinkwater's involvement with drugs would slowly allow the 'death thing' to become more dominant and invasive so that he gradually reached a situation in which Mrs Califano and he were virtually dancing a dance of death. Some vestige of self-preservation made Dr Drinkwater inflict the lethal injection to Mrs Califano and himself remain alive. Many known drug addicts have committed similar acts of violence, going through all the same preliminaries as Dr Drinkwater, but managed to stop short of murder at the last minute. Possibly it was the callous killing of the drunken man on the road and then driving on before telling the police, which made him try out another murderous situation; only this time the result was death.

17

'Like the Devil Himself'

Sarah Gibson was nineteen when she decided that she wanted
something more than the pleasantly undemanding life of county
society she had enjoyed since leaving school.

She had no need to earn a living. Her father, Colonel John
Gibson, racehorse trainer and former amateur jockey, would
have been happy for her to have stayed at home with him and
her mother, Mrs Mary Gibson, and two brothers, Martin and
schoolboy Simon, then living in that village of training stables,
Lambourn in Berkshire. Horse racing and riding inevitably
played a big part in the social scene—Martin is a well-known
National Hunt rider. But Sarah was not very happy on a horse
and perhaps became a little bored. Instead of joining in the
party-going night life of the county, fair-haired Sarah preferred
to sit at home watching television.

There was no parental objection when she announced that
she wanted to make a career for herself in the hotel and catering
world. Commendably, she felt she would be productive and
somewhat independent if she earned a living. Casting aside the
advantages of her family connections Sarah started at the bottom of the ladder. In November 1970 she left her comfortable
home to take a quite menial domestic job at the Norfolk Hotel
—since demolished—in London's West End. She worked well,
learned a lot, enjoyed the routine, and in her free time explored
the metropolis—often content, when off duty, just to amble and
gaze in the windows of the brightly lighted shops of Piccadilly
and Oxford Street.

Early in 1971 Sarah took another job and advanced a step
upwards in her chosen career. This time it was as an assistant
housekeeper at the Royal Automobile Club in Pall Mall, where

she was paid £12 a week and was one of the dozen living-in members of the staff of two hundred and sixty. The club has a restaurant for 200 people, a swimming pool and a rifle range for the 15,000 members paying subscriptions of £45 a year, and eighty bedrooms—available only to male members—at about £4 a night.

Later that year the Gibson family moved from Lambourn to a restored Georgian farmhouse at Ham, near Cheltenham, Gloucestershire, and Sarah visited them regularly once a fortnight. She told them how much she was enjoying her work and the bustle of London life. She liked her newly-found independence and was saving up for a holiday trip to Paris.

On Sunday 2nd July 1972 Sarah was off duty but was seen in the club several times during the day. She had dinner in the staff dining-room at seven o'clock and at about 7.30 walked to the Fun City bingo hall in Coventry Street a few hundred yards from the club. She was seen leaving the bingo hall at about 9.30 p.m.—alone—but nobody witnessed her return to the RAC.

Early next morning one of the housemaids went to Sarah's room—No. 519 on the fifth floor—to call her. On the bed was Sarah's naked body, her hands and feet tied with her tights and some cord, her pink and black nightdress knotted round her neck and a handkerchief and towel thrust into her mouth. She had been dead for some hours.

It was clearly a sex murder because she had been raped either just before or immediately after death. Detectives investigating the killing at first formulated the theory that twenty-one-year-old Sarah had met her killer either at the bingo hall or in the street on her way back to the club. As there was little sign of a struggle in the room, it was thought possible that she knew the man and had been taken by surprise when he attacked her.

Although Sarah was an attractive girl—a colleague described her as having 'a lovely face and big blue eyes'—she was not known to have any men friends. Her father said he was unaware of any romantic associations and was sure Sarah had no steady boyfriend, while a member of the RAC staff commented, 'She was just a happy-go-lucky, popular girl who loved having fun and going out.'

A new line of enquiry was opened when it was discovered that several items had been stolen from the girl's room. Among them were a silver locket containing a photograph of her parents, a gold charm bracelet with a heart-shaped clasp, a silver watch, gold earrings embedded with diamond chips, a Churchill crown, a mother-of-pearl cigarette lighter and a small travelling clock.

Soon after the list of stolen property was published it was discovered that the Churchill crown had been cashed at the Westminster Bank in Waterloo Place on 4th July. Three days later the bracelet and lighter were sold for £2.50 to a Soho jeweller.

Detective Chief Superintendent James Neville, in charge of the investigation, was faced with the problem of deciding whether the man who killed Sarah was a sex murderer who stole her trinkets to put the police on a false trail, or if he was a thief who raped and killed when he found a girl in the room he was ransacking.

There were other mysterious aspects of the case.

Staff at the club were emphatic that Sarah Gibson always slept with the door of her bedroom open because she could not bear to feel confined in an enclosed space. Yet Colonel Gibson was equally sure that she was not frightened in small rooms, nor was she afraid of the dark, and that she always shut the door of her room when she was staying at home. 'She was a sensible girl who never seemed frightened of anything,' he said.

Another problem to be solved was how the murderer had entered the RAC premises—by the main entrance, always guarded by a porter?, through the staff entrance fifty yards away? or by the luggage lift leading into a basement area? Nobody saw any strangers in the club that night, but nobody saw Sarah either . . .

Although the club had eighty bedrooms, only seventeen were occupied on the night of the murder. All the occupants were interviewed by detectives and plans were made to finger-print every man—including politicians, sports celebrities and titled men—who had stayed there since Sarah joined the staff. Although the bedroom accommodation for members did not extend beyond the fourth floor, it would have been a simple matter for anyone to have slipped up the stairs to the fifth floor without being observed.

A new lead put the police on a fresh trail. A porter who had formerly worked with Sarah at the Norfolk Hotel said he knew she had had one regular boyfriend for two years. This man had once stayed overnight at the Norfolk and the porter had twice seen the couple together at the RAC. The name and description of this man was circulated to every police station in the country and, because he was believed to have links with Northern Ire-land, the Ulster police were alerted.

On 7th July Superintendent Neville flew to Belfast and inter-viewed a man, but he was quickly eliminated from the enquiry.

Then as so often happens in sex killings, the police were put on the right track by the guilty man himself.

Just a week after Sarah's murder, Neville received an extra-ordinary unsigned letter which read: 'I thought you might like some help in the case as it seems you are approaching it from the wrong angle . . . I did not like the idea of Sarah's departure but it couldn't be helped, but what can be done is to stop it happening again. I found a strange sense of power in depriv-ing a body of life, though Sarah was a mistake . . . I am a lonely person and I think I may be ill. On the night Sarah died I felt no remorse or guilt so hurry up and catch me. I won't give myself up for incarceration because that would destroy me as I have a great longing for life.'

The writer offered to 'do a deal' with the police, saying that if they would provide him with a list of English drug pushers he would 'get rid of them'.

At the time the letter arrived officers in Scotland Yard's fingerprint department were checking prints found in the dead girl's room with those on record. It was discovered that the prints matched those of a man named David Charles Richard

Frooms, aged twenty-five, of no occupation and no fixed address. Little was known of his antecedents—he was apparently without family and had few friends—except that he had served several terms in prison for petty theft, later for robbery with violence, and one for an indecent assault on a girl aged thirteen. He had been released from his last sentence only six months before the murder of Sarah Gibson.

There was no doubt that Frooms was the man the police wanted. He was detained and instructed to write some words while in the charge room at Cannon Row police station. Handwriting experts then had no doubt he had penned the letter. He said: 'I am glad you have got me. I killed her, strangled her with something she was wearing and a blue cord. . . . I covered her body with a blanket and put a Do Not Disturb notice on the door.' When asked if he had had sexual intercourse with Miss Gibson, he replied, 'She was dead then . . . dead, dead, dead, DEAD!'

Mr John Mathew, appearing for the prosecution when Frooms was tried for murder at the Old Bailey in December 1972, said that the accused man had 'behaved like the devil himself' when he killed Sarah Gibson. There was no suggestion that he had killed her accidentally, no suggestion of mental incapacity with diminished responsibility, or that he was drunk or drugged.

'It is very difficult to see what defence he can have to this charge of murder,' continued Mr Mathew. 'It really was a murder most foul.'

David Frooms, a long-haired, pale-faced, bespectacled young man, pleaded Not Guilty, saying that he had no recollection of killing the girl or having any intention of doing so. He admitted that the letter received by the police was in his handwriting, but denied knowledge of having written it.

He said that on the night of 2nd July he intended sleeping in St James's Park but left when some policemen appeared. He got into the RAC through an open window and looked around for something to eat. On the fifth floor he saw the door of a bedroom open and the light on inside the room.

'I peeped in and saw a girl lying asleep on top of the bed,' he said. 'She was wearing some kind of housecoat. A handbag was on a chair. I opened it and inside was a brown purse, but all it contained were some silver coins which I put into separate pockets so they did not make a noise. I closed the door in case anyone might be wandering about the passage as I wanted to see if there was any more money in the room.'

Frooms said he then picked up a pair of tights and placed them over the girl's mouth to stop her screaming. When she opened her eyes he brandished a fish knife and told her to keep quiet. She did not struggle or make any noise. He then stuffed a handkerchief into her mouth.

'I told her to lie on her face and I tied her hands with the tights. Then I moved her on to her side because I was afraid she might suffocate. She was mumbling something like the word "stockings" and I thought they might be too tight, so I cut them loose and tied her up with some blue cord which was on the dressing-table. I also tied her ankles with the same cord because I thought she might be able to jump out of the bed.'

Frooms said he then started looking round for money and found some jewellery in the wardrobe. The next thing he remembered was being astride the girl on the bed with his hands round her neck.

Mr Cyril Salmon, QC, defending: 'What were you doing?'

Frooms: 'I don't recall doing anything. I suppose I must have been strangling her.'

Asked if he had any recollection of squeezing his hands round the girl's throat, Frooms replied 'No'. He added that he could not remember having sexual intercourse with her.

'Looking back,' he said, 'I just get a visual sort of thing of my hands round her neck. This is something I have worked out afterwards.'

Mr Salmon, asking for a manslaughter verdict, said there was no dispute that Frooms entered the club as a trespasser and stole various articles from Miss Gibson's room. To find the accused guilty of murder the prosecution had to prove either that he intended to kill or intended to cause grievous bodily harm. Frooms was suffering from a personality disorder which did not amount to diminished responsibility.

Mr Justice Forbes, telling the jury that a manslaughter verdict was open to them, said, 'No one but a monster could have done this—strangled this girl just before or after she was sexually assaulted.' He warned them, however, that because Frooms could be considered a monster, it did not follow that he was not sane.

It took the jury less than half an hour to bring in their verdict of guilty of murder. Frooms was sentenced to life imprisonment.

In Frooms there is a split between a rather inadequate psychopathic general personality and a part of himself, unknown or hardly known by him, which contains murderousness. This seems to have clicked into accessibility when he overpowered Sarah and rendered her immobile by tying her up, getting her into his power and sexually at his mercy.

His letter suggests that it was the depriving of another human being of life (which Frooms admitted was precious to him) which was his main motive. The sexual motive would appear to have been a secondary one. The fact that Frooms wrote the letter to Detective Chief Superintendent Neville is evidence of a conscience with some linkages to normality, but his failure to give himself up shows that they were rather feeble.

When at bay, his denial of memory of writing the letter would be due to a re-establishment of the split, in the interests of what he would experience as necessary self-preservation. Without a knowledge of his early childhood it is impossible to make any guess about the reasons for his murderousness.